The Classical Mexican Cinema

TEXAS FILM AND MEDIA STUDIES SERIES
Thomas Schatz, Editor

The Classical Mexican
CINEMA

The Poetics of
the Exceptional
Golden Age
Films

CHARLES RAMÍREZ BERG

UNIVERSITY OF TEXAS PRESS
Austin

Requests for permission to reproduce material
from this work should be sent to:
  Permissions
  University of Texas Press
  P.O. Box 7819
  Austin, TX 78713-7819
  utpress.utexas.edu/rp-form

The paper used in this book meets the minimum
requirements of ANSI/NISO Z39.48-1992 (R1997)
(Permanence of Paper). ∞

Library of Congress Cataloging-in-Publication Data

Berg, Charles Ramírez, 1947–, author.
    The classical Mexican cinema : the poetics of the
exceptional Golden Age films / Charles Ramírez
Berg. — First edition.
        pages   cm — (Texas film and media studies
series)
    Includes bibliographical references and index.
    ISBN 978-1-4773-0805-9 (pbk : alk. paper)
    ISBN 978-1-4773-0806-6 (lib. e-book)
    ISBN 978-1-4773-0807-3 (non-lib. e-book)
1. Motion pictures—Mexico—History.
2. Motion pictures, Mexican—History and criticism.
3. Motion picture industry—Mexico—History.
I. Title. II. Series: Texas film and media studies
series.
    PN1993.5.M6B47 2015
    791.430972—dc23
                                        2014048464

Frontispiece: Detail of figure 6.39.

doi:10.7560/302514

The University of Texas Press and the author
gratefully acknowledge financial assistance
provided for the publication of this book
from the President's Office at the University
of Texas at Austin.

An earlier version of chapter 2 was
published in Toby Miller and Robert Stam,
eds., *A Companion to Film Theory* (London:
Blackwell, 1999), 363–386. Reprinted
courtesy of Blackwell Publishers, Ltd.

An earlier version of chapter 3 was
published in Chon A. Noriega, ed., *Visible
Nations: Latin American Cinema and Video*
(Minneapolis: University of Minnesota Press,
2000), 3–32. Copyright 2000 by the Regents
of the University of Minnesota. Reprinted
courtesy of the University of Minnesota
Press.

To Cecilia—
with love
and gratitude
for everything:
your grace, beauty, charm,
poise, patience, wisdom, advice,
strength, encouragement,
understanding,
and good humor.

Everything is easier,
better, simpler,
and happier
with you around.
Thank you
for being there.

Contents

FACING: Detail of figure 3.24.

Acknowledgments

HIS BOOK would not have seen the light of day without the help of many people. I would like to thank them now.

Several experts in the field gave their time and expertise. Back in the days when the Society for Cinema and Media Studies was the Society for Cinema Studies, Ana López and I were on a conference workshop panel on Latin American cinema. Her presentation was on *La mancha de sangre*, which had just been discovered after being believed lost for decades. Ana's perceptive talk, which included handouts and clips from the film, piqued my interest and eventually led, all these years later, to the analysis of *La mancha de sangre* that I include in chapter 8.

I first saw *El automóvil gris* at a working conference on Latin American cinema that Chon Noriega organized and hosted at the UCLA Film and Television Archive in 1995. Chon asked me to lead an impromptu presentation after a screening of the film. Thank you, Chon, for forcing me to begin analyzing the film on the spot—that was the beginning of chapter 3. More thanks to Chon and the UCLA Film and Television Archive for allowing me the opportunity to view and study *El automóvil gris* at the time, before it became available on DVD.

This book would not have happened at all had it not been for Fernando Fabio Sánchez. He kindly invited me to give the keynote address at Cine-Lit VII, the international Hispanic film and literature conference held in

FACING: Detail of figure 5.30.

Portland in February 2011. It was while I was working on that keynote, a talk on the poetics of Fernando de Fuentes's Revolution Trilogy, that the idea for this book suddenly crystalized in my mind. In addition, Fernando graciously shared rare silent Mexican documentaries from his collection that helped me better understand early filmmaking in Mexico.

Patricia Torres San Martín, professor in the Department of History at the University of Guadalajara and one of the top historians of Mexican cinema, read a draft version of the Fernández chapter and provided valuable feedback on it. She also helped with the overall argument of the book, and encouraged me to include a section on *La mancha de sangre*.

I would like to thank the José Clemente Orozco Foundation, headed by Clemente Orozco, the artist's son, for permission to reproduce three of his father's lithographs.

Closer to home, I would like to thank Paul Stekler, the chair of the Department of Radio-Television-Film at the University of Texas, where I teach. It is always heartening to have the backing of your boss, and over the years Paul has enthusiastically championed my teaching, my research, and me. A tip of the hat to all my estimable colleagues in the department for their friendship and their intellectual sustenance.

Because every student touches and inspires me in one way or another, I can say that all of them helped in this project. Special thanks to those who took my Mexican film history class, read draft chapters of this book, and took the time to give me their comments and corrections. Two students assisted me directly: Isabella Cook helped during the initial writing stages, and Emily R. Pellerin did some much appreciated copyediting.

During the book's writing I was supported by a Faculty Research Assignment, sponsored by the University of Texas at Austin and administered by Roderick Hart, dean of the Moody College of Communication. My thanks to the university, the college, and Dean Hart for having faith in my project and in me. The university assisted me in another important way. Because many of the films analyzed here are little known, I wanted this book to be abundantly illustrated. A generous Book Subvention Grant from the Office of the Vice President for Research helped pay for some of the additional costs involved in reproducing those images.

As someone who does research on Mexican cinema, I am extremely lucky to have the Nettie Lee Benson Latin American Library in my backyard. It is recognized as one of the great repositories of Latin American books and materials in the world, and Margo Gutierrez, librarian for Latina and Latino studies, was extremely helpful, as was the entire staff.

A writer is only as good as his editor, and in my case I had two of the best. Jim Burr, senior sponsoring editor at the University of Texas Press, helped in countless ways throughout the process, and was particularly invaluable in getting the book from the pile of manuscript pages that I submitted to the book you hold in your hands. For the third time, I was fortunate to have a book included in the Texas Film and Media Series, edited by Tom Schatz. Tom is one of the most knowledgeable film and media historians of our time, a gifted writer, and a brilliant editor. Once again, his insightful comments helped me to say what I was trying to say.

The production team did such a wonderful job of transforming my pages into this beautiful book that I wanted to thank each one personally. A good copyeditor helps a writer look good in public and I had an excellent one, Sue Carter, who cheerfully checked details, improved wording, and pressed for clarity. Knowing the talented designers who work for the Press, I expected a nice-looking book, but when I first saw Lindsay Starr's stunning design for the cover and the book, it took my breath away. In creating this exquisite showcase for the artistry of el Cine de Oro, Lindsay created art herself. Lynne Chapman, the manuscript editor, professionally oversaw the entire process, carefully coordinating text and design while keeping me on track and on schedule. I will always be grateful to Lynne for scrutinizing every word and illustration, refining my phrasing, and providing an endless supply of ingenious solutions. My deepest thanks to you all for your expertise, good will, and creativity.

When I published my first book on Mexican cinema, I had three school-age children who provided me with lots of love, humor, and morale boosting. Now they are grown and married with children of their own. They, their spouses, and their children helped get me through the writing of this book in a million ways, large and small. They made me laugh, kept me sane, and reminded me on a daily basis how blessed I am just to know them—and especially to love and be loved by them. So thank you: Charles and Courtney, Xavi, and Santiago; Anne-Marie and Nate, Grant, and Charlie; Christina and William, Jake, Nate, Wills, and Jase.

Just before starting this book, I lost both parents in an emotionally trying eighteen-month stretch. I want to take a moment to honor them and all they did for me. They gave me life and unconditional love. They modeled decency, compassion, kindness, patience, and understanding. They were my first teachers, and I carry the lessons I learned from them into every classroom. They were my foundation, and they, too, were part of this book. Thank you, Hortensia and Gerald, for everything.

Finally, a pat on the back to my older brother, Gary, who took me to see my very first movie. When I was three years old and he was already in high school, Gary took me to the Plaza Theater in El Paso to see *Cinderella*. From the moment the lights went down and the first images appeared on the screen I fell under cinema's spell—overwhelmed, enthralled, and enchanted. That was the beginning of my lifetime love affair with the movies.

NEXT SPREAD: Detail of figure 6.51.

The Classical Mexican Cinema

CHAPTER 1

Introduction

RETHEORIZING MEXICAN
FILM HISTORY

—

N 1992, when I published *Cinema of Solitude: A Critical Study of Mexican Film, 1967–1983*, it was the first book-length critical study of Mexican cinema in English. Since then, I am happy to report, there has been a boom in the research and publishing of Mexican film history and criticism, both in English and in Spanish. It is heartening to see so much work of such high quality busily investigating Mexico's rich and fascinating cinema.

This flourishing Mexican film literature has employed numerous approaches and covered all historical periods, from the earliest days of the medium's arrival in Mexico, through the silent era, the Golden Age, the subsequent crisis in the 1960s, the resurgence (Mexico's Nuevo Cine) of the '70s, the lull in the '80s and '90s, to its current renaissance in this millennium with the rise of contemporary auteurs such as Alfonso Cuarón, Guillermo del Toro, María Novarro, Alejandro González Iñárritu, Carlos Reygadas, Luis Estrada, Mariana Chenillo, and Fernando Eimbcke, among others. Some critics and historians, myself included, have focused their attention on the Cine de Oro, the transformative two-decade-long Golden Age that lasted from the mid-1930s to the late 1950s. During that time, Mexican cinema rose from near extinction at the end of the silent era to become the most successful Latin American cinema and the leading Spanish-language film industry in the world.

FACING: Detail of figure 6.48.

But despite the flurry of research and publishing, the systematic study of the style of Mexican cinema has hardly been touched upon. Other than Eduardo de la Vega Alfaro's monograph on Sergei Eisenstein in Mexico,[1] articles I have published (which have been extensively reworked here), an essay by Evan Lieberman and Kerry Hegarty,[2] and another by Patrick Keating,[3] the investigation of the poetics of Mexican films in general and of the most honored films of the Golden Age in particular is still in its infancy. This book addresses that lack by examining the poetics of the Golden Age's Classical Mexican Cinema, the name I have given to the era's most esteemed films.

My investigation concentrates on the development of Mexican film in the first half of the twentieth century. Beginning with the pre-cinema and early cinema period at the turn of the previous century, I analyze the illustrations of the prolific artist, cartoonist, and illustrator José Guadalupe Posada to note how his engravings set the stage for the Mexican filmmakers who would soon follow. My claim is that Posada was the font from which Mexican film as a whole and what I call the Classical Mexican Cinema flowed. Then I examine the poetics of Enrique Rosas's *El automóvil gris* (1919), the crowning achievement of Mexico's silent filmmaking. Based on an infamous string of revolution-era crimes, this remarkable docudrama marked the national cinema's transition from documentaries that dominated national filmmaking from its inception in 1896 to the mid-1910s to narrative films that have commanded Mexican film production ever since. As such, *El automóvil gris* set the stage for the Golden Age films that came after the introduction of sound.

This is followed by a chapter covering the beginning of Mexican sound films in the early 1930s and the resulting rebirth of Mexico's cinema production. After that are three chapters that focus on the films produced by the predominant Golden Age auteurs of three successive decades: Fernando de Fuentes's influential Revolution Trilogy from the 1930s; the collaboration of Emilio Fernández and his filmmaking unit, especially the films they made during the 1940s; and the Mexican films of the Spaniard Luis Buñuel, who moved to Mexico in the mid-1940s, became a Mexican citizen, and directed more than twenty films there during the next nineteen years. My last analytical chapter looks at three exceptional genre films directed by three important Golden Age directors—Juan Bustillo Oro, Adolfo Best Maugard, and Julio Bracho—in the 1930s and 1940s.

Methodology: Neoformalism, Neoauteurism, and Cultural Studies
—

My analytical method combines neoformalism and neoauteurism, which will be deployed within a cultural studies framework. Neoformalist analysis is the "poetics of film" approach pioneered by Kristin Thompson in *Breaking the Glass Armor: Neoformalist Film Analysis* (1988),[4] and used extensively since then by her and David Bordwell in numerous books, articles, and blog posts.[5] In part, *The Classical Mexican Cinema* is modeled on Bordwell's *Narration in the Fiction Film* and, to an extent, his books on Yasujiro Ozu (*Ozu and the Poetics of Cinema*) and Carl Theodore Dreyer (*The Films of Carl-Theodor Dreyer*).[6] Because so little formal analysis of Mexican films exists, this approach provides me with an orderly way of detailing the style of the Classical Mexican Cinema of the Golden Age. Moreover, neoformalism has a number of other investigative benefits, enumerated by Bordwell in his second introduction to his Ozu book:

> Through the lens of poetics we can systematically study a director's subjects, themes, formal strategies, and stylistic strategies, taken in relation to the norm-driven practices of his period and place. The poetics framework is historical, because it mounts causal explanations of the movies' distinctive qualities. It's also analytical, because it asks us to scrutinize choices made by the director.[7]

Since studying the subjects, themes, and formal and stylistic strategies of the aforementioned Mexican filmmakers and their films is precisely my goal, the poetics of film approach perfectly suits my objectives here.

I recognize that some critics regard the kind of neoformalist analysis practiced by Thompson and Bordwell as ahistorical and antithetical to cultural studies,[8] but I don't see anything inherent in the method that makes it so. Indeed, as Bordwell himself states, the poetics of cinema approach is meant to investigate style within a context, "in relation," that is, "to the norm-driven practices" of the director's period and place. Properly utilized, then, neoformalism *is* historical. It situates filmmakers and their films in a particular time and place. And it is analytical—not merely descriptive—since it carefully considers the choices directors made and asks why they made them.[9]

Furthermore, there is no reason why neoformalism cannot aid in unveiling a film's ideological stance. In *Ozu and the Poetics of Cinema*, Bordwell used the results of his poetics of cinema analysis as the basis for a discussion about how those films transmitted political ideology.[10] Indeed, I did much the same thing in chapter 2 of *Latino Images in Film*, where I performed a thorough neoformalist reading of a four-minute scene in *Falling Down* (1992) in order to demonstrate how following the standardized practices of Hollywood filmmaking may inadvertently serve to perpetuate the stereotyping of ethnic minorities.[11] Of course, a lot depends on how the critical method is employed. To be sure, neoformalism can be practiced in an overly narrow, reductive, and shortsighted way—as can any analytical approach. However, applied appropriately, which I hope to do here, it need not be.

A second key analytical tool I utilize in this book is neoauteurism. Just as neoformalism is a reconceptualized version of formalism, neoauteurism is similarly a more nuanced rethinking of auteurism, the analysis of films based on who directed them. Here I take my cues from two critics whose work I deeply respect, Robin Wood and Dolores Tierney. Both of them have published significant works on individual directors[12] without resorting to vulgar auteurism of the sort whereby the critic simplistically searches for patterns of directorial flourishes that prove authorship and provide a reason for assigning directors to a cinematic pantheon. I am aware of the problems occasioned by the excesses of early examples of auteurist criticism, which are neatly summarized by Wood:

Auteurism emphasized the personal signature at the expense of everything else (sometimes valuing a director's work just because it could be demonstrated to have one) and, at the worst, claimed or at least implied that the author was solely and exclusively responsible for the meaning and quality of his texts. Its opponents countered this by pointing out that the author did not invent the language and conventions of his medium, the genre within which the work was located, the ideological assumptions inherent in the culture and necessarily reproduced . . . in the individual text; neither did the author control the conditions of production.[13]

By using the term "neoauteurism," I mean to signal the use of a more finely calibrated type of analysis of a director's body of work. Like Tierney in her masterful study of Emilio Fernández, I concede that I am taking a "director-centered approach"[14] in this book. And like Wood, in his influential book on Hitchcock, while using it I will strive "to take into account and make use of the many valuable critical developments" of the past thirty or so years in film studies, including, as Wood puts it, "work on generic convention, the principles of classical narrative, the construction of 'classical Hollywood films' both overall and from shot to shot, stars and how they signify, [and] the relations of films to our culture's construction of gender."[15]

Naturally, I'll do this within the Mexican context. And I'll take note of the play of ideology—both personal and social—within an individual film, across a body of work, within myself, and as it inflects my own critical assumptions.

Though I am still following the standard auteurist methodology—looking for stylistic patterns and their repetition within a particular director's body of work—it is my aim to be attentive enough to see the forest *and* the trees. One crippling pitfall of auteurism as it is sometimes practiced is that while going about its business of spotting an overarching directorial style across a director's filmography, it fails to fully appreciate individual works, especially when they break from established patterns. This type of auteurism thus makes criticism a self-fulfilling prophecy—finding the pattern, looking for its repetitions, and ignoring elements that don't fit. Here I have tried to be alive to patterns as well as to their absence, and to be alert to a director discarding one style in favor of another, since this might signal a new phase in an artist's work, perhaps inaugurating a new pattern. Thus, for example, I note how the exhilarating cinematic experimentation exhibited in de Fuentes's Revolution Trilogy is largely absent in the films he made afterward; how Fernández's 1950s films differ so markedly from those he made the previous decade; and how Buñuel's Mexican films evolved stylistically as they became more surreal.

I will ground my neoformalist and neo-auteurist analyses in a cultural studies approach, situating the films I treat within several contexts: historical, social, cultural, economic, industrial, ideological, and—because so much of Mexican filmmaking history revolves around its filmmakers' vexed relationship to Hollywood—global. Films are never produced in a vacuum, and it behooves the historian and critic to be aware of and sensitive to the complex network of motivations, decisions, dreams, and desires bound up in the making of each one. This is the reason I begin a book on Golden Age cinema by examining the cultural history of image making in Mexico at the turn of the twentieth century. Starting there is the best way to appreciate how the work of the prolific printmaker José Guadalupe Posada created a visual template that the next generation of artists and filmmakers would use as they set out to create authentic Mexican art forms. Posada profoundly influenced artists like David Alfaro Siqueiros, José Clemente Orozco, and Diego Rivera, and they in turn influenced filmmakers such as director Emilio Fernández and cinematographer Gabriel Figueroa. Another example highlights the discrepancy that may arise between artistic intention and viewer reception. Emilio Fernández was proud of his Kikapú Indian ancestry. So it is no surprise that what brought him to the attention of international audiences and critics was *María Candelaria* (1943), a film where two top Mexican movie stars, Dolores del Río and Pedro Armendáriz, played indigenous protagonists. And yet despite the fact that Fernández's goal was to celebrate *indios* and expose their deplorable treatment, the film's depiction of them is deeply conflicted. At best, it sent mixed messages about Mexico's indigenous people; at worst, it was yet another stereotypical representation of them.

One more example will illustrate the necessity for the film critic to be aware of multiple contexts in analyzing a director's work. This is especially important for neoformalist critics, and serves as a reminder that, from time to time, we need to step back

from our close readings and take the bigger picture into account. This case demonstrates the complexities of international political and economic dynamics, and reveals how events may push and pull filmmakers in different ways, impact filmmaking, and shape a nation's film culture. Let's consider the reopening of global film markets after World War II and the diverse effects it had on two masterful Golden Age directors, Emilio Fernández and Luis Buñuel. For the first, the change severely damaged his standing as Mexico's most lauded auteur and spelled the beginning of the end of his career. For the other, the reopened European markets brought him to the attention of international film financiers, which led to more filmmaking possibilities, reinvigorated his cinematic creativity, and helped popularize him as one of the foremost auteurs of world cinema.

After 1950, Emilio Fernández's films began looking more mainstream, containing fewer elements of the signature style he had developed in the 1940s. One reason was that he wasn't always able to work with the team of collaborators that had assisted him in his '40s films. Another was the overall decline in the quality of Mexican filmmaking in the 1950s, due to falling box office receipts, dwindling profits, and shrinking budgets. These were primarily caused by a change in Hollywood's attitude toward the Mexican movie market. During World War II, at the urging of the U.S. government, Hollywood backed off from dominating Mexico's film market. With the war over and the U.S. no longer in need of a strong hemispheric ally, Hollywood aggressively sought to recapture Mexico's screens. Its success devastated

Mexican filmmaking. Consequently, Fernández had to scramble to make films for less money and on shorter schedules than he had become accustomed to in the 1940s. His films suffered along with his reputation.

Ironically, this downturn in Mexican filmmaking had a salubrious affect on Buñuel. A disciplined filmmaker who prepared meticulously, he had learned to operate with tight budgets and on short schedules. As he gradually gained the ability to make the films he wanted to make, many of his releases were well received nationally and internationally, and his career blossomed in the 1950s. His films' increasing critical and commercial success outside of Mexico led to his securing foreign financing for his projects. Eventually, Buñuel moved his filmmaking to Europe, and the films of his second French period found a large international art film audience.

Thus a single historic event, the postwar shift in movie marketing and financing, impacted the fates of two Classical Mexican Cinema directors in contrasting ways, bad for one, good for the other. There was nothing positive about the net effect on Mexican film culture, however. It was disastrous. Mexico lost two star auteurs, the quality of films dropped significantly, the Golden Age ended, and Mexican moviegoers abandoned their national cinema. Mexican film spiraled into a long decline, the most drastic since the 1920s. As I hope this brief historical sketch indicates, as much as possible I will place my close readings within multiple contexts, and always consider the implications of my findings on the broader story of Mexican cinema—and vice versa.

Mexico's Filmic Golden Age: The Classical Mexican Cinema and the Mainstream Mexican Cinema
—

Mexico's movie industry can be traced back to the earliest days of silent film, but as the nation rebuilt after its revolution (1910–20), Mexican films were much less popular than Hollywood's with Mexican audiences. "The American-made film—of whatever quality," film historian Aurelio de los Reyes has written, "had been . . . the favorite of the entire Mexican public" since the late 1910s.[16] Hollywood overwhelmed Mexico's nascent film industry, and by the late 1920s, Mexican film production had almost completely disappeared.[17] Of the 244 films exhibited in Mexico City in 1930, for example, 196 (80.4 percent) were Hollywood films, and only four (1.6 percent) were Mexican.[18]

As we will see, Hollywood's film aesthetic became the accepted standard in Mexico— and indeed throughout the world. Though the Mexican film industry made a Phoenix-like rebirth with sound film in the early 1930s and had matured into a formidable national cinema by the end of that decade, Mexico's audiences had grown accustomed to the Hollywood way of telling stories. In the main, and to the chagrin of film aesthetes who had hoped that Mexico would develop its own national cinematic aesthetic, Mexican cinema adopted the Hollywood filmmaking paradigm.

As described by David Bordwell in *The Classical Hollywood Cinema*, the definitive study of the American studio style from 1917 to 1960 that he coauthored with Janet Staiger and Kristin Thompson, this paradigm is a set of cinematic norms for the fiction film that includes elements encompassed by three systems. First, the paradigm entails a system of narrative logic centered on cause-and-effect linkages of story events, a goal-oriented protagonist, and the adherence to Aristotelian narrative poetics. Second, it features a system of cinematic time that governs everything from shot duration to the temporal ordering of shots to favored story devices such as flashbacks and deadlines. Third, it involves a spatial system that constitutes filmic space as story space. Compositions privilege human bodies, centering and balancing them in the frame.[19]

The classical Hollywood filmmaking model, both as signifying practice and as industrial mode of production (including studio and star systems, powerful producers, well-developed distribution networks, and exhibition chains), was imitated in Mexico by the late 1930s as it embarked on what is now recognized as its cinematic Golden Age (el Cine de Oro), roughly from 1936 through 1957. Actually, most Mexican films *adopted* as well as *adapted* the Hollywood model, giving the Hollywood paradigm a decidedly Mexican inflection.[20] By and large, as far as film style was concerned, the nation's films adhered to the Hollywood model; however, there was a small but formidable filmmaking faction that rejected Hollywood's paradigm outright. As a consequence, a central feature of Mexican cinema history in the first half of the twentieth century is the dynamic tension between those that followed the Hollywood style and those that spurned it.

Accordingly, I have divided Mexico's Golden Age cinema into two groups of films: the Mainstream Mexican Cinema (MMC) and the Classical Mexican Cinema (CMC). The majority of the Golden Age movies came from the MMC, works that had clearly adopted the Hollywood style, if with a Mexican flavor.

The CMC, on the other hand, was a smaller but influential group of alternative films, many of which got noticed at home and at international festivals and are now considered canonical classics of the nation's cinema. These were films made by directors in search of a Mexican cinematic aesthetic, a distinctive film form to express *lo mexicano* (Mexicanness). Though a minority practice, they were not by any means all that esoteric or uncommon, but rather products of the same industry as the MMC. Indeed, one of the most fascinating aspects of the Cine de Oro is that the Classical Mexican Cinema contested the MMC while appearing alongside it. Mexican film culture was spacious enough to allow films such as Fernando de Fuentes's Revolution Trilogy, the Fernández unit's dramas and melodramas, Julio Bracho's searing indictment of the postrevolutionary status quo, and Buñuel's surrealist provocations to play in theaters one week and then be followed the next by conventional, largely genre-based MMC movies—comedies, melodramas, *cabaretera* films, or *comedias rancheras*. Moreover, these CMC deviations from the Mexican filmic norm also played beside the slew of Hollywood films being exhibited in Mexico at the time. These CMC films, then, offered a look at "another cinema," one that—from de Fuentes's *El prisionero 13* (*Prisoner 13*) in 1933 to Buñuel's last Mexican-made film, *Simón del desierto* (*Simon of the Desert*) in 1965—successfully established itself apart from the standard Hollywood, European, and Mexican films that commanded most of the screen time in the nation's theaters.

This heterogeneous mix of MMC's commercial films and CMC's formal experimentation was much different from the homogeneous—well nigh monolithic—U.S. Hollywood filmmaking during the same era, where cases of formal experimentation were rare. As David Bordwell famously declared about the U.S. film industry's output from 1917 to 1960: "In Hollywood cinema, there are no subversive films, only subversive moments. For social and economic reasons, no Hollywood film can provide a distinct and coherent alternative to the classical model."[21] My claim in this book is that for Mexico's Golden Age cinema the situation was just the opposite. Major film artists were energetically exploring alternatives, consciously seeking a distinctive stylistic structure for Mexican movies. The films they produced deviated from the formal norm and expressed something different thematically, stylistically, and ideologically. In addition, these films were deliberate attempts to counter the Mainstream Mexican Cinema, which Classical Mexican Cinema directors regarded as undistinguished, uninspired, and highly derivative. The Mexican case is more similar to that in France, especially the films made there between the two world wars, when the film culture spectrum was expansive enough to include experiments on one end, mainstream commercial ventures on the other, and many intriguing blends of the two poles in between. By producing films that greatly broadened the range of Mexican cinema, CMC directors successfully countered Hollywood in two ways. They made films that broke away from the Hollywood paradigm, and in so doing they established a Mexican film culture very different from that of the United States.

The MMC generally followed Hollywood's lead in everything from its star system and producer-based industrial organization down to shooting, editing, and lighting styles, set design, costuming, and makeup, as well as scripting and acting conventions. Since MMC films adhered so closely to the classical Hollywood cinema, a style that has been thoroughly explicated by Bordwell, Thompson, and Staiger,[22] I feel that a neoformalist examination of those movies would be redundant and unnecessary.

What does need to be analyzed, however, is the poetics of the Classical Mexican Cinema. Though these films were a numerical minority, their impact on Mexican film history was at least equal to and arguably greater than the majority MMC. These vibrant and significant movies were exceptional, a term I use in my title in two senses. First, I mean to indicate those Mexican films that were deemed extraordinary by virtue of their garnering worldwide attention, critical acclaim, and awards both at home and at international festivals—films, that is, like Fernández's *María Candelaria* (1943), which put Mexican cinema on the international moviemaking map, and like Buñuel's *Los olvidados* (1950) and *Él* (1953), which kept it there. Second, I use "exceptional" to point out that in the context of Mexican Golden Age filmmaking the CMC films were the exceptions, not the run-of-the-mill industrial product. They intentionally did not look or feel like mainstream Mexican films, and proudly stood apart stylistically and ideologically.

This meant that their domestic reception was often mixed. Some CMC films were critically and commercially successful at home and abroad, like Fernández's first films with Dolores del Río, *Flor silvestre* and *María Candelaria* (both 1943). Others failed at the box office and were shunned by local critics, only to be lauded overseas or rediscovered by a later generation, reevaluated, and eventually added to the canon of great Mexican films. This was the case with de Fuentes's *¡Vámonos con Pancho Villa!* (1936) as well as Buñuel's *Los olvidados* (1950), two first-run failures that would rank #1 and #2 in a 1994 poll of Mexican filmmakers, critics, and historians conducted by *Somos* magazine.[23] Just as some of the CMC films were immediately popular and others were not, some were genre films, and some were more difficult to categorize. But they were just as unmistakably Mexican as the MMC films (though we might have to exclude Buñuel's literary adaptations, *Robinson Crusoe* [1954] and *Abismos de pasión* [*Wuthering Heights*, 1954]). Formally, however, they were definitely idiosyncratic—vigorously accentuating a distinctive cinematic style in order to assert *mexicanidad* (Mexicanness).

The CMC was mostly the work of three auteurs: Fernando de Fuentes, Emilio Fernández's filmmaking unit (comprised of Fernández, screenwriter Mauricio Magdaleno, cinematographer Gabriel Figueroa, and editor Gloria Schoemann), and, interestingly enough, the Spanish-born Luis Buñuel. Besides the works of these directors, in chapter 8 I'll discuss three more exceptional films, directed by Bustillo Oro, Best Maugard, and Bracho.

How were the CMC films, which are the focus of this book, different from the Mainstream Mexican Cinema? A short list of CMC characteristics will help explain the distinction I am making. As I work my way down the list,

keep in mind that it wasn't so much that the elements present in CMC films were entirely absent in the MMC. Rather, it's that all three of these features were *regularly present* in CMC films, and present *to a greater degree* than in their MMC counterparts, and that they were *deliberately placed there by their directors.*

First, the CMC was self-consciously auteurist—carefully planned and executed by filmmakers with an explicit aesthetic and ideological agenda. It's fair to say that most of the MMC films were quickly made entertainments produced to clear a profit. Similarly, many CMC films were made by frugal producers hoping to make money. But the difference was that CMC directors were thinking beyond their films' commercial potential. They had something to say, wanted to say it in a special way, and wanted viewers to take notice. Fernando de Fuentes's Revolution Trilogy was the director's harshly critical commentary on the failure of the 1910–20 revolution. Unlike the majority of the happily resolved films of the MMC, de Fuentes's trilogy was composed of tragedies that raised the chilling possibility that the disappointing and dispiriting outcome of the revolutionary war might have been due to an inherent flaw in the Mexican character. As de Fuentes said at the time of the release of *El compadre Mendoza* (1934), the second film of the trilogy:

It would have been easy to narrate the plot [of *El compadre Mendoza*] in such a way that the conclusion was a happy one like we are used to seeing in American films; but it is our opinion that Mexican cinema ought to be a faithful reflection of our way of being, bleak and tragic, if what we are attempting is to present truthful profiles of ourselves, rather than making a poor imitation of what we are given by Hollywood.[24]

Similarly, Emilio Fernández's films that he made with Gabriel Figueroa and the other members of his filmmaking team were a direct attack on the MMC, which Fernández derided as hardly Mexican at all, and little more than Hollywood in Spanish. Fernández and Figueroa's shared ambition was to create a uniquely *Mexican* cinema, films that unambiguously and unmistakably explored Mexican themes, portrayed Mexican characters, and were set in a landscape that would be recognized by filmgoers the world over as—and only as—Mexico.[25]

For his part, Luis Buñuel worked out an informal arrangement with his first producer, the Russian émigré Oscar Dancigers, by which he agreed to direct commercial projects in exchange for the chance to make more personal films.[26] In these productions he slowly but surely brought his surrealism to the fore, employing it to skewer machismo, burlesque the bourgeoisie, and challenge the narrative bedrock of Hollywood and MMC filmmaking—the happy ending. But even in his more commercial outings, Buñuel, the most consistently surrealist filmmaker in the history of cinema, found ways to smuggle in his irrational, dreamlike imagery.

Second, CMC films purposely drew attention to their style. A fundamental aspect of the Hollywood paradigm was the understanding that a film's style should never call attention to itself, an unwritten rule adopted by MMC directors and producers. CMC filmmakers, by contrast, produced films with formal elements that were meant to stand out and be noticed. As mentioned above and as will be discussed in chapter 5, de Fuentes intentionally gave all three films of the Revolution Trilogy tragic endings that he felt were truer to the Mexican experience. Consequently, the dramatic structure of these films was emphatically unlike that of the MMC and resulted in a different viewing experience for audiences. Fernández and Figueroa were so staunchly opposed to MMC filmmaking that they developed a nationalistic cinematic style to depict Mexico visually, one heavily influenced by Mexican painters, graphic artists, and muralists. The whole point of their formally ambitious project was for audiences to notice that their films looked different. As I'll show in the three films I analyze in chapter 8, directors Juan Bustillo Oro, Adolfo Best Maugard, and Julio Bracho operated out of the same desire to experiment beyond the paradigmatic bounds of mainstream films. As far as Buñuel was concerned, he was busy developing his new, smoothly inconspicuous cinematic style and seemingly following Hollywood's and the MMC's "unobtrusiveness principle." Until, that is, he tossed in another of his recurring "irrational sparks" and derailed a film's narrative flow. Ever the wily surrealist, Buñuel used the MMC style in order to sabotage it.

Third, CMC was ideologically oppositional. In large measure, the CMC's opposition stemmed from a nationalistic impulse that was rooted in the 1910–20 revolution and that led to a corresponding revolution in the arts. Turning their backs on European and North American influences, Mexican artists sought to discover, define, and promote a native aesthetic. CMC filmmakers followed suit. As such, the CMC style was a declaration of cinematic independence whose overarching goal was to create movies that proclaimed *mexicanidad*. Aligning itself with contemporaneous nationalistic movements in all the Mexican arts, the CMC aesthetic in effect asserted that its films had succeeded in capturing the authentic Mexico, while MMC moviemaking—for all its Mexican characters, colorful colloquialisms, familiar locales, popular songs, and folkloric costumes—had not.

From the vantage point of CMC filmmakers, the MMC had failed because its films were imitative of—one could even say infected by—the dominant Hollywood filmmaking paradigm. After all, Hollywood's was a foreign style, developed to depict American characters engaged in the American experience, and never meant to convey *lo mexicano*. This difference becomes strikingly evident in the analysis of the dramatic structure of CMC films, which reveals how many were tragedies that broke away from Hollywood's and the MMC's standard three-act, happy-ending formula. The CMC was more pro-Mexican than rabidly anti-American, however. For Mexico to flourish after the revolution, the thinking went, it needed to find its true identity. This was as true of national politics as it was of the arts. Consequently, Mexican cinema, as de Fuentes, Fernández, and Figueroa argued, must be part of that nationalistic identification effort.

The subjects of my analyses, artist José Guadalupe Posada and filmmakers Enrique Rosas, Fernando de Fuentes, Emilio Fernández and Gabriel Figueroa, Juan Bustillo Oro, Adolfo Best Maugard, and Julio Bracho, were all involved in this nation-defining mission, either implicitly (Posada and Rosas) or explicitly (the others). Luis Buñuel, however, the focus of chapter 7, was a special case. Though

just as subversive, oppositional, and anti-establishment as the rest—if not more so—he was not part of the nationalistic project. Rather, his ideological opposition stemmed from a lifelong commitment to surrealism, whose primary motivation was the dismantling of the bourgeois status quo. "The real purpose of surrealism," Buñuel wrote, "was . . . to explode the social order, to transform life itself."[27] Still, Buñuel was allied with the other CMC filmmakers because in attacking the status quo, he challenged the MMC.

Of course, every film carries ideological content, wittingly or not. What I want to suggest is that the Classical Mexican Cinema's ideological program was explicit, whereas the politics of the MMC were typically implicit and unthinking. Moreover, the ideology embedded in the MMC's narratives typically celebrated the Mexican status quo—not surprising, since it was conveyed via a filmic style that was adopted from Hollywood. From the Classical Mexican Cinema perspective, then, the Mainstream Mexican Cinema was hopelessly conservative and retrograde. In effect, the CMC was filmmaking that said, "We fought a revolution to blaze new artistic trails and create a new form of cinematic expression for Mexico, not to revert to the status quo ante and copy foreign filmmaking models." The CMC point of view was that filmmakers who relied on conventional filmmaking imitative of the Hollywood paradigm were merely another sign of how thoroughly the revolution had failed.

These, then, are the defining characteristics of the Classical Mexican Cinema, the films and filmmakers that I analyze in this book. Not every film the CMC auteurs made was memorable, commercially or artistically successful, cinematically innovative, or ideologically confrontational. But many were, and focusing on the groundbreaking films from these filmmakers' output reveals their individualistic styles, their aesthetic goals, and their ideological intentions. This book is dedicated to analyzing those films that exhibited these three characteristics, were aesthetically significant, and were cinematically exhilarating. The films, that is, that were artistically and ideologically special: the exceptional films of the Golden Age.

Distinguishing between the MMC and Classical Mexican Cinema in this way means that I had to omit many popular and beloved Cine de Oro films—movies that are commonly accepted as part of Mexico's cinematic canon, feature popular stars of the time, and appear on the *Somos* list of the best Mexican films of all time. In excluding these films, I'm neither disregarding their importance nor questioning their stature in Mexican film history. And I'm certainly not denying the fact that they are immensely entertaining, important, and enjoyable. They are all those things, something that the appearance of so many of them on the *Somos* list confirms. They are absent here because stylistically they adhered to—rather than deviated from—dominant Mexican and Hollywood filmmaking norms of the time.

My focus here is the Classical Mexican Cinema, a remarkable body of work made by filmmakers consciously striving to forge a native cinematic form, express *lo mexicano*, and avoid imitating Hollywood. This book is the story of how, against the odds, they succeeded in finding a *Mexican* way to say something memorable, meaningful, and true about the national experience.

CHAPTER 2

Every Picture Tells a Story

JOSÉ GUADALUPE POSADA'S
PROTOCINEMATIC GRAPHIC ART

—

OSÉ GUADALUPE POSADA (1852–1913) is Mexico's best known and most prolific turn-of-the-century engraver, an image-making genius who created thousands of penny press illustrations. Many of them, like his signature *calaveras* (skeleton figures), are still recognized today. But he never made a film, had little if any known association with filmmakers, and died twenty years before the appearance of the Classical Mexican Cinema in 1933. So why begin a book on Mexican cinema with a chapter on him? The reason is that Posada is *essential* to understanding the history of Mexican film. In both formal and ideological terms, Mexican cinema begins with Posada.

Formally, Posada's art is the fountainhead of visual narration in Mexico. He provided a pictorial model for depicting Mexican life that would be studied and adopted by the next generation of painters, graphic artists, muralists, and film directors, particularly Classical Mexican Cinema filmmakers. Thus it is crucial to appreciate the linkages between Mexico's early cinema and the array of journalistic images available at the time, especially those created by Posada, who for more than forty years was the nation's most productive mass media illustrator. During that time he discovered and developed representational techniques we would call "cinematic," techniques that would be available for incorporation into modern Mexican cinema, which for me begins in 1919 with *El automóvil gris* (*The Gray Automobile*), the subject of my next chapter. The visual language he developed was similar to film's, and encompassed shot selection, framing, composition, and the use of diagonal lines to accentuate depth.

The second reason to begin with Posada is an ideological extension of the first and the one that most directly links him to the Classical Mexican Cinema. It is the fact that his art was regarded as the precursor of the nationalistic art movement, a crusade that drove Mexican art for the first half of the twentieth century. Posada's inexhaustible production and propagation of Mexican imagery served as a seminal example for artists and muralists like Dr. Atl, Diego Rivera, David Alfaro Siqueiros, and José Clemente Orozco. Not only did Posada's art demonstrate that Mexico was a worthwhile subject, it also inspired them to reject hegemonic European artistic traditions and establish a native aesthetic. The work of these artists and their admiration for Posada's body of work in turn had an effect on Soviet filmmaker Sergei Eisenstein while he was making *!Que viva México!* in 1931–1932. Eisenstein's appropriations of Posada motifs along with the muralists' establishing a nationalistic aesthetic provided an aesthetic template for CMC filmmakers in their quest to create a distinctive and authentic national film style.

A perfect example of why Posada's work was so pivotal for artists, Eisenstein, and CMC filmmakers is shown in fig. 2.1, a striking illustration depicting the miraculous appearance of the Virgin of Guadalupe. The next generation of Mexican artists must have marveled at how economically, effortlessly, and effectively it proclaimed its *mexicanidad*.

By combining the Virgin de Guadalupe, the nation's spiritual patroness, and the ubiquitous maguey plant, Posada situated this event in only one place in the world—Mexico. As we will see, this was not lost on an artist like Orozco, a director like Eisenstein, and CMC filmmakers Emilio Fernández and Gabriel Figueroa, all of whom would make the maguey a prominent compositional feature in their work.

And beyond its effective nationalism, much of Posada's imagery penetrated beneath the surface of things and provided commentary on the Mexican status quo. Obvious examples are his *calaveras*' playfully mocking Mexican high society. But there was a no-nonsense, journalistic side to Posada too, a tough-mindedness that informed his imagery as he chronicled the entire spectrum of Mexican life—good and bad, flattering and

FIG. 2.1. José Guadalupe Posada, *Sorpredente Milagro. Segunda Aparición de Nuestra Señora la Virgen Santísima de Guadalupe, entre la Hacienda de la Lechería y San Martín* (*Amazing Miracle. Second Appearance of Our Lady the Most Blessed Virgin of Guadalupe, between the Hacienda of the Dairy and San Martin*), 1893. (Courtesy the Nettie Lee Benson Latin American Collection, University of Texas at Austin)

The Classical Mexican Cinema

shameful. This ability to see Mexico without illusions gave a sting to his cultural critique, and that refusal to look away became a fundamental characteristic of the Classical Mexican Cinema.

Though Posada's combination of native subject matter and critical perspective deeply affected the style of the CMC, it did not have the same effect on the Mainstream Mexican Cinema. Because it adopted and adhered to the Hollywood filmmaking paradigm, stylistically the MMC would very likely have developed as it did with or without the existence of Posada. But it is impossible to imagine the existence of the Classical Mexican Cinema—in form or content—without Posada's formidable example serving as a guiding star.

I will use the formal/ideological rationale I have just laid out to structure this chapter. After a close analysis of Posada's images to note their cinematic qualities, I will explore the similarities between his cultural criticism and the ideological stance characteristic of CMC films. But before doing that, let me briefly position Posada within Mexico's turn-of-the-century journalistic world, just at the time when it was joined by a new image medium—*el cine*.

The Penny Press, Posada, and *el cine* in Turn-of-the-Century Mexico
—

At the time that cinema was first becoming popular, the rich mix of image-containing media available in Mexico was very different from that in the First World. When it was introduced in Mexico in the mid-1890s, cinema joined a larger, well-established representational system that included the fine arts (painting, sculpture, drawing, etching, engraving, printmaking) and the popular media (photographs and illustrations in newspapers, pictorial magazines, advertisements, slideshows, dime novels, posters, handbills, and broadsides).

Of these, the penny press ruled. In the early 1900s, it was the most popular image medium in the country, and Posada was its master graphic artist. From the 1890s to the rise of newspapers and other mass media in the first part of the 1920s, the penny press was the most widespread, accessible source of images for the Mexican public. In Mexico City in the 1890s, for example, at least eighteen such presses were in operation, and from 1900 well into the 1910s, a period considered the heyday of the medium, there were more than forty.[1] During this time, these presses mass-produced countless one-sheet broadsides and small newspapers, with pressruns in the hundreds or thousands and sometimes in the millions.[2] Agents, newsboys, and hawkers sold these for one or two centavos[3] "on street corners, in market places, at fairs, ranches and haciendas."[4] In addition, these editorial houses printed a number of other image-containing items such as board games, cookbooks, songbooks, storybooks, and chapbooks.

There has been a fair amount of research into the reciprocal influences of image media and the beginnings of First World moving pictures.[5] But as of yet, no one has made more than a passing commentary on these mediated cross-fertilizations in Mexico's early cinematic history.[6] From this perspective, Posada is a central figure. In his own way, he was as important to the unfolding of Mexican cinema as Winsor McCay and his comics were to the early development of U.S. film. To begin with, there is the length and breadth of his career. The prolific Posada was an illustrator for more than forty years, from the pre-cinematic era (he began illustrating in León in the 1870s and moved to Mexico City around 1887) until well into Mexico's initial documentary film stage (roughly 1896–1916). Moreover, his etchings and engravings encompassed an impressively broad range of subjects, from religious portraits to carefully drafted views of Mexico City to depictions of news events, satirical *calavera* drawings, and miracles. Posada documented Mexican life, legend, and folklore by creating thousands of images (most estimates have put the total at between fifteen and twenty thousand, though the actual number will never be known)[7] in various media: woodcuts, type-metal engravings, and zinc relief etchings.[8] These were published in popular Mexican journalistic forms—broadsides and chapbooks—that "had virtually disappeared in Europe and the United States."[9]

When moving pictures arrived, the new medium established a built-in kinship with journalism. From 1896, when the Lumières' and Edison's representatives introduced moving pictures to the nation, until 1917, when Mexican filmmaking turned away from documentaries and embraced fiction films, the national cinema was predominantly documentary. The new medium was considered a branch of journalism and generally understood as a moving variant of illustrated magazines, which were gaining popularity in Mexico in the 1890s. Though at first these periodicals were exclusively foreign, Mexico's own production of such magazines began in 1895 with the publication of *El mundo ilustrado*, which combined engravings, lithographs, and photographs.[10] In those early

decades of cinema, then, Posada and Mexican filmmakers saw themselves—and were seen by others—as essentially in the same business: reportage. Twenty years later that same impulse was one of the main characteristics of CMC filmmaking. Like Posada, CMC directors were using a mass communication image medium to depict the national experience and report on problems in the system.

Mexican Cinema's Documentary Stage (1896–1917)
—

One distinguishing feature of Mexican cinema is the fact that for its first twenty years, from 1896 until 1916, Mexican film production was almost exclusively a documentary practice. In contrast, both European and North American cinemas gravitated toward narrative much earlier: U.S. films, for example, made the transition during the 1903–1907 period.[11] And during the 1910s, a time when foreign films—mainly French, Italian, and North American—commanded more and more attention from filmgoers in Mexico, the onset of the Mexican Revolution (1910–20) provided an impetus for domestic documentary production to continue, as newsreel footage brought events of the civil war to life for the nation's moviegoers.

But the rush to capture current events was not the only reason that Mexican cinema remained almost entirely documentary, despite the unrelenting trend toward narrative films in First World cinema. First of all, Mexican documentaries were enormously popular. Second, they provided native filmmakers with a ready-made market niche. Third, documentaries were cheap to make and economical to market—entrepreneurs like

Enrique Rosas and Salvador Toscano shot, edited, promoted, and exhibited their films in their own theaters.[12] Fourth, they fed the desire of Mexicans to see themselves on the silver screen.[13]

Fifth, from the 1870s on, Mexico—through its intellectual and political leadership—was under the sway of positivism. As promoted by Gabino Barreda, who transplanted the French philosophical movement to Mexico, positivism was touted as a means of moving Mexico from anarchy to liberty. This belief was based on two assumptions: first, that economic evolution preceded political evolution (and ultimately liberty), and second, that the proper means of achieving economic evolution was through order. Order, organization, a scientific approach to the nation's problems, and education of the masses were the cornerstones of Mexican positivism.[14] "In that context," writes film historian Aurelio de los Reyes, "fiction cinema was rejected because of its potential to dupe the public: the cinema was a science and as such should show truths."[15]

Finally, a nationalistic side effect of positivism led artists in the last decades of the nineteenth century toward a celebration of lo mexicano and away from the imitation of foreign traditions. As part of this movement, the representational arts, from paintings to illustrations to photographs, were called upon to depict Mexico, its people, and its culture.[16] To the degree that cinema in Mexico was regarded as a science as well as an art (early comparisons likened it to etchings, painting, and theater),[17] it was clear that it should promote nationalism, like the other representational arts. Mexico's twenty-year

documentary-film stage, therefore, was not simply a case of arrested development, but rather the result of the convergence of complex technological, political, economic, philosophical, and nationalistic factors.

The decline of the Mexican documentary came in 1915, when interest in nonfiction films waned significantly. By 1916, revolutionary documentaries—along with domestic documentaries in general—had all but disappeared from Mexican movie screens.[18] Shortly thereafter, in 1917, a small band of enterprising Mexican filmmakers initiated Mexico's first sustained fiction-film stage by producing story films. While there had been sporadic attempts at el filme de argumento (scripted fiction films) before, there had never been a sustained effort of the kind that began in that year. Only a fragmentary record of this early wave of narrative films survives, but it seems that they took two forms, one derivative and the other nationalistic. Among the first were imitations of Italian melodramas, which were very popular in Mexico at the time. For example, Mexico's first narrative feature, La luz (The Light, 1917), was a faithful reconstruction of the Italian film Il fouco (1915), which had enjoyed enormous success in Mexico in 1916. The five films starring the Mexican stage actress Mimí Derba and produced by documentarian Enrique Rosas in 1917 were also clearly under the spell of Italian melodramas. A second group of "truly nationalistic" films was also produced; these were movies that would exhibit the landscape, folkways, and customs of Mexico (such as the first film version of Federico Gamboa's popular 1904 Mexican novel Santa in 1918).[19]

This brief experimental-fiction stage culminated in the national cinema's first legitimate narrative blockbuster, the 1919 docudrama *El automóvil gris*. As I will discuss in more detail in the next chapter, the film was originally released as a twelve-part serial, and only survives as a partial version. Nevertheless, it is so accomplished cinematically that it can be said to be the bellwether of the Golden Age, an important precedent for both the CMC and the MMC.

Narrational Representation in Turn-of-the-Century Mexico
—

In the discussion that follows, I am not looking for causal links between penny press illustrations and cinema. Given the fact that of the twenty-four feature fiction films made in Mexico up to 1919, only a few remain, that a similarly high percentage of the documentaries are also lost, and that only about a thousand Posada images of the many thousands he produced have survived,[20] such an argument would be difficult to support. Nevertheless, I am intrigued by the intertextual evolution of image narration in both print and moving pictures in Mexico from the 1890s to the release of *El automóvil gris* in 1919. I am seeking a better understanding of the dynamic, cross-pollinating influences that must have flowed among the media as filmmakers, still photographers, and graphic artists alike worked toward a coherent narrational system by which images could clearly and efficiently relate a tale. Artists like Posada learned how to utilize images narratively and helped develop a visual storytelling syntax. Early illustrations like Posada's, along with moving images from Mexican documentary films

and foreign fiction and nonfiction movies, all provided a foundation from which Mexican filmmakers must have learned to transmit comprehensible, coherent narratives.

Before I begin my analysis, a word on the use of the term "narrative" in relation to Posada. I use "narrative" in the Bordwellian sense, as "the activity of selecting, arranging, and rendering story material in order to achieve specific time-bound effects on a perceiver."[21] And although useful in categorizing the two general types of emerging early film, I deemphasize the nonfiction/fiction dichotomy when speaking of Posada's imagery because, by Bordwell's broad definition, all of his illustrations were narrations: that is, each drawing required him to select, arrange, and render story material—whether real or imagined—clearly, coherently, and emphatically, in order to provoke an interested response from a potential customer.

Finally, it is known that Posada did create at least two film advertisements. They took the form of handbills, and probably doubled as small posters. One was for the 1905 French film *La poule aux oeufs d'or* (*The Hen That Laid the Golden Eggs*, directed by Gaston Velles), and the other for a fight film of a bout between Bob Fitzsimmons and Jack O'Brien.[22] The first contained an image from the end of the French film, one of the most popular movies of its day (fig. 2.2). It is so detailed that Posada probably copied it from existing promotional materials that may have come with the film, rather than sketching it from repeated viewings of the movie (fig. 2.3). The second contained an image from the fight, plus two small portraits of the boxers. Again, the likelihood is that Posada based his poster on supplied promotional materials for the

Mexico City exhibition. In the analysis that follows, I am omitting these two illustrations because I am not interested in Posada's abilities as a copyist, which is what he appears to have done in these two engravings. Rather, I am focusing on the way Posada imagined and visualized scenes for events he was called on to narrate—not ones he copied from other sources—and the way his resulting images anticipated film language.

Posada's Cinematic Techniques
—

Surveying the work of Posada, one notes several cinematic techniques that would become part of what is now called "film language." By "cinematic" I mean characteristics unique to moving pictures, techniques that could not be duplicated by other media, that were not common practice in other media at the

time, or that would be extremely difficult to achieve in other media. For example, when watching a play on a stage, a spectator is presented with the entire proscenium view. Cinema is able to capture that in a long shot (LS), and in fact much of early cinema framed the action from such a front-row-center proscenium vantage point. Later, however, cinema began to enter the narrative space to record closer shots via the medium shot (MS) and the close-up (CU). Providing more detailed information with these shots is something cinema can do that stage drama cannot and is one example of a cinematic feature of the medium. Others include cinema's capturing of serial motion through still photographs, the manipulation of time and space via editing, various moving camera shots (pans, tilts, and tracks), and dissolves and fades between one scene and the next.

LEFT | FIG. 2.2. Posada's 1906 illustration for the handbill promoting the Mexico City screening of the Pathé studios blockbuster *La poule aux oeufs d'or* (*The Hen That Laid the Golden Eggs*, 1905). As can be seen by comparing it with a still from the film, it depicts a scene copied from the movie's ending. (Courtesy the Nettie Lee Benson Latin American Collection, University of Texas at Austin)

ABOVE | FIG. 2.3. The final scene from *La poule aux oeufs d'or*.

Here, then, is a summary of Posada's cinematic pictorial techniques, which he pioneered and made available to both CMC and MMC filmmakers.[23]

NEARER VANTAGE POINT TO PROVIDE PARTIAL-FIGURE AND FACIAL REPRESENTATIONS

In film partial-figure and facial representations would be called medium shots and close-ups. They became prevalent with the advent of analytical editing, one of the hallmarks of Hollywood's and the greater Western cinema's classical style. It involves breaking down the action of a scene into separate shots: LSs to establish the setting, MSs to place the subject within the context of his or her immediate environment, and CUs to provide a significant detail of the subject or action. Early on in Western cinema history, films were made up almost exclusively of frontal, proscenium-like, full-figure LSs or medium long shots, and it was not until the mid-1910s that films began using a wider array of shots with any regularity. However, it appears that Posada created medium and close-up images of subjects frequently before they became standard cinematic practice.

Posada's *Gran Fandango y Francachela de Todas las Calaveras* (*Happy Dance and Wild Party of the Skeletons*, no date), shown in fig. 2.4, gives an example of the frontal, proscenium style common to both illustrations and early cinema. The image is self-contained in that the entire scene is depicted, and the diegetic world—as well as the narrative—ends at the image edge.

Contrast this image with those in figs. 2.5 and 2.6, two of thirteen images from the front and back pages of a two-sided

FIG. 2.4. *Gran Fandango y Francachela de Todas las Calaveras* (*Happy Dance and Wild Party of the Skeletons*, no date). (Courtesy the Nettie Lee Benson Latin American Collection, University of Texas at Austin)

TOP | FIG. 2.5. Aurelia the fish vendor. (Courtesy the Nettie Lee Benson Latin American Collection, University of Texas at Austin)

BOTTOM | FIG. 2.6. Doña Antonia the butcher. (Courtesy the Nettie Lee Benson Latin American Collection, University of Texas at Austin)

broadside, *Una calavera chusca* (*A Funny Calavera*, no date), in which Posada and his *corrido* (ballad) lyricist poked fun at local market vendors. While some of the *calavera* characters are drawn in full figure, many are drawn in "medium shot." Of course portraits were a common artistic genre, and Posada produced many in his time. But these pictorial MSS are not so much posed, formal portraits as they are shots of active individuals caught in the middle of a working day—almost snapshots. As such they have a documentary immediacy, and despite being *calavera* figures, they possess recognizable human characteristics. These MSS approach the cinematic by providing closer details of the vendors that identify them not only by the foods they sell but also by costume and utensil (the fish, striped skirt, and apron-vest of Aurelia the fish vendor [fig. 2.5]; the large knife of Doña Antonia the butcher [fig. 2.6]). This sort of indication of individual traits was something that evolved in Hollywood and Western cinema throughout the 1910s and was standardized by around 1917.

One of Posada's best-known engravings is the close-up *calavera* of the fashionable lady, *La catrina* (fig. 2.7). This, we could say, is a portrait, not of a particular person, but of a class of women. Posada's commentary—death overtaking wealth—is much more forceful in this near view, which allows the viewer to see how she clings to the pretensions of her upper-class standing, even beyond the grave: plumes and flowers decorate her fancy hat and ribbons adorn her bony, hairless skull.

A fascinating example of another Posada "medium shot" is a cinema-style two-shot in a skeleton composition (fig. 2.8) included in the *Corrido aquí la calavera está, señores, de*

toditos los buenos valedores (*Here Is the Calavera, Gentlemen, of All the Good Friends*, 1910). Interestingly, these figures can be found as separate subjects in other broadsides (for example, *Calavera de cupido*, 1913). Someone—Posada, Vanegas Arroyo, or the person composing the later page—realized that the two-shot image could be manipulated and re-purposed as individual CUs, prefiguring cinematic shot selection (over-the-shoulder shots) and editing (cutting from a MS two-shot to individual CUs).[24]

Another Posada MS is of the strange case of a man who was said to have a foot protruding from his side (fig. 2.9, not dated or otherwise identified). Obviously the nearer vantage point is called for in order to provide important details of the freak occurrence and to satisfy viewer curiosity.

The Classical Mexican Cinema

OFF-SCREEN SPACE: FRAMING TO IMPLY A STORY WORLD EXISTING BEYOND THE COMPOSITION

One additional feature of medium and close-up images is that their partial views insinuate a diegetic world beyond the "frame." In the shot from *Alegoría de revolucionarios* (*Allegory of the Revolutionaries*, no date) shown in fig. 2.10, we see the crouched, full body of one soldier, but only three-quarters of the wounded man he is protecting. The compact composition's limited information, together with the gaze of the soldier toward the upper right part of the composition, imply the existence of what in cinema is called "off-screen space." Another characteristic of the maturing cinematic style, the acknowledgment of and reference to off-screen space goes hand in hand with advancements in editing. Were this an image from a Golden Age film, we would expect it to be part of a scene whose progression of shots would typically begin with a LS (establishing the location), then this image, then probably glance-object cutting (the next shot might well be of the person or object holding the soldier's gaze). In addition to editing, another cinematic option from this shot would be camera movement (a pan, tilt, or tracking shot) that would also provide important information and thus be well motivated.

ENTERING THE NARRATIVE SPACE

From 1909 and throughout the 1910s, in both Hollywood cinema and, as we will see, in Rosas's *El automóvil gris*, cameras were sometimes positioned closer to the subject in order to feature details of a scene. The camera's entry into the space of the narrative is another clearly cinematic trait. A good example of Posada doing the same thing is shown in fig. 2.11, an undated, unnamed image of women who have gathered to observe conjoined twins. Viewers are placed at a very near vantage point, one that has clearly placed them inside the narrative space, perhaps even closer to the twins than the women.

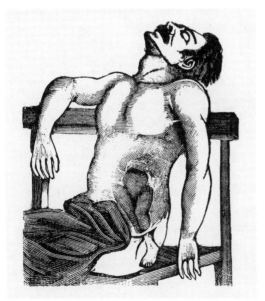

LEFT | FIG. 2.9. *El fenómeno* (*The Phenomenon*, no date). (Courtesy the Nettie Lee Benson Latin American Collection, University of Texas at Austin)

ABOVE | FIG. 2.10. *Alegoría de revolucionarios* (*Allegory of the Revolutionaries*, no date). (Courtesy the Nettie Lee Benson Latin American Collection, University of Texas at Austin)

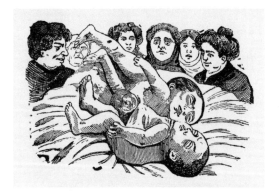

ANGLED COMPOSITIONS TO ACCENTUATE DEPTH

Two typical characteristics of early cinema compositions were their frontal, front-row-center perspective and their shallow depth, both of which drew considerably from stage conventions. By shooting actions at an angle, filmmakers began emphasizing depth, something the camera could capture but that was severely limited on the stage. While Posada, in figs. 2.4 and 2.20, for example, did sometimes rely on this head-on proscenium style, he often broke with it to compose the action on an angle, using strong diagonal lines to

add depth. The broadside image in fig. 2.12, *Los patinadores* (*The Street Cleaners*, 1890), presents the action at an angle along a receding diagonal as films would gradually begin doing, particularly in the first decade of the new century. In those early films—Edwin S. Porter's *The Great Train Robbery* (1903) is a good example—a pattern of shooting was adhered to by which interior shots maintained the frontal, flattened, proscenium perspective while exteriors were angled. Interestingly, although Posada began angling on action much earlier than cinema, as with *Los patinadores*, or with fig. 2.13, *¡Terribles y espantosísimos estragos! Habidos por la suma escasez de semillas y el terrible TIFO . . .* (*Terrible and Frightful Ravages Caused by a Grain Shortage and the Terrible Typhus . . .*, 1893), he appears to have followed the same proscenium interior/angled exterior representational practice.

MULTIPLE IMAGES TO PROVIDE SHIFTS IN TIME AND SPACE

In narrativizing events, Posada sometimes found that one image was not sufficient to relate the tale he had to tell. This is the case with fig. 2.14, from a broadside with the headline *Tristísimas lamentaciones de un enganchado para el Valle Nacional* (*Very Sad Lamentations of a Contracted Laborer at National Valley*, 1903). The broadside is an exposé of the oppression of humble Mexicans kidnapped or hired under false pretenses to work in the plantations of the Valle Nacional region, a common practice during the dictatorship of Porfirio Díaz. In a LS on the left, Posada illustrates a survivor relating his cautionary tale to a crowd of astonished listeners. Then, in an extreme LS enclosed in an oval bubble, he depicts the laborers working the fields. The broadside image provides views not only of two different locations, but also possibly of different times. (Is the balloon showing what occurred in the past? What is still occurring? Or warning his audience what may befall them in the future if they are not careful?)

A similar example is found in fig. 2.15, *Un sentenciado en capilla* (*A Prisoner in Solitary Confinement*, no date). Here there is more ambiguity (which the accompanying text, now unavailable, may have clarified). It is not clear in the leap in space and time from the main illustration to the bubble image whether the execution is that of the prisoner or the man's imagining of it. Similar problems in transmitting plot information existed in cinema as primitive narrational systems struggled with standardizing conventions (like thought and dream balloons) and ways to denote a character's thoughts as distinct from simultaneous or subsequent actions.

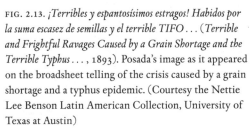

FIG. 2.13. *¡Terribles y espantosísimos estragos! Habidos por la suma escasez de semillas y el terrible TIFO . . .* (*Terrible and Frightful Ravages Caused by a Grain Shortage and the Terrible Typhus . . .*, 1893). Posada's image as it appeared on the broadsheet telling of the crisis caused by a grain shortage and a typhus epidemic. (Courtesy the Nettie Lee Benson Latin American Collection, University of Texas at Austin)

TOP | FIG. 2.14. *Tristísimas lamentaciones de un enganchado para el Valle Nacional* (*Very Sad Lamentations of a Contracted Laborer at National Valley*, 1903). (Courtesy the Nettie Lee Benson Latin American Collection, University of Texas at Austin)

BOTTOM | FIG. 2.15. *Un sentenciado en capilla* (*A Prisoner in Solitary Confinement*, no date). (Courtesy the Nettie Lee Benson Latin American Collection, University of Texas at Austin) ·

Sometimes Posada used several illustrations to tell a complex story, the equivalent of separate film shots to capture a scene. The three images in figs. 2.16 to 2.18, for example, all appeared on a two-sided broadside entitled *Gran chasco que se pegó Don Chepito Mariguana: Por andar en amores con una mujer casada* (*The Great Joke Played on Don Chepito Mariguana: Because He Pursued a Married Woman*, no date). The comical *corrido*, featuring one of Posada's recurring characters, Don Chepito, tells of his ill-fated attempts to woo a married woman. Don Chepito first flirts with her on the street (fig. 2.16), then is knocked down by the woman's husband (fig. 2.17), and is finally arrested (fig. 2.18). Of interest here is first of all Posada's rendering of sequenced events, which required him to isolate and dramatize the key incidents of the story. But beyond that is the fact that in the broadside they appeared in a different order, beginning in medias res on the front side with the image in fig. 2.17, then continuing on the back with fig. 2.16, the start of the tale, and fig. 2.18, the end of it. This order in effect creates a flashback from the middle of the narrative, then a flash-forward to its conclusion, and anticipates complex movie narratives that later would be common in cinema.

TOP | FIG. 2.16. *Gran chasco que se pegó Don Chepito Mariguana: Por andar en amores con una mujer casada* (*The Great Joke Played on Don Chepito Mariguana: Because He Pursued a Married Woman*, no date). Don Chepito declares his love. (Courtesy the Nettie Lee Benson Latin American Collection, University of Texas at Austin)

MIDDLE | FIG. 2.17. Don Chepito is accosted by the woman's husband. (Courtesy the Nettie Lee Benson Latin American Collection, University of Texas at Austin)

BOTTOM | FIG. 2.18. Don Chepito taken to jail.

The Classical Mexican Cinema

A variation of Posada's representation of sequenced events is an illustration in which he collected four different actions in successive panels, as in a comic strip. Fig. 2.19, *De nuestros dibujantes, momentos antes de los acontecimientos* (*From Our Artists, Moments before the Event*, 1903), showing the attempted theft of a clock, is an illustration Posada did for a small penny periodical called *El diablito bromista*.[25] In the first panel, a garbage collector empties a customer's household waste. In the second, he presents the bill inside to the lady of the house. When she leaves the room to get the money (panel three), he tries to steal the clock, but just then it chimes and he is caught and attacked (fourth panel).[26]

FRAMING WITH PARTIALLY SHOWN FIGURES IN THE FOREGROUND

Posada's crowd scenes generally have one interesting detail in common: they have foreground figures that are cut off by the bottom edge of the composition. For example, though one of Posada's courtroom drawings, fig. 2.20, *Jurado* (*Trial*, no date), has the typical frontality of many of his interior drawings, it varies from the proscenium style in the way the soldiers and onlookers at the bottom of the drawing are cut off above or at the waist (even the two witnesses or defendants, seen at the center bottom, are cut off at the ankles).

FIG. 2.19. *De nuestros dibujantes, momentos antes de los acontecimientos* (*From Our Artists, Moments before the Event*, 1903). (Courtesy the Nettie Lee Benson Latin American Collection, University of Texas at Austin)

Compositions like these possess several cinematic qualities. They give viewers a privileged view they could only have if they were so close to the scene that they couldn't see the entire bodies of the nearer people: that is, it positions them either within or very near to the narrative space and gives the picture documentary immediacy. In addition, the foreground figures frame the action occurring in the middle and background, thus accentuating depth in the frame and taking viewers' eyes from fore- to mid- to background. Moreover, they are composed in depth, a key characteristic of both Hollywood's and Mexico's Golden Age cinema, beginning, as we will see in the next chapter, with *El automóvil gris*. As a quick point of reference, I include a shot from the trial of the bandits at the end of *El automóvil gris* (fig. 2.21), a still that exhibits the same pictorial qualities as the Posada print.

Posada's Bequest to the Classical Mexican Cinema

In general, and at least indirectly, all Cine de Oro filmmakers owed a debt to Posada. Like him, they worked in a popular, not elitist, visual medium. They were commercial artists and their job, like his, was to create images that related stories to viewers clearly, concisely, and unambiguously. But as I mentioned at the start of this chapter, Posada's influence on Classic Mexican Cinema filmmakers, though posthumous, was much more direct and explicit. He had practiced what they sought: a way to produce work that was thoroughly Mexican in both form and content. He left behind a clear-eyed record of the entire spectrum of the turn-of-the-century Mexican experience—good, bad, and ugly. At its best, his was a tough-minded art that refused to look away. Delving into the core of Mexican life, he bore witness to all that he found. For all these reasons, when CMC moviemakers were pursuing a national film aesthetic a generation after his death, Posada was their touchstone.

Let me give some examples to draw out the sort of influence Posada had on the Classical Mexican Cinema. Although many of his

TOP | FIG. 2.20. *Jurado* (*Trial*, no date). (Courtesy the Nettie Lee Benson Latin American Collection, University of Texas at Austin)

BOTTOM | FIG. 2.21. *El automóvil gris* (1919). The trial of the robbers at the end of the film has a very similar composition to that shown in fig. 2.20.

The Classical Mexican Cinema

illustrations dealt with lurid crimes—after all, robberies, suicides, kidnappings, and murders were the penny presses' stock-in-trade[27]— occasionally more mundane wrongs were featured. And in the depiction of little-noted, everyday injustices, Posada's social critique could be scathing. For example, there is this unsettling domestic scene of a drunken man, presumably the household's husband and father, raging on as his son cowers beneath him and his wife prays to the Virgin of Guadalupe (fig. 2.22).

Compare that image with fig. 2.23, a scene of domestic abuse from Luis Buñuel's *La hija del engaño* (*Daughter of Deceit*, 1951). The similarity between the two images, right down to the men's unhinged behavior and the Virgin of Guadalupe on the walls, is striking. But despite such neat parallels, I'm not making the argument that Posada's influence on CMC filmmakers was a matter of their imitating specific details from his engravings in their films. The point I want to make is that the key link between Posada and the CMC is their shared critique of Mexican *machismo*. Both images decry Mexican patriarchy's tolerating the sort of physical, psychological, and emotional abuse depicted here. That my example comes from a Luis Buñuel film is significant, since the inanity of *machismo* was one of his favorite targets. (I'll have more to say about *La hija del engaño* in chapter 7.)

Or compare the two images in figs. 2.24 and 2.25. The first is one of many Posada engravings depicting firing squad executions, most of them capturing the moment of death. This one, however, focuses on a painful scene just before the execution, when the prisoner's disconsolate family holds on to their father and husband. Fig. 2.25 is from the tragic

TOP | FIG. 2.22. *Woman Praying to the Virgin of Guadalupe as Her Husband Rages Madly.* This image was also known as *Milagro de la Virgen de Guadalupe* (*Miracle of the Virgin of Guadalupe*), which interprets the scene as the Virgin's miraculous appearance at the wife's time of need; see Berdecio and Appelbaum, 32, 149. (Courtesy the Nettie Lee Benson Latin American Collection, University of Texas at Austin)

BOTTOM | FIG. 2.23. Domestic abuse in Luis Buñuel's *La hija del engaño* (*Daughter of Deceit*, 1951). A daughter tries to prevent her abusive, alcoholic father from whipping her stepsister.

climax of Emilio Fernández's first major hit, *Flor silvestre* (1943). The main male character, José Luis (Pedro Armendáriz), is about to be executed by order of a bandit leader. It is interrupted when his wife (Dolores del Río), carrying their baby boy in her arms, rushes to his side. She is forcibly pulled away and José Luis is killed.

TOP | FIG. 2.24. *Fusilamiento del capitán Calapiz* (*Execution of Captain Calapiz*). (Courtesy the Nettie Lee Benson Latin American Collection, University of Texas at Austin)

BOTTOM | FIG. 2.25. The tragic ending of Emilio Fernández's *Flor silvestre* (1943). Just before José Luis (Pedro Armendáriz) is killed by a bandit firing squad, his wife, Esperanza (Dolores del Río), holds their baby boy in one arm and clings to her husband with the other. She must be forcibly torn from his side before the execution can proceed.

Once again there is a compositional affinity between the two depictions, which in this case was neither indirect nor coincidental, but explicit. According to the film's cinematographer, Gabriel Figueroa, this execution scene was directly "inspired by José Guadalupe Posada" (though he doesn't refer to any specific engraving).[28] And once again, I want to emphasize their shared critical perspective. Both explore the uncomfortable spectacle of death to reveal the pain involved in any killing; this is especially true for Fernández, who extends the scene considerably. With such a protracted, graphic treatment of the execution, Fernández was using the form and feeling of a familiar Posada motif to express one of the great themes of CMC films—the consequences of the revolution's brutality on succeeding generations. Furthermore, both instances raise what became a major question for the CMC: To what degree does such savagery define the Mexican character?

The Classical Mexican Cinema

I will continue the story of the emergence of the CMC in the next chapter by discussing how Mexican film went from its twenty-year-long documentary stage to the creation of its first masterpiece, a fictionalized version of a real-life crime spree entitled *El automóvil gris* (1919). I will analyze director Enrique Rosas's style and argue that it was a complex synthesis of five different influences: four national cinemas (Mexico's documentaries plus Hollywood, Italian, and French fiction films) along with the penny press graphic arts tradition of Posada. As I make my case, I will show that the development of Mexican cinema in general and the Classical Mexican Cinema in particular involved a mix of imitation, innovation, and inspiration.

CHAPTER 3

Enrique Rosas's
El automóvil gris (1919)
and the Dawning of
Modern Mexican
Cinema

—

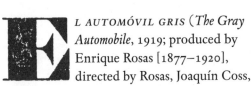L AUTOMÓVIL GRIS (*The Gray Automobile*, 1919; produced by Enrique Rosas [1877–1920], directed by Rosas, Joaquín Coss, and Juan Canals de Homs) is one of the few surviving examples of Mexican silent narrative film, and has been called "the most famous [Mexican] movie of the period."[1] Originally released as a twelve-episode serial with an estimated running length of between three and four hours, it was based on a notorious series of robberies that occurred in Mexico City in 1915. These crimes were unusual because of the robbers' distinctive modus operandi. Taking advantage of the chaos brought on by the Mexican Revolution, the thieves disguised themselves as soldiers and displayed signed search warrants to gain entry to the houses of some of the wealthiest families in Mexico City. They terrorized the inhabitants, robbed them, and made their escape in a gray Fiat.[2]

Though it is the first Mexican docudrama, *El automóvil gris*'s re-creation of actual events is impressive. It was based on two sources: newspaper accounts of the affair by Miguel Nicoechea, a reporter who covered the crimes; and case notes taken by Juan Manuel Cabrera, the assistant chief of police for the military's Special Services, who was in charge of the investigation and was said to have made most of the arrests in the case.[3] Nicoechea and Cabrera coscripted the film with Rosas, and Cabrera played himself in the film. Furthermore, according to the film's prologue, it was shot in the locations where the events had occurred.[4] Finally—and most dramatically—rather than staging the climactic execution of six of the bandits, Rosas, who oversaw the editing, inserted documentary footage of the actual firing squad execution, which he himself had photographed in 1915.[5]

This canny combination of authenticity and sensationalism appealed to audiences, contributing to the film's enormous popularity. When it was released in December 1919, it broke all of Mexico's established box office records, including those for most theaters to exhibit the same film on one day (19), most single-day admissions (40,233), and biggest opening day outside of Mexico City (4,012 pesos, in Veracruz).[6]

After the coming of sound, the serial was re-edited twice, in 1933 and 1937. Dialogue, music, and sound effects were added, and it was condensed to feature length (reportedly 111 minutes, though the DVD of the film, issued by the National University of Mexico [UNAM], runs 105 minutes). This renewed its popularity, extended its exhibition life, and made it one of the longest-running, most-viewed films in Mexican cinema history.[7] In the process, however, this reconstruction completely destroyed the original. In order to conform to emergent two-hour feature-length norms, Rosas's heirs deleted scenes, characters, plot threads, and the entire last episode. What remains for today's viewers can be confusing, especially if they are not familiar with the events depicted.[8] And as far as is known, the excised elements from the serial version are gone, making the reconstruction of the original impossible.

But even given all the problems with the film that survives, it remains a seminal text in which a number of formative cinematic currents converge, making it crucial to the understanding of the development of Mexican cinema. To begin with, because of its subject matter, it conveniently satisfied the nationalistic urge emerging in Mexican arts at the time. Moreover, *El automóvil gris* contains an early expression of twin themes—the corruption of revolutionary ideals and the accompanying remorse over the loss of the unique opportunity the revolution afforded—that would haunt the nation's cinema for the next seven decades.[9] Additionally, the symbiotic relationship between political leaders and the film's producer set a precedent for state involvement in motion picture production that characterizes Mexican filmmaking to this day.[10]

Furthermore, *El automóvil gris* holds a unique place in Mexican film history as the crucial link between Mexico's turn-of-the-century image making—Posada's illustrations and the early documentaries—and the Golden Age cinema that arose in the 1930s. At the same time, Rosas was borrowing from other national cinematic traditions. Formally, then, *El automóvil gris* resulted from the blending of these five influences:

1. the visual storytelling system established by Posada's penny press illustrations;
2. Mexico's rich documentary tradition, which thrived for the first twenty years of the nation's film history by feeding its audience's appetite for images of Mexican current events;
3. Italian cinema, known for its melo-dramas, attention to period detail, and mobile camera;
4. French cinema, especially, in the case of *El automóvil gris*, the crime serials of

Georges Feuillade (such as *Fantômas* [1913–1914], *Les vampires* [1915–1916], *Judex* [1916], and *La nouvelle mission de Judex* [1917]), with their extensive use of location shooting and fast-paced cops-and-robbers narratives; and

5. the emerging Hollywood paradigm, with its goal-driven protagonist, causally linked narrative, and evolving rules of editing, lighting, and shooting based on character psychology.

The merging of these disparate influences made it possible for Mexico's narrative film to keep pace with European and American filmmaking in the 1910s, despite Mexican cinema's near-exclusive concentration on documentary production. Instead of finding itself hopelessly behind other national cinemas in the world, Mexican filmmaking— spurred by talented filmmakers like Rosas— proved nimble and inventive enough to catch up by 1919, and seemed poised to enter a silent golden age.

One of my goals here is to detail the complex story of the evolution of Mexican film from its inception to the Golden Age. This is necessary because at first glance it may appear that, stylistically at least, Mexico's Cine de Oro arose by simply imitating U.S. film and becoming a Spanish version of Hollywood. It's true that after the coming of sound many Golden Age films (the Mainstream Mexican Cinema) were formally identical to U.S. movies. However, as this chapter will show, the way that Mexican films arrived at that style was complicated—combining, as I've said, influences from five sources, only one of which was Hollywood. In the time between the release of *El automóvil gris* in 1919

and the first flowering of the Golden Age more than a decade later, four of those five vanished, leaving the Hollywood paradigm as the best—and only—remaining option. I will discuss how this came to pass at the end of this chapter, after undertaking a formal analysis of *El automóvil gris*. But first we must familiarize ourselves with the beginnings of movies in Mexico, with the infamous "gray car" crimes themselves, and with the production of the film.

Mexican Film Culture, 1896–1917

Owing to a distinct set of factors, Mexico's cinema development was unique. As I mentioned in chapter 2, one key difference was that until 1916, Mexican films were almost exclusively documentaries. Representatives of the Lumière brothers shot and exhibited their *actualités* (brief documentaries) in Mexico in 1896, and when Mexican film entrepreneurs like Salvador Toscano Barragán and Enrique Rosas began producing their own films, they found a lively market for such views of the nation. In contrast, both European and North American cinemas would gradually gravitate toward narrative; in the case of U.S. films, this was especially true after 1907.[11] And while these foreign films commanded more and more attention from filmgoers in Mexico, apart from a few isolated attempts at *el filme de argumento*, Mexican cinema production remained a resolutely documentary practice.[12] The onset of the Mexican Revolution (1910–1920) only bolstered this trend, as newsreel footage brought the civil war to life for thousands of Mexican spectators.

But interest diminished after 1915, and by 1916 revolutionary documentaries were almost completely absent from Mexican movie screens.[13] What caused the decline? For one thing, by this time documentaries were chronicling a revolution that Mexicans were growing increasingly tired of. For another, the availability of European films was dwindling because of World War I. Energetic Hollywood entertainments—comedies, chase films, melodramas—took up the slack and increased their Mexican market share. But the rising prominence of American films was not without its problems. Often captivated by Hollywood cinema, Mexican viewers were also distressed by its derogatory representation of Mexico and Mexicans.[14] Such imagery helped foster the desire to create a national cinema that could compete with Hollywood on the one hand and counter negative images on the other. An additional factor leading to the decline of the nonfiction film may have been the impression on the part of Mexican moviegoers that documentaries were far from impartial and had turned into political propaganda for those in power.[15] For all these reasons, Mexican viewers' growing appetite for narrative films together with their waning interest in newsreels provided the catalyst for the rise of Mexican narrative filmmaking.

El automóvil gris was only the thirty-ninth Mexican feature (defined as a film longer than forty minutes) produced in Mexico, and only the twenty-fourth narrative film.[16] Still, it demonstrated a sure grasp of narrative and a sophisticated understanding of cinematic form. In large measure this was due to the filmmaking expertise of Enrique Rosas, a former newsreel cinematographer, producer, and exhibitor who was not only the film's codirector but also its producer, coscriptwriter, cinematographer, chief editor,

and promoter. For Rosas, *El automóvil gris* was the perfect vehicle for making the transition to longer form narrative filmmaking. Because of his extensive background in reportage, it is hard to imagine a more suitable project than the cinematic reconstruction of the scandalous case of "la banda del automóvil gris" (the Gray Car Gang).

The Infamous Impostors in
the Gray Getaway Car
—

The wave of thefts and assaults that served as the basis for Rosas's film began in April 1915. According to published accounts, the robberies were extremely lucrative for the thieves, netting them jewels, clothes, and cash. At one house, they stole 200,000 pesos, at another 78,000 pesos' worth of bank notes. But the assaults could turn extremely violent, sometimes deadly. Just after midnight on May 25, for example, Manuel Taliabue surprised two gang members as they were about to break into a house. They killed Taliabue, robbed him, and proceeded to enter the house. There they murdered a young boy in front of his mother and sister.[17] The gang's activities lasted several months, until eighteen alleged members, accomplices, and associates were arrested, tried, and variously pardoned, imprisoned, or executed in December of that same year.[18]

The criminals exploited the disorder caused by the revolution, as rival factions fought over control of the government and the capital city, which changed hands five times in the first five years of the revolt. In the year the robberies took place, 1915, the government—and the capital—was controlled first by Emiliano Zapata, and then by his rival, Venustiano Carranza, whose counter-revolutionary forces gained control in August.[19]

The bandits' successful operation during the rule of two opposing leaders is significant because of the widely held suspicion that the outlaws were in league with high-level government officials. This was based on the bandits' possession of two signs of authority that gave them carte blanche: authentic military uniforms and signed and sealed search warrants. Thus one of the most fascinating elements of the case, and one that added to the notoriety of the crimes as well as to the success of the film, is completely lost to modern viewers—the belief that the thieves were associated with government officers of two competing regimes. And though it is not clear how high the government cooperation went, there was in fact some government complicity.[20]

Whether or not this collusion led to police negligence in the pursuit and capture of the gang is unknown, but the investigation was hampered by other factors. Chief among them was that Mexico City's infrastructure had, for all intents and purposes, collapsed. For example, because of a coal shortage, the capital's city council ordered that streetlights be lit only from 7 to 10 p.m. This allowed the band an ideal cover for their crimes: pretending to be protecting the peace, they could ride the dark streets late at night unimpeded.

But there was mounting public pressure to find the criminals, and, all things considered, arrests were expeditiously made. By June 1, four ringleaders had been captured. Here fate, in the form of the shifting winds of the revolution, intervened. General Pablo González, the leader of Carranza's troops,

engaged Zapata's army several times in June and July within Mexico City's limits. During one of those battles, the jail and penitentiary were damaged, and all the prisoners, including the band members, escaped. This led to a second round of Gray Car Gangster robberies.

When General González finally occupied Mexico City for Carranza in August 1915, he found a weary citizenry on the verge of starvation and a society on the brink of collapse. His occupation did not improve the situation. Carranza's soldiers were probably feared more than they were respected by *capitalinos*, because renegade military units were known to sack houses almost at will. Higinio Granda, a member of the original gang, exploited the general lawlessness and the pervading ambivalence toward authority for his own ends; he headed a new gang that began its criminal activities soon after González's occupation. The chief of Special Services of the military police probably aided them by providing search warrants signed by General González. As a result, rumors began spreading that González was the evil genius behind the gang's operations. Some even claimed that his lover, stage diva and movie star Mimi Derba, wore stolen jewelry.[21]

This second series of robberies lasted from August until December 12, 1915, when Federal District police arrested thirteen male and five female suspects in the case. Although more suspects would be arrested in the following days, including Rafael Mercadante, Granda's second-in-command, Granda would not be among them (he was arrested and imprisoned nine months later). A few were not implicated and were released. The five women, evidently the lovers of some of the gang members, were sentenced to ten years in prison; the remaining ten men were sentenced to death. At the last minute General González pardoned four of the condemned prisoners, including Mercadante; the remaining six were executed by firing squad on December 20.

The Production and Release of
El automóvil gris
—

The major shift in the Mexican filmmaking paradigm that occurred in 1916–17, away from documentary and toward narrative, called for a corresponding change in the Mexican mode of production. No longer could a single enterprising individual like Rosas fulfill all the necessary roles of producer, cinematographer, distributor, and promoter. Narrative films required the collaboration of specialists in a number of key areas: acting, writing, cinematography, editing, directing, and producing, as well as set design, construction, and art decoration. The entrepreneurs who made the first Mexican cinema were forced either to leave the business or, like Enrique Rosas, to join with others to form production companies.

Together with singer and stage star Mimi Derba, Rosas formed Azteca Films in 1917. General González, romantically involved with Derba at the time, was a silent partner. Azteca Films was a significant enough concern to have its own studio and to release five melodramas in 1917. These films were evidently influenced by Italy's "diva genre," "stories of passion and intrigue in upper-middle-class and aristocratic settings."[22] Rosas photographed them and Derba starred in four of the five, and they shared creative duties,

both contributing as screenwriter, producer, director, and editor. Evidently the films didn't do well commercially and the company's production of narrative movies ceased soon afterward. Derba returned to the stage, and Rosas returned to making documentaries. For example, he released one on the assassination of Zapata in April 1919, a week after the rebel leader was killed.[23]

Rosas had already begun shooting *El automóvil gris* in March of that year, having once again secured the backing of General González. Drawing on the experiences of Nicoechea and Cabrera, he had written the script with the poet Juan Manuel Ramos.[24] Filming continued until November, and the film was released on December 11, 1919. Though it appears that he was assisted in directing by two of the actors, Joaquín Coss (who played one of the victims, Vicente González, who pursues the gang with the police) and Juan Canals de Homs (who played the gang leader, Granda), Rosas is the film's auteur, since as producer he personally contributed to and oversaw all stages of the production: creative (scripting and directing), technical (shooting and editing), financial, and promotional.[25] But his artistic autonomy was compromised, first by his association with General González, and second by Carranza's government.

In 1919, González was entertaining presidential ambitions. Probably not coincidentally, on the very day that *El automóvil gris* premiered in Mexico City, he accepted the candidacy in the upcoming elections. Naturally, González would have wanted to set the record straight with a filmed illustration not only of his innocence but also of his active pursuit, capture, and punishment of the gang. No doubt Rosas was eager to demonstrate that his friend and business associate was in no way implicated in the crimes. He had already produced a documentary film in 1916 celebrating González (which included the same execution footage that concludes *El automóvil gris*),[26] so it is not surprising that *El automóvil gris* exonerates González by showing that Granda acted independently of high-ranking government officials. This is demonstrated in one fictionalized sequence where Granda refers to a mastermind who planned and coordinated the gang's activities from a secret office. But this "Mr. Big" is later revealed to be merely a mannequin in a back room, thus "proving" that Granda acted alone.[27]

Political exigencies and governmental censorship—either direct or indirect—must also have colored Rosas's film. In subtle ways, the responsibility for the crimes was shifted to the Zapata regime. For one thing, the eleven gang robberies were condensed to five, with three of them occurring during the Zapata era (though official records revealed that of the eleven robberies, five occurred during Zapata's rule and six during Carranza's). For another, *la banda*'s escape from prison was portrayed as resulting from a deliberate act of the retreating Zapata troops ("On their way out of the capital," a title card relates, "the Zapatista forces open the penitentiary doors") rather than from the random vicissitudes of war.[28] Moreover, the film glosses over the military abuses of the Carranza era. General González and the other Carranzista officials were depicted as proactive investigators, the police as tireless public servants. Furthermore, in the film's version of events, the search warrants used by the gangsters

were fraudulent, which was not the case in actuality. The reconstruction of the film in the 1930s blurred and diminished some of this propagandizing. González's influence had declined considerably since 1919 (he was not elected president), and his role in the sound version of *El automóvil gris* was reduced to a single scene in which he was not identified. Overall, however, the sound-era feature version maintained the positive depiction of the Carranza government.

Rosas, who knew the value of well-orchestrated ballyhoo, announced in September that the film he was preparing would be unprecedented in Mexican cinema: a serial with forty-five episodes requiring three successive evenings of screenings. Though the twelve-episode serial that he actually released by year's end was much more modest, it was quite an accomplishment nonetheless.[29] Along the way, Rosas also had to fight off competition from distributors and exhibitors who were eager to capitalize on the well-known case of "*la banda del automóvil gris*." Consequently, a flurry of films were released with that or similar titles in the fall of 1919. The most serious challenge came from another enterprising Mexican filmmaker, Germán Camus, whose company began filming its own serial. Since the film no longer exists, it is difficult to say how similar it was, but based on the chapter titles (for example, "The Robbery of the Banker's House"), Camus's appears to be a thinly disguised knockoff of Rosas's serial. The two films were even scripted by the same screenwriter, Juan Manuel Ramos. Though Rosas tried to shut down Camus's project through legal means, he was unsuccessful. Camus's film, entitled *La banda del automóvil* (*La dama enlutada*) (*The*

Automobile Gang, or *The Lady in Mourning*), was finished and exhibited on September 11, well before Rosas's was completed and, from all indications, had a successful run.[30]

In addition, a twelve-episode Vitagraph serial, *The Scarlet Runner* (1916), was being distributed by Jacobo Granat under the title *El automóvil gris* (*The Gray Automobile*). Rosas immediately published an announcement that Granat's *El automóvil gris* was a U.S. film that had nothing to do with the nefarious crimes of 1915 and was in violation of patent laws, and that Rosas's "real" *Automóvil gris* would soon be available for viewing. When the exhibition of the U.S. film with the title *El automóvil gris* was suspended by a judge's order, Rosas may have thought he was vindicated. But the crafty Granat responded by simply changing the name of the American serial to *El automóvil rojo* (*The Red Automobile*).[31]

In order to appreciate the pivotal role *El automóvil gris* played in the evolution of Mexican cinema, let me briefly place it and Mexican filmmaking in general within the context of the development of film in the U.S. and Europe, the two major competing film traditions in the 1910s. With that in hand, we can then begin an analysis of the formal characteristics of Rosas's film.

El automóvil gris and the Development of Mexican Narrative Film
—

The first years of American and European cinema were characterized by non-narrative *actualités*. Throughout the early 1900s, these short documentary "views" gradually gave way to narrative films. In large measure, the first story movies adhered to the theatrical, proscenium-arch filmmaking tradition, recording the action from a stiff, front-row-center vantage point. Beginning around 1909 and lasting through most of the next decade, movies moved into a transitional stage where filmmakers left theatrical influences behind and explored more cinematic narration by utilizing staging, camera placement, and editing. This evolved into a classical stage, which began in the late 1910s in the U.S. and by the early 1920s in Europe. On both continents, narrative film development that eventually blossomed into classicism was the result of an extensive process of trial and error from 1895 to 1917 as filmmakers first produced thousands of short *actualités*, followed by a steady stream of split-reel, one-reel, two-reel, serial, and feature films.[32]

Mexican cinema leapfrogged to roughly the same point in its narrative filmmaking evolution at around the same time, and *El automóvil gris* was the reason. Rosas's achievement was remarkable, especially given that Mexican filmmaking had so much catching up to do. After all, Mexico had produced far fewer films, most of them short documentaries, and, by 1919, only two dozen story films. Moreover, the nation's filmmaking was steeped in a well-established tradition of journalistic—not fictional—narration that included Posada's prints and newsreels by Rosas and other Mexican documentarians. But Rosas had to have been a student of film—as well as a quick study—and rapidly absorbed the narrational lessons of Italian, French, and American cinema. The result of that mix was his production of *El automóvil gris*, a long-form narrative film that conformed very well to contemporary cinematic storytelling norms in 1919.

Looking at the trajectory of the nation's film history, we can divide the evolution of Mexican cinema into three stages of its own, all drastically different from the American and European experiences. The initial documentary phase lasted two decades (1896–1916). The next, transitional, stage was short (1917–23) and heavily affected by Italian cinema, represented by films such as the Rosas-Derba melodramas,[33] and by another key European influence, the French serials of Louis Feuillade. Though the third stage, the Cine de Oro (the Golden Age, 1936–56), began nearly a decade after the end of the second, it was ushered in by *El automóvil gris*. Linking Mexico's second and third stages, Rosas's docudrama is a watershed Mexican film that exhibits all five of the formative cinematic influences—penny press illustrations, early documentary reportage, the melodramatic strain of Italian cinema, the vitality of Feuillade's French crime serials, and some of the conventions of Hollywood's burgeoning narrative paradigm.

El automóvil gris consolidated all the narrative gains made by Mexican cinema up to the end of the 1910s, and at the same time set the stage for the Cine de Oro era that was to follow. Its full effect, however, was delayed and blunted because Mexican film production declined precipitously in the mid-1920s, practically disappearing by the end of the decade. Consequently, the third phase of Mexican filmmaking would not materialize until the national cinema was revived by the arrival of sound in the early 1930s. One way to appreciate how Mexican cinema built on the advancements of *El automóvil gris* and used it as a springboard to arrive at its Golden Age is to compare its formal characteristics with those of the European film style of the 1910s, represented by Feuillade's serials, together with some of the stylistic and narrative characteristics enumerated by Kristin Thompson

and David Bordwell in their description of Hollywood's classical stage.[34]

In order to avoid the ethnocentric trap of positing Hollywood or European cinema as formal ideals to which Mexican cinema was obliged to conform to earn legitimacy, I will organize my comments around the question of narrative intelligibility. Since record numbers of Mexican viewers—familiar with Mexican documentaries as well as U.S. and European fiction films—obviously made sense of the film, it seems fair to ask how and by what cinematic means this clear transmission of narrative information was achieved. My one caveat is that I am forced to make my analysis based on the fragments that remain: the feature version of *El automóvil gris*; an incomplete draft of the original treatment;[35] contemporary accounts of the film; a few short fragments from the serial included on the DVD; and stills from the serial (many of which are promotional production photographs and not frame enlargements from the actual film) that may offer clues to omitted scenes.

Obviously, there are pitfalls here. To begin with, we cannot know if the missing sequences in the treatment were ever scripted, or, if written, ever filmed. Furthermore, the shooting script prepared from the treatment is lost; presumably it would have incorporated numerous changes that remain unknown to us. Finally, an incident's inclusion in the treatment does not necessarily mean it found its way into the finished script, that it was filmed, and if filmed was part of the released serial.

On the positive side of the ledger is that, on the whole, the integrity of the original serial seems to persist in the surviving feature. Although some threads of the narrative were deleted and others abbreviated during the re-editing and sonorization process, the basic story is intact and is presented in the same order. And though some shots are extremely brief, making it appear that they may have been trimmed or that frames from the original were lost, it's highly unlikely that any new footage was shot or added when the sound version was made. Thus, the 644 shots that comprise the extant feature film most likely exhibit enough of the cinematic characteristics of Rosas's original for us to judge the state of Mexican cinema in 1919.

The Poetics of *El automóvil gris*
—

BLENDING HOLLYWOOD CONTINUITY AND EUROPEAN TABLEAU STYLES

According to de los Reyes, just before making *El automóvil gris* Rosas had learned Hollywood's recent advancements in film language. Particularly, I would say, he learned the basics of the emerging continuity style, which utilized analytical editing to break a scene into separate shots. On a trip to New York in 1917, Rosas realized that if he wanted to export his films successfully he would need to adopt some of Hollywood's storytelling techniques.[36] And he would have been able to study the latest developments in Hollywood filmmaking closely by watching two exemplars of the emerging paradigm—D. W. Griffith's *The Birth of a Nation* (1915) and *Intolerance* (1916), both of which were released in Mexico in 1918.[37] As we will soon see, in *El automóvil gris* Rosas ably employed the principles of the incipient American continuity system.

But not exclusively. Rosas was also deeply influenced by Feuillade's crime serials, and used elements of the French filmmaker's style

too. This is interesting because, as Bordwell has shown, Feuillade employed a narrational method that was different from Hollywood's continuity style. Rather than break a scene into separate shots, following Hollywood's far-to-near, LS-MS-CU analytical shooting and editing pattern, the makers of Europe's transitional 1910s films opted for longer takes with much less cutting and, in interior scenes especially, played out "most of the action . . . in a single orienting view, called in France the *tableau*." Bordwell defines the characteristics of the European tableau style:

> The nearest characters would be framed from the thighs or knees up. The director might cut in a close-up to show a letter or newspaper article or visiting card, since such items were too small to read in a master view. At a point of intense drama there might be a medium shot of a character's reaction. Such a cut-in would probably be axial—that is, taken right along the lens axis of the tableau framing rather than from the oblique angles on display in many American scenes.[38]

Although they might be considered competing and in some ways oppositional narrational methods, Rosas mixed both continuity and tableau styles in *El automóvil gris*.

Indeed, there are many signs of the Feuillade influence on *El automóvil gris*. And it's perfectly understandable on many levels. To begin with, there were so many similarities between Feuillade's films and the events of the gray car gang story that it made perfect sense for Rosas to use the crime serials as a kind of narrative and stylistic template. In several respects, *la banda del automóvil gris* was a true-life version of "Les Vampires," the nefarious fictional criminal gang who are the villains in Feuillade's ten-part serial of the same name released in 1915–1916 (fig. 3.1). Like Les Vampires, the Mexico City band preyed on the wealthy, used clever disguises, and struck quickly and without warning. The dual crime fighters were also alike: the good guys in *Les vampires* are an intrepid newspaper reporter and his comic sidekick; in *El automóvil gris*, they are the chief of police and Sr. González, a victim-turned-volunteer vigilante. And like Feuillade, Rosas would shoot in real locations, which is a great part of the charm of both films.

But beyond that, I believe Rosas was simply a Feuillade fan. As a moviegoer and a filmmaking professional, he no doubt delighted in the exuberant dynamism of Feuillade's films, in the unexpected twists and turns of the stories, and in their seemingly endless rooftop escapes, car chases, and improbable last-minute rescues. Rosas's eagerness to apply many such devices in his serial raises the question of how much he played with history in making *El automóvil gris*. Nevertheless, there was a definite "Feuillade effect" evident in his serial. Two of the more striking ones are illustrated in figs. 3.2–3.5.

FIG. 3.1. The "Feuillade effect" in *El automóvil gris* (1919). Higinio Granda (Juan Canals de Homs, center), the gang's leader, asks *banda* members to take a pledge of allegiance by placing their hands above his pistol before going on their first job. In its organization and method of operation, the gray car gang resembled a real-life Mexican version of the fictional criminals in Feuillade's *Les Vampires* (1915–16).

TOP | FIG. 3.2. *Les vampires*. In one of several rooftop escapes, one of the vampires, dressed in his stealthy, all-black vampire outfit, and his female accomplice, Irma Vep (Musidora), disguised as a maid, make their getaway.

BOTTOM | FIG. 3.3. *El automóvil gris*. One of the incarcerated prisoners, Francisco Olviedo (Ángel Esquivel), attempts to escape the penitentiary from its rooftop, but encounters a sentry at the outer wall.

The Modified Continuity Style: Analytical Editing

Sometimes, Rosas follows the analytical editing pattern. Such scenes typically begin with a long shot (LS) or medium long shot (MLS) to establish location. As the scene proceeds, there eventually is a medium close-up (MCU) and sometimes a full close-up (CU), usually of one key character as he or she speaks or notices something. Then there is a return to the original LS or MLS to close the scene. A scene near the end of the film where one of the robbers is brought before the chief of police shows Rosas's adherence to this basic shot progression (figs. 3.6–3.9).

A longer scene is a good example of a slightly more complex use of the Hollywood continuity style, and shows how Rosas mixed it with elements of the European tableau style. It's a sequence of five shots from a scene earlier in the film, again in the police chief's office. Vicente González, one of the gang's victims, is going over some details with the Zapata-era detectives when he discovers that one of the bandits, Granda, is working for the police.

The scene opens with a long MLS take [length in minutes:seconds, 1:08] in the detective's office. Granda's assistant is alone in the room, rifling through the detective's desk. Using his key to open a drawer, he takes out several sheets and then stamps them with a seal from the desktop. Granda enters (fig. 3.10) and the assistant shows him the forged search warrants he's stealing for the gang's use. The chief inspector enters frame left and asks Granda's assistant to open the door. As the inspector sits at his desk, a group of agents enter, including Granda, who stands on the right, framed by the doorway. González enters frame left and shows some papers to the chief inspector (fig. 3.11).

So far, the scene has adhered to the tableau system, but it will shift to the continuity style when Rosas cuts to a MCU of González as he spots Granda (fig. 3.12). Rosas cuts to a MCU reaction shot of Granda realizing he's been discovered (fig. 3.13). But though Rosas has shifted to the continuity style, he uses the tableau method for cutting in to a closer shot. That is, the tighter shots of González and Granda are axial MSS. Rosas moved the camera

LEFT | FIGS. 3.6–3.9. One of the captured thieves, Chao (Manuel de los Ríos), is brought into the police chief's office. Here Rosas follows what was becoming the standard Hollywood continuity shot progression: LS—MS—CU (or MCU) with a slight difference. To end the scene, Rosas pulls back to the MS, rather than all the way back to the first establishing LS.

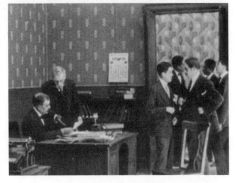

ABOVE | FIGS. 3.10 AND 3.11. *El automóvil gris.* Two frames from the scene's long initial take.

MIDDLE | FIG. 3.13. [:03] MCU. Granda realizes González has spotted him. It's evident that this is an axial cut because he is still framed by the open office door, as he was in the wider shot.

BOTTOM | FIG. 3.14. [:12]. Rosas cuts back to a MLS, which appears to be slightly closer than the one in fig. 3.11. González attacks Granda, who takes out his pistol and fires, but the shot is wild. The other agents hold Granda while González explains that he is one of the bandits.

closer but stayed on the invisible axis line between the camera lens and González from the wider shot.[39] In the Hollywood continuity system, cut-ins were typically shot from an angle off that axis line, usually 30 degrees off of the lens-subject axis.[40]

Rosas now pulls back to a shot that appears slightly closer to the actors than the original MLS to show González's reaction: he suddenly pounces on Granda, who fights back, pulls his pistol and fires (fig. 3.14). After the two are separated and Granda is disarmed, González explains his actions by identifying Granda as the leader of the gang (figs. 3.15–3.16).

Tableau Style: Staging in Depth with Long Takes

Like a European filmmaker, Rosas sometimes moved his actors to alter the nature of the shot without resorting to editing. By blocking the actors toward (or away from) a static camera, Rosas could, for example, transform a LS into a MS (or vice versa). A good example of his use of the tableau style comes during the robbery of González's house. To force González to tell where his money is hidden, Granda and his accomplices take him out to the patio and threaten to kill him. In a LS and in one long take (52 seconds), González is given an ultimatum and then blindfolded and readied for execution (fig. 3.17). Suddenly Mercadante, Granda's second-in-command, pulls Granda aside to suggest torturing González instead. Without cutting to a different shot, Rosas has the two walk into the foreground—and into a MS—as they discuss the matter, while the other gangsters and González remain in the background (fig. 3.18). Once Granda agrees, they join the others, walking back into a LS.

The Classical Mexican Cinema

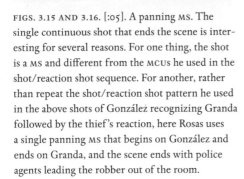

FIGS. 3.15 AND 3.16. [:05]. A panning MS. The single continuous shot that ends the scene is interesting for several reasons. For one thing, the shot is a MS and different from the MCUs he used in the shot/reaction shot sequence. For another, rather than repeat the shot/reaction shot pattern he used in the above shots of González recognizing Granda followed by the thief's reaction, here Rosas uses a single panning MS that begins on González and ends on Granda, and the scene ends with police agents leading the robber out of the room.

FIGS. 3.17 AND 3.18. Tableau style. In a single unedited shot, Granda has Sr. González blindfolded and is about to give the order for his men to execute him when Mercadante halts the proceedings. They walk into the foreground, creating a MS where Mercadante proposes suspending González from his thumbs to make him talk.

FRAMES WITHIN THE FRAME

A time-honored practice in art and graphic design, a frame inside the larger picture frame adds visual interest, directs the viewer's eye by isolating a particular part of the frame, and increases the sense of depth in the composition. Of course, to a certain extent such framing is unavoidable—in the course of narrative events, characters will naturally walk under archways, pass through doorways, and look out of windows. But Rosas had a good eye for composition and staged action within existing frames (doorways, windows, gate entrances, archways) in an organic way to direct viewer attention (as we saw in fig. 3.10, where he highlighted Granda by placing him within a doorway frame) as well as accentuate depth (figs. 3.19–3.24). As we will see in the next three chapters, it's a practice that would also be employed in slightly different ways by Fernando de Fuentes, Emilio Fernández, and Luis Buñuel, assisted by the cinematographer they shared, Gabriel Figueroa.

FIGS. 3.19 AND 3.20. In a shot that also utilizes the long-take tableau style staging, Rosas frames Sr. González arriving at the entrance of the police building in a LS and asking directions to the chief's office in a MS.

FIGS. 3.21 AND 3.22. *Top*, the band loading up the stolen goods. *Bottom*, the chief of police on the trail of the gang.

INCORPORATION OF LOCAL COLOR

Rosas was not only a gifted filmmaker but also an experienced film exhibitor who knew what Mexican movie audiences responded to. The enduring success of Mexican documentaries, several of which he filmed, promoted, and exhibited (he projected films in *carpas* [theatrical tent shows] as early as 1899, and he opened his own nickelodeon in 1908),[41] confirmed one thing: Mexican audiences liked seeing Mexico on the screen. Thus *El automóvil gris* included sequences shot in Puebla, Ápam, and Almoloya, as police tracked down fleeing gang members (fig. 3.25). While some of these scenes were motivated by the facts of the case, others, particularly an extended, to-the-death cockfight near the end of the film (fig. 3.26), seem to be included mainly for their value as Mexican spectacle. In the bargain, such scenes helped validate local folkways and boost national pride. As early Mexican cinema struggled to differentiate itself from Hollywood and European film, such sequences stamped *El automóvil gris* as uniquely *mexicano*.

The Classical Mexican Cinema

REVERTING TO REPORTAGE: DOCUMENTING—NOT DRAMATIZING— THE EXECUTION AND THE REFUSAL TO LOOK AWAY

As has been noted, a major selling point of the serial and feature versions of *El automóvil gris* was Rosas's decision to include the documentary footage he himself had shot of the 1915 execution of the gray car gang (figs. 3.27 and 3.28). The executions provide a somber, crime-does-not-pay ending for the film, of course, and using the actual filmed recording of the deaths rather than re-enacting them

with actors makes for an even more sobering conclusion. But in using the documentary footage, Rosas included a grisly but routine detail of executions seldom seen in staged re-enactments—the coup de grâce. After the first volley of shots by the firing squad, the soldiers approach the wounded prisoners and shoot them point-blank in the head or heart to ensure that they are dead.

FIGS. 3.23 AND 3.24. *Top*, a priest ministers to one of the incarcerated prisoners, Risco (Carlos E. González), in a room that serves as a makeshift confessional. *Bottom*, a variation of the frame-within-the-frame technique, bookending, in which elements of the composition, in this case beer bottles on either side of the prisoner, Mercadante (Miguel Ángel Ferríz), are arranged to frame a character.

FIGS. 3.25 AND 3.26. Rosas shot in real locations and claimed to have shot the robberies where they actually occurred. *Top*, during a battle between Carranza and Zapata forces, prisoners escape from the main jailhouse. *Bottom*, on the trail of one of the gang members in Ápam, the inspector, in the light-colored attire, attends a cockfight.

FIG. 3.29. Untitled and undated Posada engraving showing the coup de grâce.

FIGS. 3.27 AND 3.28. The execution, ending with the coup de grâce.

Rosas's coverage of the execution bears a striking resemblance to several execution engravings by Posada (fig. 3.29), and juxtaposing these images is a reminder that for a time the two were contemporaries working in what was understood as the same business—news reporting. And as leading practitioners in their respective fields, their job was to report events as accurately and completely as possible.

As I argued in the previous chapter, this combination of graphic pictorial documentation and fierce honesty is one of the fundamental characteristics of the exceptional filmmaking of the Classic Mexican Cinema. All of the films I analyze were produced by filmmakers who, in one way or another, at one time or another, shared the same belief: that the mainstream national cinema was not telling the whole, true national story. Fernando de Fuentes's Revolution Trilogy, the Fernández unit's nationalistic films of the 1940s, Luis Buñuel's surrealist view of Mexican society, Juan Bustillo Oro's double narrative in *Dos monjes*, Adolfo Best Maugard's proto-neorealist *La mancha de sangre*, and

Julio Bracho's noirish *Distinto amanecer*—all these were produced because, like Posada and Rosas, these filmmakers refused to look away.

The Legacy of *El automóvil gris*

The film was an immediate, unqualified, and unprecedented commercial and critical success. Silvestre Bonnard (Carlos Noriega Hope), the astute film reviewer for *El Universal*, singled out its "splendid cinematography" and praised *El automóvil gris* as clearly better than other contemporary Mexican films. He concluded with a prediction that Rosas would soon produce the definitive Mexican film.[42]

It was not to be. Rosas died on August 20, 1920, without having directed another film, and *El automóvil gris* would have to stand as his final filmmaking statement. Its impact was unmistakable and enduring. To Juan Bustillo Oro, a prolific director of Mexico's Golden Age cinema (he scripted *El compadre Mendoza* [1933], discussed in chapter 5, and directed many other films, including *Dos monjes* [1934], which will be analyzed in chapter 8), Rosas's achievement was an "everlasting triumph."[43] Historians Federico Dávalos Orozco and Esperanza Vázquez Bernal called it "the most ambitious and perhaps the most important [Mexican] film of the silent era,"[44] and it is now generally regarded as a landmark that surpassed all the cinema that preceded it.[45]

Beyond that, it also sheds light on the complex nature of media dependency in the development of Third World cinemas. In the case of Mexico, *El automóvil gris* reveals a hearty fusion of native creativity and foreign influences, rather than the crushing result of First World cultural imperialism. Indeed, this study demonstrates how deterministic and oversimplified media imperialism theory can sometimes be.[46] Enrique Rosas was not simply copying the emerging Hollywood paradigm or mindlessly imitating the declining European ones. On the contrary, this analysis of Rosas's poetics argues from internal evidence that this experienced filmmaker synthesized his documentary experience with the exuberance of Italian cinema, the jaunty unpretentiousness of French crime serials, and Hollywood's continuity system and narrative economy. Rosas combined these influences in such a way that *El automóvil gris* became far more than the sum of its parts—it was the first step toward Mexico's Cine de Oro.

El automóvil gris influenced both types of Golden Age movies. For Mainstream Mexican Cinema filmmakers, it introduced the use of Hollywood techniques of editing and narration. In fact, Rosas could be regarded as a pioneer whose early implementation of the Hollywood style in 1919 placed him in the vanguard of the international move toward the adoption of the continuity system.

But *El automóvil gris* was a powerful model for the Classic Mexican Cinema's auteurs as well. Rejecting the adoption of the Hollywood style and opposing the imitative MMC, this small band of defiant filmmakers dedicated themselves to forging an authentic Mexican cinematic form to faithfully express *lo mexicano*. Just as they were inspired by Posada's work, they must have appreciated how Rosas had achieved the goal they were aiming for—telling Mexican stories for Mexican audiences in a Mexican way. Those filmmaking rebels and the classic Mexican films they made are the focus of the rest of this book.

CHAPTER 4

The Adoption of the Hollywood Style and the Transition to Sound

—

IVEN THE RICH and varied streams of influence on Mexican film that we saw in the previous chapter, one question remains to be answered. Why did the majority of the Golden Age films—what I'm calling the Mainstream Mexican Cinema—end up adopting the classical Hollywood cinematic style? Why didn't the MMC follow the lead of *El automóvil gris* and retain at least some traces of the other four influences?

A major factor was the decline of Mexican filmmaking in the 1920s, a crisis so severe that the nation's cinema very nearly disappeared due to the onslaught of American films screened in Mexican theaters. Of a total of 5,044 films exhibited nationally

during the decade, Hollywood movies accounted for 78.9 percent of them (3,981), while Mexican films amounted to only 1.3 percent (64).[1] Compounding the problem was the lack of interest shown by the nation's moviegoers for Mexican cinema. Of the few made-in-Mexico feature-length films that were produced—only forty from 1923 to 1930—none were commercially successful.[2] "From 1921 to 1932," wrote director Juan Bustillo Oro of this period, "our cinema was reduced to isolated and frustrated attempts by heroic filmmaking aficionados, and Mexican films completely disappeared from the daily lives of Mexicans."[3] As a result, there was a thirteen-year gap between *El automóvil gris* and the release of *Santa*, the first sound film. If Mexican filmmaking had blossomed in

FACING: Detail of figure 4.1.

the 1920s instead of waning, it might have entered a silent golden age, just as national cinemas in the U.S., France, Germany, and the Soviet Union did. Had that occurred, Mexican directors might well have been more influenced and inspired by Posada and Rosas.

But that did not happen and the resulting time lag meant that the rebirth of Mexican cinema would fall to a new generation of filmmakers. For many of those young founders of Mexican sound film, the engravings of Posada and the newsreels of pioneers like Rosas would be little known, and very possibly unseen, relics of the past. And by the 1920s and early 1930s, when these budding cineastes would have become seriously interested and involved in cinema, Italian melodramas had disappeared from movie screens, and the heyday of serials was coming to an end. Feuillade, for example, turned from serials to directing melodramas in the 1920s, and made his last film in 1924. By that time, according to Bordwell, he had begun employing "something close to découpage [analytical editing] in the American manner."[4]

Feuillade and Rosas were not alone in the gradual adoption of the Hollywood style—this happened worldwide after the war. As Bordwell writes,

> American films swept the globe in the wake of World War I, and the découpage methods they employed soon became a cinematic lingua franca. Feuillade and his contemporaries adjusted to the new norms, and a younger generation—Abel Gance, Jean Epstein, Carl Dreyer, Fritz Lang, F. W. Murnau, and many others—embraced them eagerly.[5]

The Hollywood continuity system was gradually adopted by directors the world over, and regarded as simply the accepted, modern manner of making movies.

Still another factor was that many young Mexicans, who would eventually become the actors, technicians, editors, directors, and producers in Mexico's nascent sound film, had gone to Los Angeles in the 1920s and 1930s and had firsthand exposure to the Hollywood system. Gabriel Figueroa studied cinematography in Hollywood, and Emilio Fernández and his editor, Gloria Schoemann, both worked there as extras. Many others who would become Cine de Oro filmmakers worked in the American studio system as well: actors like Dolores del Río, Lupita Tovar, and Emma Roldán, for example, as well as future directors Carlos Navarro, Tito Davidson, Roberto Gavaldón, Chano Urueta, Gilberto Martínez Solares, and René Cardona. Some filmmakers went the other way. Three of the leading cinematographers of Mexican sound films, Ross Fisher, Jack Draper, and Alex Phillips, were transplants from Hollywood. There were indirect Hollywood influences as well. Julio Bracho and Emilio Gómez Muriel, who would become two of the most successful and prolific Golden Age directors, began their movie careers codirecting *Redes* (1936) with Fred Zinnemann. An Austrian who had migrated to Hollywood and was making films there, Zinnemann came to Mexico to direct Paul Strand's production of *Redes*. Thus, many of those who were instrumental in initiating the modern era of Mexican filmmaking were affected either directly or indirectly by the Hollywood system, and were familiar with its style, technology, and mode of production.[6]

The Classical Mexican Cinema

Still, there were a couple of filmmaking alternatives available to Mexico's up-and-coming filmmakers at the beginning of the 1930s. Soviet cinema was a leading possibility. It was cinematically lively, and its oppositional stance coincided with Mexico's postrevolutionary pro-worker ethos. Additionally, many Mexican artists and intellectuals, some of whom were calling for the development of an authentic Mexican cinema, were Communists, leftists, or left leaning. Moreover, when Sergei Eisenstein arrived in Mexico in December 1930 and began making ¡Que viva Mexico! the following spring, it clearly demonstrated how the Soviet filmmaking style could be tailored to the Mexican experience. Indeed, according to historian Emilio García Riera, ¡Que viva Mexico! exerted the most influence on Mexican filmmakers and critics at the time.[7]

But not those interested in film as a business. Eisenstein never completed ¡Que viva Mexico!, and its failure must have served as a cautionary tale to many Mexican filmmakers—and especially potential producers. Visually, of course, the footage was stunning. Eisenstein's ability to capture *mexicanidad* by incorporating Mexican cultural motifs and celebrating indigenous mexicanos was extraordinary. In the chapters that follow, we will see that García Riera's assessment was correct: at a formal level Eisenstein's film was immensely influential to some Mexican filmmakers, principally those of the Classical Mexican Cinema. However its experimental structure—described as a "cinematographic mural" and a "filmic symphony" that combined Mexican history, art, folkways, and landscapes[8]—set ¡Que viva Mexico! apart from the majority of popular commercial films and

would likely have made it difficult to market had it ever been finished.

Worse, from a producer's bottom-line perspective, Eisenstein's filmmaking method of letting the structure and meaning of the film emerge as he shot—and shot, and shot—was unwieldy and expensive. He began filming in April 1931 and was still shooting nine months later, in January 1932, when the film's American backers, who included Upton Sinclair, shut down the project. Eisenstein was not allowed to complete the shooting and never had a chance to edit the tens of thousands of feet of film he had exposed.[9] Fragmentary versions of the film were released at the time, but they were edited by others: Sol Lesser's *Thunder over Mexico* and *Death Day* (both 1934), and Marie Seton's *Time in the Sun* (1939). To recoup expenses, Sinclair even sold off some of it for use as stock footage.[10] Future film producers looking for practical modes of sound film production must have looked on in horror. Seeking to establish a vital national cinema that would attract Mexican viewers and compete commercially with Hollywood and European films, they needed an economically feasible moviemaking business model. Clearly, ¡Que viva Mexico! was not it.

The dark, brooding films of German expressionism presented another filmmaking option. They certainly had their followers among aspiring Mexican filmmakers during the 1920s and 1930s. For example, we will see how the expressionist style was employed in Juan Bustillo Oro's *Dos monjes* (1933) in chapter 8, and note its influence on the chiaroscuro lighting of de Fuentes's Revolutionary Trilogy (1933–1936) discussed in the next chapter—especially evident in the haunting final shot in the last of the three films, *¡Vámonos con Pancho Villa!* (1936, figs. 5.9–5.16). But these proved to be isolated cases. Though he was fascinated by German expressionism in his youth, director and writer Bustillo Oro, who would go on to direct, produce, and write dozens of Golden Age films, ultimately turned his back on it, recognizing that "it was not, nor could it ever be popular. It was difficult to understand and stirred up extremely disturbing things in the back of one's conscience."[11]

He was right. Mexican filmmakers—and audiences—preferred sunnier films with happy endings. For all its artistry, *¡Vámonos con Pancho Villa!* was a box office disappointment. But de Fuentes's next film, *Allá en el Rancho Grande* (1936), which ends not in darkness but with a fanciful triple wedding that neatly resolves the story's class tensions, was the most commercially successful film made in Mexico up to that time, a popular hit at home and abroad. During the Golden Age, expressionism's shadowy visual style was used, but selectively—just as it was in Hollywood: as a shorthand device to add suspense or mystery to the proceedings or as a way to emphasize the psychological plight of characters inhabiting a treacherous world. In the Classical Mexican Cinema, besides de Fuentes's use of it in the Revolutionary Trilogy, it was employed effectively by the Fernández unit in *Río Escondido* (1948) and *Salón México* (1949), in Buñuel's *Los olvidados* (1950) and the nightscapes of *El bruto* (1953), and in Julio Bracho's memorable film noir, *Distinto amanecer* (1943)—all shot by cinematographer Gabriel Figueroa.

In short, the appeal of the Soviet and German traditions faded fairly quickly, the other four influences receded in time, and as one

commentator put it in 1931, American films of any kind were the favorites of Mexico's moviegoing public during the 1920s.[12] Not surprisingly, then, the majority of Mexican producers who bankrolled the films and the filmmakers who made them opted for the Hollywood paradigm.

And given the scant film evidence available, it appears that since the mid-1920s Mexican filmmakers had already begun using the Hollywood style. It is difficult to generalize about Mexico's film style in the '20s, however, given the fact that roughly 90 to 95 percent of the Mexican films made between 1896 and 1930 are lost.[13] Nevertheless, an analysis of the only surviving 1920s films, *El tren fantasma* (*The Phantom Train*, 1927) and *El puño de hierro* (*The Iron Fist*, 1927), both directed by Gabriel García Moreno, tells us what we need to know.[14] Namely, that the film language being developed by Hollywood and adopted by the world's filmmakers was also implemented in Mexico. Indeed, *El tren fantasma* is described on the Universidad Nacional Autónoma de México (UNAM) film archives online site as a film made "in the style of American thrillers of the time."[15] Another assessment notes how the film blends the advances of *El automóvil gris* with influences from "contemporary Hollywood productions."[16] And, as Eduardo de la Vega Alfaro says, both *El tren fantasma* and *El puño de hierro* are the work of a director possessing a firm grasp of the elements of the Hollywood style and reflect the direct influence of American filmmaking.[17] In particular, I would cite the films' use of the following techniques: the LS—MS—CU progression, analytical editing, shot/reverse shot, screen direction, match-action cutting, and the use of CUs for important details (figs. 4.1–4.10). The adoption of the Hollywood style in Mexican sound films appears to be a continuation of a well-established filmmaking practice.

Sound Saves Mexican Cinema

The revival of Mexican filmmaking came about as a result of the medium's transition to sound, beginning in Hollywood in 1927 and in Mexico in the early 1930s. Sound's arrival created an international marketing problem for Hollywood but an opportunity for Mexican cinema. In Mexico, a few businessmen and filmmakers felt that the time was ripe to reestablish a national film industry. They saw an opening created by Hollywood studios' awkward attempts to hold on to their Spanish-speaking markets in Latin America and Spain by producing "Hispanic films." These low-budget, short-schedule sound productions made with Spanish-speaking casts were sometimes original films and sometimes remakes of Hollywood fare (*The Big House* [1930] became *El presidio*, for example, and Universal made a Spanish-language *Dracula* [1931]). Initially well received, Hispanic films' popularity was short lived. One problem was their low production values. Another was Latin American audiences' preference for the original Hollywood films with A-list Hollywood stars, not poorly made copies with unknown actors.[18] Aspiring Mexican producers realized that they could beat Hollywood by producing Spanish sound films and creating their own stars.[19]

The *Santa* Precedent: Mexico's Adoption of the Hollywood Style

A good way to understand the development of Mexican filmmaking in the shadow of Hollywood's cinematic dominance is to think of it as a dynamic relationship of the kind Michael Curtin has described. He proposes thinking about the circulation of film, television, and other media as the "globalization of media." Rather than understanding it "reductively as cultural homogenization or western hegemony," Curtin suggests that we consider it instead as "part of a larger set of processes

FIGS. 4.1 AND 4.2. *El puño de hierro* (1927). Use of a close-up to isolate an important detail. *Top*, medium shot: three-shot in a drug den, where two men, center and right, attempt to convince the man on the left to inject himself with the drug. *Bottom*, CU of the syringe.

FIGS. 4.3–4.7. *El puño de hierro* (1927). LS—MS progression. *Top left*, long shot: Perico (Manuel Carrillo) and his young assistant, Juanito (Guillermo Pacheco), come upon a street fight. *Top right*, mid-shot: getting closer, they continue watching. *Middle left*, MS: Perico and Juanito notice something on the sidewalk. *Middle right*, slightly closer MCU: a box. *Bottom*, MS: they inspect its contents (drug paraphernalia).

that operate translocally, interactively, and dynamically at a variety of levels: economic, institutional, technological, and ideological."[20] In our case, while it's true that most Mexican filmmakers adopted the U.S. model, a few of them implemented it in distinctive ways, transforming it to express *lo mexicano* within the Classical Mexican Cinema. Cinematographer Gabriel Figueroa, for example, took what he learned from his Hollywood mentor, Gregg Toland, and fashioned it into a unique visual style that became emblematic of Mexican cinema. One of the directors he worked with, Emilio Fernández, based many of his films on Hollywood movies, but deftly placed them within a Mexican context to express *mexicanidad*.

A perfect example of the complex globalization process that Curtin defines is the development of Mexico's early sound cinema, beginning with the nation's first optical

The Classical Mexican Cinema

sound film, *Santa* (1932). Though Mexico turned to Hollywood for help, there was an element of Mexican ingenuity that contributed significantly not just to the development of Mexico's first incursion into sound filmmaking, but also to the first wave of the nation's talkies produced during that decade.

The coming of sound to Mexican cinema is mainly the story of the Rodríguez brothers, Roberto (1909–95) and Joselito (1907–85),

who were born in Mexico City and went to Los Angeles in 1923—while in their teens—to study film. Roberto found a job at MGM and worked his way up to camera operator and Joselito worked in a film lab.[21] Incredibly, by 1929, though still only in their early twenties, they had developed the Rodríguez Sound Recording System, a successful optical (sound-on-film) technology distinctive for its size (it weighed only twelve pounds while their competitors' machines weighed over two hundred pounds), portability, and ease of use. Among the advances that set their sound system apart from others at the time was their invention of a pre-amplifier to aid in using microphones at a distance from the camera and the recording console, and a noise reduction process to eliminate hiss from recordings. Additionally, the Rodríguez Sound Recording System was said to be better and more accurate at lip-synching, achieving a much higher percentage of perfectly synchronized sound than competing systems. It was so good, in fact, that it soon drew the attention of Lee De Forest, the American pioneer of early film sound, who threatened to sue the Rodríguez brothers for infringing on his sound-on-film system, Phonofilm. But when they demonstrated their system to him, he realized that theirs truly was a different system, reportedly

FIGS. 4.8–4.10. *El puño de hierro* (1927). Match-action cutting. In a LS, one of the bad guys pushes Perico aside, scoops up the box, and runs toward the car to make his getaway. Matching the action from the previous shot, there is a cut as he jumps into the car in a MS. It is important to note that this is not an axial cut; director García Moreno changed the angle of shooting as he brought the camera closer, an advance over Feuillade's and Rosas's axial cut-ins. In the same long take, the car drives off, with the bad guys unaware that the two amateur detectives have climbed aboard. The shot ends with the car driving away, concluding the scene.

remarking that "it would never have occurred to me to do it that way."[22]

Around the same time in the early 1930s, Juan de la Cruz Alarcón, head of the newly formed Compañía Nacional Productora de Películas, was embarking on the business of making sound movies in Mexico. Coming from a background as a Mexican distributor of foreign films, he now wanted to make a sound film to revive the moribund national film industry. For the company's inaugural production, Cruz Alarcón decided to remake *Santa*, which had previously been made in a silent version in 1918, and was based on a popular Mexican novel by Federico Gamboa. He traveled to Hollywood to secure stars, technicians, and the recording technology.[23] Cruz Alarcón hired the Spanish actor Antonio Moreno, a heartthrob in Hollywood's silent cinema, to be *Santa*'s director.

Moreno was steeped in the Hollywood system, with nearly twenty years of experience there. Working his way up from bit parts (he had a minor role, for example, in D. W. Griffith's *The Musketeers of Pig Alley* [1912]), by the 1920s he was a celebrated matinee idol. Moreno had starred as the romantic lead alongside the likes of Greta Garbo (*The Temptress*, 1926), Clara Bow (*It*, 1927), and Pola Negri (*The Spanish Dancer*, 1924), and besides working for Griffith, he had acted for other top silent-era directors such as Fred Niblo and Rex Ingram.

Moreno's first assistant on *Santa* was another emigrant, director Ramón Peón (1887–1971). Before coming to Mexico, Peón had made ten films in his native Cuba; one of them, *La virgen de Caridad* (1930), is generally considered to be the best silent Cuban film. After a short stay in Hollywood, where he directed two films, he went to Mexico, where he would eventually become one of the most prolific filmmakers, directing some forty-six films, in addition to acting, writing, and producing.[24] Still another non-Mexican lured from Hollywood to work on *Santa* was its Canadian-born cinematographer Alex Phillips (1900–1977). By the time he came to Mexico to photograph *Santa*, he had ten years' of experience in Hollywood as a director of photography of comedy features and shorts for the Christie Corporation. Phillips made Mexico his home and went on to become one of the industry's busiest cinematographers. For the next forty-four years, he photographed more than two hundred films and worked with some of the top directors, such as Luis Buñuel, Ismael Rodríguez, Emilio Fernández, and Fernando de Fuentes, shooting the latter's *La zandunga* (1938) and *Doña Barbara* (1943).[25] In retrospect, it seems likely that a primary reason the Compañía Nacional hired two Mexicans, de Fuentes and Carlos L. Cabello, as second assistant directors was to help ensure that *Santa* would maintain its local flavor. Rounding out the talent Cruz Alarcón brought from Hollywood were two Mexican actors working in Los Angeles, Lupita Tovar and Donald Reed (born Ernesto Guillén in Mexico City), for two of the main roles.[26]

As far as the sound technology was concerned, Cruz Alarcón found that it basically came down to two options: RCA and Western Electric. However, neither company was willing to sell him their equipment outright. Instead, Cruz Alarcón would have to rent it, along with the operators (who did not speak Spanish). In addition to the rental price, he would be required to pay a royalty of roughly

$500 per year for each film he made with the system, a fee to be paid in perpetuity. The brothers Rodríguez tracked down Cruz Alarcón—the story is they caught him just as he was boarding a plane back to Mexico City—and demonstrated their system to him. On the strength of their presentation, they were hired to record the sound for *Santa* and returned to Mexico. The Rodríguez Sound Recording System was used not only for Mexico's initial sound film but also for the majority of the films made in Mexico for the next ten years.[27] Following that, the brothers went on to become prolific directors, producers, and screenwriters of Golden Age films (Joselito directed 33 films and produced 36; Roberto directed 40, produced 29, and was involved in the writing of 47).

Mexico's first sound film, then, was a blending of U.S. and Mexican talent and technologies. In terms of stylistics, technology, and mode of production, *Santa* set a precedent for Mexican filmmaking and cinematic narration that would be followed by the majority of Cine de Oro films for decades. But its content was not particularly Mexican. In fact, in the opinion of historian García Riera, importing so much Hollywood-linked talent "infected" *Santa*, making it seem more like one of Hollywood's Hispanic films than a Mexican one.[28]

He has a point. Even though it is one of the foundational works of the *cabaretera* genre, *Santa* is not a uniquely Mexican narrative. An examination of the wretched treatment of women within patriarchy, its story might have taken place in any Spanish-speaking country, from Spain to Latin America. The same holds true of *La mujer del puerto* (1933), another important early *cabaretera*

film. In contrast, the Fernández unit's *Salón México* (1948) contains explicit Mexican references, tying its protagonist specifically to Mexico, its government, and its history, as does another Fernández unit prostitute film, *Las abandonadas* (1944), both of which I discuss in chapter 6.

A more complete story of Mexican cinema's adoption of the Hollywood mode of production, therefore, obliges us to consider what filmmakers did with it. Most, it's true, simply utilized it, perhaps "spicing it up" by adding some Mexican elements—language, slang, humor, music, folkloric dress, traditions, and the like. Stylistically, though, they adhered to the key elements of the Hollywood paradigm—the norms of scripting, shooting, editing, lighting, acting, as well as the three-act structure and the happy ending. This majority practice resulted in the films that comprise what I term the Mainstream Mexican Cinema.

But there were countercurrents. Some cineastes believed that the Hollywood paradigm should be spurned and that national filmmakers ought to formulate a distinctive Mexican cinematic style. As Adolfo Fernández Bustamante wrote in 1931:

> If it hopes to succeed, Mexican cinema should be Mexican art; it should employ national motifs, which we have by the hundreds; natural settings, which are abundant in our country; stars who embody our distinct racial characteristics different from Hollywood's "beautiful models." . . . Eisenstein . . . has given us the template for our cinematic future, has marked the path we should follow; he has been a guide . . . who did not seek

the beautiful boy or the Yankee-looking girl, but cast *indios* instead, selected the most Mexican landscapes and has produced the wonder of an authentic work of Mexican art, profoundly nationalistic and beautiful.[29]

A handful of filmmakers agreed, and set about developing a national film style.

Cultural imperialism—the pressure on developing countries to conform culturally, technologically, and ideologically to developed ones—does exist. It is evident in the international acceptance of the Hollywood paradigm. At the heart of Fernández Bustamante's call for the creation of a national film aesthetic was the fear that adopting Hollywood's style would mean that Mexican film—and Mexico itself—would lose its identity. But the flip side of media colonialism is that it has the potential of planting the seeds of cultural revolt. Ironically, then, the adoption of the Hollywood filmmaking model by the majority of Mexican directors prompted a small minority to reject it and set off on a different creative path. The films they made formed the Classical Mexican Cinema.

CHAPTER 5

Mexican Cinema Comes of Age

FERNANDO DE FUENTES IN THE 1930S

—

ITH THE emergence of sound films in the 1930s, a new generation of Mexican filmmakers busily explored various cinematic approaches, leading to the formation of two distinct branches of Mexican Golden Age films. Some producers and directors were simply attempting to turn out popular, commercially successful productions, and drew on the internationally pervasive Hollywood model as a handy template. This was the beginning of the Mainstream Mexican Cinema, which by the mid- to late 1930s became the dominant filmmaking practice. Other moviemakers, looking to create an independent, homegrown cinema, sought alternatives to the Hollywood paradigm. This smaller but enormously influential branch was the Classical Mexican Cinema.

One of the first and most important CMC directors was Fernando de Fuentes, generally regarded as "the most gifted filmmaker of the early Mexican sound cinema."[1] Though he directed thirty-seven films during a career spanning twenty-two years, his best known, most honored, and most formally daring films were three that he made at the start of his career, between 1933 and 1936. They all centered on the revolution, and together formed an informal trilogy that many at the time considered the apogee of Mexican filmmaking. For example, upon the release of the first of the three, *El prisionero 13* (*Prisoner 13*,

1933), director and screenwriter Juan Bustillo Oro published a long tribute, declaring it the first truly Mexican film and one that marked a watershed in the nation's movie history. "From now on," he wrote, "our filmmakers will be divided into two periods: before and after *El prisionero trece*."[2] The Revolution Trilogy continues to be highly esteemed today. In a 1994 survey of Mexican film critics and historians (and one celebrated filmmaker, the cinematographer Gabriel Figueroa) conducted by the periodical *Somos* to determine the country's best one hundred films, the last movie of the trilogy, *¡Vámonos con Pancho Villa!* (*Let's Go with Pancho Villa!*, 1936), was deemed number one. The middle film, *El compadre Mendoza* (*Godfather Mendoza*, 1934), was voted number three.[3]

Upon completing the Revolution Trilogy, de Fuentes directed *Allá en el Rancho Grande* (1936), which at the time was the most financially successful Mexican film ever made. It was also the first Mexican film to win an international award: a prize at the Venice Film Festival for Gabriel Figueroa's cinematography. Due in large measure to the critical and commercial success of these four de Fuentes films, then, Mexican cinema rose from obscurity to a secure place on the global cinematic map.

De Fuentes's Early Film Career
—

Fernando de Fuentes (1894–1958) was born in Veracruz, the son of the manager of the National Bank of Mexico in Monterrey. In college, he first studied engineering and then majored in philosophy at Tulane University in New Orleans. Afterward, he worked at a number of different jobs, working in a bank,

as an assistant to General Venustiano Carranza, and on the staff of the Mexican embassy in Washington, DC, in 1919. Returning to Mexico City, he published articles and poetry in capital city newspapers.[4]

In the 1920s he entered the film business, gaining experience in distribution (he worked six years in the Mexico City office of the agency that handled films for Paramount Studios) and exhibition (he ran a chain of theaters, the Circuito Máximo, and then managed the Cine Olimpia, a top-flight, first-run Mexico City theater). After the transition to sound, he took credit for solving a major problem that had stumped Hollywood studios and exhibitors alike—how to screen English-language films for non-English-speaking audiences. De Fuentes claimed that he "invented" the eventual solution: subtitling.

He gravitated to film production in 1931 as second assistant director on *Santa*; he then edited director Antonio Moreno's next film, *Águilas frente al sol* (*Eagles Facing the Sun*, 1932). Though officially credited as coscriptwriter and dialogue director on *Una vida por otra* (*One Life for Another*, 1932), he later maintained that he in fact directed the film, since the director of record, John H. Auer (1899–1981), was Hungarian and didn't speak Spanish.[5] "In my opinion," de Fuentes told an interviewer three years after the film's release, "it was the first film that I directed, because directing the dialogue in a case like that called for arranging the entire scene and obtaining the necessary reactions from the actors."[6]

After another uncredited stint as assistant director on the first Mexican film directed by the Russian actor and director Arcady Boytler (1895–1965), *Mano a mano* (*Hand* to Hand, 1932), de Fuentes finally received screen credit for writing and directing *El anónimo* (*The Anonymous One*, 1933), made for Compañía Nacional. The following three-year period was a time of intense creativity in which de Fuentes directed nine features and two documentary shorts, interspersing the films of his Revolutionary Trilogy with various genre films: a tragic love story (*La Calandria* [*The Lark*, 1933]), a swashbuckling adventure (*Cruz Diablo*, 1934), a horror film (*El fantasma del convento* [*The Phantom of the Convent*, 1934]), a costume melodrama (*El tigre de Yautepec* [*The Tiger of Yautepec*, 1933]), a family melodrama (*La familia Dressel* [*The Dressel Family*, 1935]), and the film that initiated the *comedia ranchera*, *Allá en el Rancho Grande* (which, though shot after *¡Vámonos con Pancho Villa!*, was released before it).

Nationalistic Art, *¡Que viva México!*, and the Classical Mexican Cinema
—

At about the same time, there was a strong impulse toward nationalism in Mexican art. In essence, an artistic revolution had accompanied the political one. Serious Mexican artists of every stripe rejected the prevailing Eurocentrism of Mexico's prerevolutionary artistic mainstream, began exploring Mexican themes, and sought a native aesthetic to express them. The bridge connecting Mexican art and cinema was Sergei Eisenstein. He befriended Diego Rivera (1886–1957) when the Mexican painter visited Moscow in 1927. Rivera showed Eisenstein pictures of his murals, photographed by Tina Modotti (1896–1942), and the director was captivated by Mexican visual culture. When the Soviet filmmaker arrived in Mexico in 1930, he

studied the nation's artistic traditions, old and new, from pre-Columbian times to the etchings of Posada to the work of contemporary muralists such as Rivera, José Clemente Orozco (1883–1949), and David Alfaro Siqueiros (1896–1974).[7] The influence of Mexican art history is evident in *¡Que viva México!*, the film Eisenstein began shooting in the spring of 1931.

In turn, *¡Que viva México!* profoundly influenced nascent Mexican directors, particularly those of the CMC. If the MMC had the Hollywood paradigm as their model, Eisenstein's film was the prototypical CMC film, a perfect fusion of striking cinematic technique and Mexican culture. In it, Eisenstein synthesized centuries of art, history, and culture, and fashioned an eye-opening spectacle out of familiar elements that Mexican directors had ignored or taken for granted. For budding filmmakers, *¡Que viva México!* was a compendium of Mexican imagery and themes as well as a handbook of practical cinematic techniques and visual tropes that could be utilized to represent Mexico. It inspired a few Mexican directors, like de Fuentes, Fernández, and Figueroa, to produce films that told stories about the inhabitants of a place that in the hands of a filmmaker like Eisenstein looked unlike anyplace else in the world.

Here an interesting question arises. If *¡Que viva México!* was never finished, how could it have inspired Mexican filmmakers? After all, as we saw in the previous chapter, Upton Sinclair, the film's financial backer, pulled the plug on the project and kept all the footage in Los Angeles, where it had been sent to be processed. Brokenhearted, Eisenstein returned to Russia, never to complete the film. How, then, did it serve as a touchstone for a new generation of Mexican filmmakers, particularly two pantheon directors of the Classical Mexican Cinema like de Fuentes and Fernández?

There are several ways budding filmmakers might have been exposed to Eisenstein's film and its imagery. First, anyone interested in film or the arts would have been aware of the Russian filmmaker's arrival in Mexico, of his friendship with Rivera and other artists and muralists, and of his film project, all of which were well covered by the press. Moreover, once the film was in production, there were pictorial spreads in newspapers such as *El Universal* and arts publications like *Orbe, Sur,* and *El Universal Ilustrado,* the most prestigious cultural magazine of its time.[8] These typically contained production shots from the filming along with images from the film itself.[9]

For his part, Fernández said that he first saw footage from *¡Que viva México!* in an editing room in Hollywood while he was working there as an extra. Though Fernández is known to have invented large chunks of his life story, this claim is credible because Fernández was indeed in Hollywood in 1932 and 1933, when independent producer Sol Lesser was editing a Sinclair-approved version of Eisenstein's film entitled *Thunder over Mexico.* It was released in the U.S. in 1933, another way Fernández might have seen it. In 1935 it was exhibited in Mexico City,[10] and doubtlessly was seen by young filmmakers and cineastes. It's fair to assume that de Fuentes and Figueroa (and possibly Fernández, too, who by that time had moved back to Mexico City) would have seen it at that time. One way or another, then, young aspiring Mexican filmmakers would have been well aware of *¡Que viva México!* and Eisenstein's cinematic celebration of Mexico, its people, culture, and history.

A beneficial side effect of the connection between Mexican muralists, Eisenstein, and CMC directors was the enhancement of the filmmakers' stature. The fact that muralists and CMC directors shared the same aesthetic goals placed them on the same plane as artists. In the egalitarian postrevolutionary atmosphere, this meant that the highbrow/lowbrow distinction that characterized American arts for decades and stigmatized movies as strictly popular entertainment rather than art was absent in Mexico. The cultural equivalence of muralists and directors was further strengthened by the fact that Mexican art and movies both targeted the same mass audience, just as Posada's engravings had decades earlier. The same populist impetus that led painters like Rivera, Orozco, and Siqueiros to fill the walls of government buildings with their monumental murals drove CMC directors to light up the nation's screens with their visions of Mexico. CMC films were the illuminated murals of the nationalistic art movement.

Mexican Film Culture in the 1930s
—

The arrival of sound had the desired effect of spurring growth in the Mexican film industry. In the wake of *Santa*'s success, other production companies sprang up (the major ones were México-Films and Industrial Cinematográfica, S.A.),[11] and in the following year, 1933, Mexico released twenty-one feature-length films—a stunning turnaround from the single film made in 1931—suddenly becoming the world leader in Spanish-language filmmaking.

Government support of—and involvement in—the film business began in earnest in 1934, the first year of the *sexenio* of leftist president Lázaro Cárdenas. His administration subsidized the construction of CLASA (Cinematográfica Latino Americana, S.A.) studios, and generously assisted the shooting of CLASA's first film, de Fuentes's *¡Vámonos con Pancho Villa!*, by providing an entire army regiment, a military train, and supplies and equipment. It was the most expensive Mexican film made up to that point, costing an estimated 1 million pesos at a time when the budget for an average film was between 20,000 and 30,000 pesos. When it performed so poorly that CLASA declared bankruptcy, the government stepped in and covered the cost of the film, preventing the studio from going under.

But if de Fuentes's revolution tragedy nearly took down a major studio, his next film, the sunny musical melodrama *Allá en el Rancho Grande*, was so profitable that, in the words of film historian Emilio García Riera, it single-handedly established the modern Mexican film industry.[12] Made at a cost of between 65,000 and 85,000 pesos, the film reportedly collected an estimated 100 million pesos in box office receipts, a remarkable 1,333 percent return on investment.[13] It launched Mexico's cinematic Golden Age, a quarter century of unprecedented film production. In a remarkable turn of events, by the 1940s, in terms of quantity, quality, and profitability, Mexico had become the world leader of Spanish-language filmmaking, the Hollywood of Latin America.

The Revolution Trilogy
—

Cinematically, thematically, and ideologically, the Revolution Trilogy—*El prisionero 13*, *El compadre Mendoza*, and *¡Vámonos con Pancho Villa!*—is de Fuentes's boldest work, and I will devote the rest of the chapter to these three films, all set during the 1910–20 Mexican Revolution. By examining their cinematic style and dramatic structure I hope to show just how exceptional they were.

SUMMARIES OF THE FILMS

Knowing their tales will facilitate the formal discussion that follows, so let me briefly relate each of them. As I do so, I will take the opportunity to explain some of the basic history of the revolution, common knowledge for Mexican viewers at the time of their release, so that readers can appreciate the devastating critical commentary de Fuentes's films were making about those events.

El prisionero 13: The Sins of the Father

El prisionero 13 begins before the revolution, sometime in the early to mid-1890s, during the Porfiriato (1876–1910), the regime of dictator Porfirio Díaz (1830–1915). It centers on Colonel Julián Carrasco (Alfredo del Diestro), a drunken, abusive, and philandering husband. When his wife, Marta (Adela Sequeyro), begs him to stop drinking, he refuses; he tells her she is free to leave, but forbids her taking their young son, Juan (fig. 5.1). In their fight over the custody of the boy, Carrasco threatens to kill her but is restrained by a friend. She secretly flees with Juan and disappears.

Years go by and Juan grows into a young man (Arturo Campoamor). Col. Carrasco, unaware that his estranged wife and son live in the same city, is now the commander of the army's battalion headquarters during the administration of General Victoriano Huerta (1850–1916). This places the action in 1913 or 1914, when Huerta served as president after having betrayed and very likely murdered President Francisco Madero (1873–1913), the revolutionary leader who overthrew Díaz.

Carrasco arrests thirteen revolutionaries, imprisons them in the garrison, and receives orders to execute all of them at dawn the next morning. After accepting a bribe to free one of the prisoners, Carrasco orders his assistant to replace the freed prisoner by arresting a young man at random off the street. As fate would have it, Juan is picked up. Learning what has happened, Marta hurries to the garrison to beseech her husband for their son's life. But by the time she finds him, the executions have already begun, and Carrasco and Marta race to save Juan's life. Juan is lined up facing the firing squad, and just as the commander is about to give the order to fire, Carrasco wakes up—the whole thing, the entire film up to this point, has been a bad dream. Flinging a bottle of tequila to the floor, he swears off alcohol for good (fig. 5.2).

This improbable deus ex machina happy ending was not the film's original conclusion, but one added shortly after *El prisionero 13*'s initial release. According to one of the actors, Emma Roldán, in the original version (which has been lost) the firing squad executes Juan before Carrasco can save him;[14] contemporary film reviews confirm her claim.[15] Evidently objecting to the film's depiction of the military, the government had the film pulled from exhibition until the ending was changed.[16]

I will analyze the narrative structure and ideological implications of the film's two endings later in the chapter, but for now let me focus on the government's censorship, which is telling. It reveals just how sensitive government officials were about realistic—that is, unflattering—portrayals of the revolution, even though the fighting had been over for more than a decade and the film's negative depiction was of Huerta's regime, a leader generally considered a prime villain in the popular narrative of the revolt. Censoring the film was a signal to filmmakers that sanitized accounts of the ten-year civil war were a much safer storytelling strategy. Interestingly, however, de Fuentes ignored the warning, and his next two revolution films were just as critical as the first one—if not more so. Knowing the risks involved only makes de Fuentes's accomplishment in completing the trilogy as honestly as he did that much more extraordinary.

El compadre Mendoza: The Compromised Morality of Going Along to Get Along

Like *El prisionero 13*, *El compadre Mendoza* takes place during Huerta's presidency, 1913–14, when Emiliano Zapata and other rebel leaders revolted against him. It concerns a well-to-do *hacendado*, Rosalío Mendoza (again Alfredo del Diestro) who opportunistically sides with whichever revolutionary faction appears at his doorstep. When it's the Zapatistas, his assistant replaces Huerta's picture with a portrait of Zapata, and Mendoza greets them with open arms. When the government's forces arrive, the Huerta picture goes back up. And when Venustiano Carranza defeats Huerta and becomes the new president, it's down with Huerta and ¡Viva Carranza! (figs. 5.3–5.6).

Mendoza marries Dolores (Carmen Guerrero), the young daughter of a business acquaintance, and a Huertista officer,

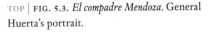

TOP | FIG. 5.3. *El compadre Mendoza*. General Huerta's portrait.

BOTTOM | FIG. 5.4. *El compadre Mendoza*. Huerta's portrait is replaced by Emiliano Zapata's.

TOP | FIG. 5.5. *El compadre Mendoza*. Mendoza (Alfredo del Diestro, center) greets two Zapatista generals, including Felipe Nieto (Antonio R. Frausto, *right*), who befriends Mendoza and becomes his son's godfather.

BOTTOM | FIG. 5.6. *El compadre Mendoza*. When Huerta is deposed and Carranza becomes president, his portrait goes up: ¡Viva Carranza!

Colonel Martínez (Abraham Galán), is an honored guest at the wedding party. The Zapatistas make a surprise nighttime attack, capture Col. Martínez, and are just about to execute Mendoza for colluding with the enemy when their leader, Gen. Felipe Nieto (Antonio R. Frausto), intervenes and saves his life. They become close friends, and the Mendozas name their first child after Nieto, who becomes the boy's godfather. But when Mendoza's business fortunes take a turn for the worse and he is at the brink of financial ruin, a Carranza officer proposes a deal—money in exchange for betraying Nieto to the Carranzistas. Mendoza agrees, Nieto is assassinated at the hacienda, and his body is left hanging at its entrance (fig. 5.7).

¡*Vámonos con Pancho Villa!*: Chastened Idealism, Broken Dreams, and Mexico's Dark Night of the Soul

¡*Vámonos con Pancho Villa!* takes place in 1914 and tells the story of a group of six friends, all rancheros, who have sat out the first four years of the revolution. Finally, out of patriotic fervor, they decide that they must do the honorable thing and join the rebel army of Pancho Villa (Domingo Soler) (fig. 5.8). When they locate Villa's army to volunteer, they find him distributing maize to peons from a freight train (fig. 5.31). This introduction to Villa immediately casts him as a true reformer, a sort of second coming of Robin Hood, and seemingly validates their idealistic but impetuous decision to enlist.

Gradually, however, reality sets in. Five months later, the six "Leones de San Pablo" ("the San Pablo lions"), as Villa has dubbed them, have become frustrated by the war's tedium. The revolution drags on and they

have yet to distinguish themselves. When their chance finally arrives, they prove their bravery in successive battles, but two of them are killed. A third is slain by friendly fire. The surviving Leones are rewarded for their bravery and appointed to *los dorados*, Villa's elite bodyguard detail. One day in a bar they partake in a Russian-roulette contest of bravery with other *dorados*. The happy-go-lucky Melitón, nicknamed Panzón (Big Belly, played by Manuel Tamés), is seriously wounded and, to prove his manhood, commits suicide.

TOP | FIG. 5.7. *El compadre Mendoza*. Betrayed by Mendoza, Gen. Nieto is killed by Huerta's soldiers, and his body is displayed at the entrance to Mendoza's hacienda.

BOTTOM | FIG. 5.8. ¡*Vámonos con Pancho Villa!* The six friends, later nicknamed Los Leones de San Pablo, decide to join Villa's army.

The youngest of the two remaining Leones, Miguel Ángel (Ramón Vallarino), contracts smallpox and is cared for by the other, Tiburcio (Antonio R. Frausto), in an isolated freight car. When a doctor and one of Villa's generals learn of Miguel Ángel's infection, they order Tiburcio to cremate him—alive. Tiburcio returns to the freight car, kisses Miguel Ángel on the forehead, and then shoots and kills him. Alone in the dark, Tiburcio creates a makeshift funeral pyre of Miguel Ángel's corpse and his belongings, and salutes him in farewell. Villa arrives and, fearful of contamination, quarantines Tiburcio until further notice and leaves for battle. "All right, here's where it ends," Tiburcio says to himself, renouncing the revolution. In the film's brilliant final shot, a single forty-seven-second-long take, Tiburcio walks toward and then away from the camera, retreating into darkness (figs. 5.9–5.16).

As powerfully elegant as this ending is, it was one of several options. Once again, the government may have suppressed the finale that de Fuentes originally shot.[17] An ending that was shot, but remained unseen for decades, was a brutal epilogue that was discovered on a deteriorated 16mm copy of the film by the Filmoteca de la UNAM (the film collection at the Universidad Nacional Autónoma de México) in 1973. It has been included in the Filmoteca's DVD of the film, released in 2010 as part of the centennial celebration of the revolution. This ending is set years after Tiburcio leaves Villa's army. Villa and the rag-tag remnants of his rebel forces, now considered bandits rather than revolutionaries, arrive at Tiburcio's ranch, where he lives with his wife, son, and daughter. Desperately in need of men, Villa asks Tiburcio to join

him. Tiburcio begs off, saying he can't leave his family. After enjoying a taco, Villa agrees that Tiburcio should not leave his wife and daughter—and he kills them in cold blood. Enraged, Tiburcio draws a rifle on Villa but is killed by the same general who ordered Miguel Ángel's cremation. Villa and his men ride off, taking Tiburcio's newly orphaned son with them.

Unlike the case of El prisionero 13, cutting that last sequence does not reverse—or even blunt—the film's message. With or without that ending, the film still portrays the revolution as a barbaric tragedy that cost too many lives and changed too little. Furthermore, Tiburcio's fading into darkness is by far the more eloquent conclusion. Yes, the omitted scene would have added another layer of brutality and further chipped away at Villa's reputation as revolutionary idol, but the film as released was a savage enough depiction of the revolution and did plenty to demystify Villa's image as romantic bandit-turned-rebel hero.

THE POETICS OF THE REVOLUTION TRILOGY

Let me now turn to the description of de Fuentes's Classical Mexican Cinema style, which he developed over the course of making the trilogy. His style, distinct from other Mexican filmmakers of the time, was a unique combination of several cinematic elements, enumerated below. The formal choices de Fuentes made and the cinematic techniques I discuss were not merely ornamental; rather, as we'll see, each had a clear narrative function and added ideological dimensions and emotional textures to his storytelling.

FIGS. 5.9–5.16. The last shot of Fernando de Fuentes's
¡Vámonos con Pancho Villa!.

Low-Key Lighting

De Fuentes's fascination with moody German expressionist lighting was in full display in the trilogy. He experimented with it sporadically and tentatively in his earlier films, but used it confidently and extensively in the trilogy—to such a degree that it's sometimes difficult to discern the action. In the films he made afterward, it appears much less frequently (with the exception of the ending of *Doña Barbara* [1943]). How did he employ low-key lighting? Occasionally the way the German filmmakers did, to accentuate the existential predicament of characters caught at a moral crossroads. In *¡Vámonos con Pancho Villa!*, for example, de Fuentes stages a scene where, in a moment of introspection, Los Leones discuss death sitting around a campfire at night, each one, save Tiburcio, unknowingly foretelling his own demise (fig. 5.17). Another example is the scene where Tiburcio is given the order to cremate Miguel Ángel (fig. 5.18).

At other times, de Fuentes used low-key lighting in the manner being adopted around the same time by John Ford—to indicate and underscore sorrow. Just before the slaughter of Gen. Nieto in *El compadre Mendoza*, for instance, Mendoza sends his wife and child away from the hacienda so they won't witness the atrocity about to take place. Close-up shots of them riding away in a coach in the shadowy darkness heighten her sense of loss (fig. 5.19).

De Fuentes also used low-key lighting in the manner utilized by German directors that would later be appropriated by film noir: darkness as an indicator of impending doom,

TOP | FIG. 5.17. *¡Vámonos con Pancho Villa!* Low-key lighting is used to stress the plight of characters caught in an existential situation. Around a campfire, the six Leones talk about how they would like to die, foreshadowing their own deaths later in the film. Here, Panzón (Manuel Tamés) declares that he wants to "die like a man" (*morir a lo macho*). The worst thing, he proclaims, presaging his own death, would be for people to say he died like a coward.

MIDDLE | FIG. 5.18. *¡Vámonos con Pancho Villa!* Low-key lighting is used at a low point for a character. Tiburcio is given the order to kill and cremate his last remaining friend.

BOTTOM | FIG. 5.19. *El compadre Mendoza.* Low-key lighting is used to accentuate sadness. Mendoza sends his wife, Dolores, and her son away from his hacienda just before the murder of Nieto. She knows intuitively that something bad is about to happen, possibly even guessing it will be the killing of the boy's godfather.

a sign of characters' helplessness and loss of agency. Tiburcio's concluding march into darkness in *¡Vámonos con Pancho Villa!*, signaling just how completely the cruelty of the revolution has crushed him, is a perfect example (figs. 5.9–5.16). Another is de Fuentes's staging of the mother's vigil in *El prisionero 13*, on the night before Juan's execution, as she waits for a chance to see Carrasco and plead for their son's life (fig. 5.20).

Related to this was his ominous use of low-key lighting to signal the presence of evil. In de Fuentes's universe, many a corrupt government official's most reprehensible deeds occur in darkness, including the murder of Gen. Nieto in *El compadre Mendoza*, and Villa's command that Tiburcio kill and cremate his friend in *¡Vámonos con Pancho Villa!*

Frame within the Frame

As with Enrique Rosas, a favorite de Fuentes technique was creating frames within the film frame. But in the trilogy de Fuentes used it much more regularly, insistently, and sometimes excessively. Keep in mind that the elimination of extraneous visual information had become a fairly common technique in

FIG. 5.20. *El prisionero 13*. Low-key lighting is used when Marta, Juan's mother (Adela Sequeyro, *right*), and Juan's girlfriend wait all night for an audience with Col. Carrasco.

silent films via the use of irises, vignettes, and masks. Rosas was edging away from this tradition when he used the frame-within-a-frame technique in *El automóvil gris*. In the Revolution Trilogy, however, de Fuentes broke with the silent era's obtrusive guiding-eye composition methods of masks or moving irises in or out, which may have begun to seem mechanical and heavy handed. Very likely influenced by Eisenstein, as I will discuss below, de Fuentes used the frame-within-the-frame technique to feature important details and deemphasize unimportant ones.

Sometimes a frame within the frame was simply an artistic embellishment, a clever visual ornamentation that called attention to itself. During Mendoza's wedding celebration in *El compadre Mendoza*, for instance, de Fuentes first surveys the listless party of the swells going on inside. It's a dull, lifeless party, and the musicians aren't even playing. Then he cuts outside to the farmworkers' much livelier festivities, where camaraderie and music are abundant and liquor flows freely. The contrast makes his ideological point: authentic *mexicanidad* resides with the common people, not with the pretentious bourgeoisie inside. To highlight this idea, among the shots of the working-class revelers de Fuentes includes one of a smiling young woman framed inside the curved arm of the man dispensing drinks to the guests (fig. 5.21).

Another example from the same film is partly directorial flourish, but also an adroit variation on the over-the-shoulder shot that adds dramatic emphasis. It comes when Mendoza's wife, Dolores, first meets General Nieto and thanks him for saving her husband's life. Nieto, out of gentlemanly respect, reaches to take off his sombrero, and

The Classical Mexican Cinema

de Fuentes captures her face in the resulting frame (fig. 5.22). It's a way of indicating their mutual love at first sight. For the rest of the film, Dolores and Gen. Nieto share a platonic love affair, which makes his murder at the end all the more heart wrenching for her.

De Fuentes obviously enjoyed such doubled framing, and looked for imaginative ways to do it. He found an unusual one in an early battle sequence in *¡Vámonos con Pancho Villa!* when he placed Tiburcio and Miguel Ángel within the spokes of a wagon wheel. To our eyes it may seem forced, but it might have looked fresher to moviegoers in 1936, who may well have appreciated it as a clever alternative to "old" silent-era devices like irises and masks (fig. 5.23).

There are, however, numerous cases of de Fuentes creating frames within frames more traditionally and less self-consciously. An effective example occurs in the same battle scene in *¡Vámonos con Pancho Villa!* (fig. 5.24).

TOP | FIG. 5.21. *El compadre Mendoza.* Frame within the frame: the extended arm of the man pouring a drink forms a circular frame around the young woman's face.

BOTTOM | FIG. 5.22. *El compadre Mendoza.* For the scene where Gen. Nieto meets Mendoza's wife, Dolores, de Fuentes creates a frame-within-the-frame variant of the standard Hollywood over-the-shoulder shot that underscores their love at first sight and the beginning of their platonic love affair.

TOP | FIG. 5.23. *¡Vámonos con Pancho Villa!* Tiburcio and Miguel Ángel in a frame-within-the-frame composition from a battle scene.

BOTTOM | FIG. 5.24. *¡Vámonos con Pancho Villa!* A more traditional example of a frame within the frame during a battle sequence.

Frame within the Frame Variant: Bookending

De Fuentes created an organic type of frame-within-the-frame composition by bookending. In this case, de Fuentes divided the frame into vertical thirds, placed the important action in the middle, and filled the outer two-thirds with less important information, drawing and holding viewers' attention on the center. A perfect example occurs in an early shot of Villa, seen between the figures of two of the Leones in *¡Vámonos con Pancho Villa!* (fig. 5.25).

Some of de Fuentes's most notable examples of bookending occur in *El prisionero 13*: the shot of men on the street discussing the arrest of the revolutionaries (fig. 5.26), the sentry's waking the troops at dawn on the morning of the execution (fig. 5.27), the revolutionaries, tightly flanked by columns of soldiers on either side, being led to the firing squad (fig. 5.28), and Carrasco awakening from his nightmare (fig. 5.10). In the first three of these compositions de Fuentes

TOP | FIG. 5.25. *¡Vámonos con Pancho Villa!* Villa meets Los Leones de San Pablo in a shot that illustrates bookending, a frame-within-the-frame variant.

BOTTOM | FIG. 5.26. *El prisionero 13.* Bookending combined with vignetting highlights the conversation of the two men in the center.

TOP | FIG. 5.27. *El prisionero 13.* The sentry alerts the troops the morning of the execution. Here de Fuentes's frame-within-the-frame strategy combines bookending and vignetting. The addition of a low camera angle makes the soldier more imposing and creates a sharp contrast with the helplessness of the doomed prisoners.

BOTTOM | FIG. 5.28. *El prisionero 13.* The revolutionaries, flanked by the army troops, are led to their execution (bookending and vignetting).

The Classical Mexican Cinema

combined bookending with vignetting—making the center brighter than the rest of the frame—to draw the viewers' gaze there.[18] And since the center of de Fuentes's frames contained the most interesting information, it tended to linger there.

Use of Diagonals

Another technique borrowed from painting and graphic design that de Fuentes favored was the use of diagonals in his compositions. A diagonal line may be thought of as graphically restless, midway between the strong solidity suggested by a vertical line and the stable equilibrium of a horizontal one. In a way, the diagonal seeks graphic resolution—either all the way up and vertical or all the way down and horizontal. Because it is suspended between, it adds dynamism and energy to the frame, and as an "unresolved" graphic component, it introduces a note of visual tension. As such, the diagonal as used by de Fuentes was a graphic element that added to his narration in several compositions of the trilogy films. For instance, diagonals appear in *¡Vámonos con Pancho Villa!* to convey the energy and excitement of the revolution. Diagonal compositions are part of the film's visual rhetoric, particularly early in the film, where they are used to depict the revolution as an undeniable force whose momentum swept across the nation and captivated Los Leones (figs. 5.29–5.30).

In another example, de Fuentes cleverly matched a diagonal composition across two shots in the same scene. As mentioned earlier, an early shot of Villa in *¡Vámonos con Pancho Villa!* shows him dispensing maize to a crowd from inside the freight car, a shot that works on several levels at once (fig. 5.31). It's a

TOP | **FIG. 5.29.** *¡Vámonos con Pancho Villa!* The connecting rods of the train's running gear create a dynamic diagonal, suggesting the powerful forward thrust of the revolution.

BOTTOM | **FIG. 5.30.** *¡Vámonos con Pancho Villa!* This diagonal shot shows Villa's army on the move.

frame-within-the-frame composition that introduces Villa as the revolution's Robin Hood, stealing from the rich to give to the poor. The interior frame accentuates depth as our eye travels diagonally from the soldier's bandolier at the right bottom foreground up to Villa leaning out to distribute the corn, then out to the sea of outstretched sombreros beyond. De Fuentes links this diagonal composition with another right-to-left upward diagonal in a shot of a woman in the throng extending her *olla* so that Villa can fill it with maize (fig. 5.32). The two shots epitomize the democratic idealism that motivated the early days of the rebellion and caused the six friends to join Villa's army.

FIG. 5.31. Diagonal composition combined with frame within the frame, emphasizing depth in *¡Vámonos con Pancho Villa!*.

FIG. 5.32. A second diagonal composition from the same scene in *¡Vámonos con Pancho Villa!* matches the right-to-left upward line of the shot of Villa.

Diagonal Compositions in *El prisionero 13*'s Execution Scene

TOP | FIG. 5.33. *El prisionero 13*. A soldier tries to wake an unresponsive prisoner only to discover that he has committed suicide.

BOTTOM | FIG. 5.34. *El prisionero 13*. The rebels' final roll call before their execution.

TOP | FIG. 5.35. *El prisionero 13*. The revolutionaries are led to the firing squad.

BOTTOM | FIG. 5.36. *El prisionero 13*. Juan, lined up next to another prisoner, braces himself as he is about to be executed by the firing squad (the final diagonal).

De Fuentes used diagonal compositions in *El prisionero 13* for a different effect, to add tension in the execution scene. As the prisoners are taken from their cell and led to the firing squad, the suspense mounts as to whether Carrasco and Juan's mother will be able to save Juan. De Fuentes uses a series of diagonals to visually underscore the tension (figs. 5.33–5.36). The strong horizontal line created by the aimed rifles of the firing squad ultimately resolves the series of pre-execution diagonals (fig. 5.37).

Editing: The Faces of Mexico Montage

One of de Fuentes's favorite devices was a montage of brief shots to give a quick cross section of the Mexican people. Liberty, equality, and democracy for all Mexicans were key tenets of the revolution, and artists from Posada to the muralists celebrated the nation's social variety, with filmmakers following suit. Thus in scenes where a crowd is gathered, de Fuentes would take the opportunity to present a series of quickly edited portraits of the nation's populace, usually favoring the peons and working classes (figs. 5.38–5.40; figs. 5.41–42, and 5.43–46). Significantly, there were no montages of the bourgeoisie in de Fuentes's films.

Editing: Analog Montage

De Fuentes's favorite scene-to-scene transition, the analog montage (a term coined by García Riera),[19] was a graphic match on action that moved the story ahead in time and shifted to a different space. For instance, in *El prisionero 13* de Fuentes showed the growth of Juan from a small child to a young man by repeating the action of his mother knotting his tie at three different times (figs. 5.47–5.49).

FIG. 5.37. *El prisionero 13.* The rifles' repeated horizontal lines provide a stark resolution to the previous series of diagonal compositions.

FIGS. 5.38–5.40. *El compadre Mendoza.* Faces of Mexico: some of the partygoers at the outdoors workers' celebration.

FIGS. 5.41 AND 5.42. *¡Vámonos con Pancho Villa!* Faces among the throng gathered to receive corn from Villa.

Like the wagon spoke frame-within-a-frame in *¡Vámonos con Pancho Villa!*, analog montage has not worn well. One problem was that the edits were not always smooth, and their lack of fluidity often impeded rather than facilitated the narrative's time-space shift. Whatever the case, analog montage joined several other short-lived editing techniques in vogue in the 1930s such as wind-blown calendar pages and the use of various exotic types of wipes—both of which de Fuentes used in *El compadre Mendoza*—that did not endure in film language. As fades and dissolves became the standardized time-place transitions, unsuccessful experiments like flashy wipes and analog montage were relegated to the cinematic dustbin. However, this kind of trial and error was characteristic of late 1920s and early 1930s cinema and

FIGS. 5.43–5.46. *¡Vámonos con Pancho Villa!* Faces in a cantina visited by the Leones.

The Classical Mexican Cinema

FIGS. 5.47–5.49. *El compadre Mendoza.* De Fuentes favored analog montage to shift the story in time and space. Here, time passes and Juan grows into manhood. Although these are brief shots and come in quick succession, they are linked differently. A dissolve joins the first two, and a fade-to-black the next two.

demonstrates that de Fuentes was not afraid of using the medium in new and interesting ways. Emerging developments in montage by the Soviets, along with innovations by directors like French auteur Abel Gance, prompted young, adventurous filmmakers like de Fuentes to experiment with editing. But later in his career, when analog montage didn't catch on, he dropped it.

The Long Take with Moving Camera

De Fuentes sometimes departed from the analytical editing style that gradually came to dominate Hollywood and international filmmaking. At times de Fuentes would follow the standard long shot (LS)—medium shot (MS)—close-up (CU) progression, but at others preferred moving the camera to capture entire scenes in one long take. This certainly had a European flavor, a fusion of the longer take tableau style of the 1910s and the gracefully moving camera of a filmmaker like F. W. Murnau, which, as we'll see, was a favorite of de Fuentes.

The most impressive example of the extended take and moving camera technique in the trilogy occurs in *El prisionero 13*, in the pivotal scene where the prisoners become aware that they are about to be executed. De Fuentes captures the entire scene, which includes LSs, MLSs, and several MSs, in a single 102-second mobile shot (figs. 5.50–5.55).

THE EISENSTEIN INFLUENCE

Now that we have described de Fuentes's visual style, and before we proceed to analyze the narrative structure of the trilogy films, it may be beneficial to pause and speculate on the degree to which he may have been

FIGS. 5.50–5.55. *El prisionero 13*. The long take with moving camera. In one 102-second take, de Fuentes begins with an establishing LS of the rebels gathering around Juan, then moves the camera closer for a MLS of the group. Moving in tighter, he isolates Juan being questioned by the revolutionary leader (Antonio R. Frausto, *right*) in a MS two-shot, tilts up for MS commentary from some of the rebels, then back down to the MS two-shot as the leader realizes that they are about to be executed and announces the news to the others. To conclude the scene, de Fuentes tracks the camera back to the initial LS position. Since LSS often connote sadness, it is the ideal emotional ending to the scene.

affected by Eisenstein's unfinished Mexican film project. Earlier in this chapter I repeated a commonplace precept of Mexican film history that Eisenstein's unfinished *¡Que viva México!* influenced Cine de Oro filmmakers. Not being able to find an instance of de Fuentes mentioning it, however, prompted me to search for correspondences between the two filmmakers in their films. Accordingly, I created a side-by-side comparison of some of Eisenstein's imagery in *¡Que viva México!* with de Fuentes's trilogy to see what affinities might reveal themselves. Here are some of the more striking similarities from Eisenstein's *¡Que viva México!* and de Fuentes's trilogy (figs. 5.56–5.65).

The Classical Mexican Cinema

A couple of important points need to be made here. The first is a caution about the nature of Eisenstein's effect on Cine de Oro filmmakers. Thinking of it as going in only one direction is too reductive. The trail of inspiration and influence was richer and more complicated than that, and is better described, in the words of Eduardo de la Vega Alfaro, as an "aesthetic praxis" of Mexican visual arts that Eisenstein became aware of, then participated in.[20] As de la Vega Alfaro argues, Eisenstein's imagery in *¡Que viva México!* was inspired by a host of sources, most of them Mexican: Posada; the muralists and other artists; Anita Brenner's 1929 anthropological study of Mexican history,

society, and culture, *Idols behind Altars*;[21] the illustrations in that book, which included photography by Edward Weston and Tina Modotti; and what Eisenstein discovered with his own, very alert, eyes. And, as film historian Aurelio de los Reyes has made clear, he was also influenced by the revolution, seeing it as another instance of the class struggle.[22] The best way to appreciate the Eisensteinian effect on Mexican cinema, then, is not to see it as a straight line from *¡Que viva México!* to el Cine de Oro, but instead as a circle of influence. It originated with Mexico, its people and artists; it was absorbed by Eisenstein into *¡Que viva México!*; that in turn affected Mexican film artists and seeped into

FIGS. 5.56 AND 5.57. Frame within a frame: *top*, *¡Que viva México!*; *bottom*, *El compadre Mendoza*.

FIGS. 5.58 AND 5.59. Frame within a frame: just as Eisenstein used a cactus to frame a revolutionary firing his rifle, so too de Fuentes used one to frame Panzón taking target practice in *¡Vámonos con Pancho Villa!*.

FIGS. 5.60 AND 5.61. Bookending: *top, ¡Que viva México!; bottom, ¡Vámonos con Pancho Villa!*

FIGS. 5.62 AND 5.63. Diagonal compositions: the diagonal is omnipresent in Eisenstein's films, including *¡Que viva México!* Compare this image with that of the woman already discussed in *¡Vámonos con Pancho Villa!*

their films, where, finally, it was returned back to Mexico and Mexicans, who were the movies' primary audience. In the next chapter we will see how Emilio Fernández and Gabriel Figueroa also adapted Eisenstein's style to create their own.

The second point is that however much de Fuentes consciously adopted some of *¡Que viva México!*'s visual imagery, what he took from Eisenstein was selective. For instance, he rejected Eisenstein's dialectical montage, with its emphasis on colliding shots against each other. It is of course impossible to know how and to what degree dialectical montage would have figured in *¡Que viva México!*, since Eisenstein never had the chance to edit

it. Moreover, scholars like David Bordwell and Masha Salazkina have argued convincingly that Eisenstein's Mexican experience marked a turning point in his theory and filmmaking practice, away from his montage-as-collision films of the 1920s, where clashing images were central, and toward editing as synthesis, where "the conflicts of montage are absorbed into a harmonic unity," as Bordwell puts it.[23] So it's difficult to say whether *¡Que viva México!* would have been the last of his "collision films" or the first of the "synthesis" ones (like Bordwell and Salazkina, I suspect the latter).

But what is clear is that de Fuentes spurned Eisenstein's collision editing. The

The Classical Mexican Cinema

obvious place for any semblance of that to appear would have been in de Fuentes's faces of Mexico montages. But while those series of shots may possess the rapid rhythm of dialectical montage, de Fuentes was not colliding images here. The variety and contrast as he cut from one face to the next was not meant to be jarring but rather celebratory of Mexico's diverse society, specifically its working class. On the whole, de Fuentes's editing was more in tune with V. I. Pudovkin's notion of montage as linkage—whose function was to guide a viewer through the narrative—rather than as collision. This was certainly the logic behind analog montage. Regarding his overall cinematic style, as we've seen, de Fuentes's long take plus mobile camera method was firmly in the tableau tradition filtered through F. W. Murnau, very likely a favorite of the director's.[24]

NARRATIVE STRUCTURE OF THE FILMS

All the films of the trilogy are tragedies, stories about the downfall of a protagonist as a result of a fateful decision. Shakespeare's tragedies are the classic models. Hamlet decides to kill his uncle, the king, out of a sense of honor. Due to the corrosive combination of moral weakness and ambition, Macbeth decides to kill the king and take his place. The tragic structure of Shakespeare's tragic plays and de Fuentes's trilogy is shown in fig. 5.66.

This graph of the tragic dramatic structure is known as Freytag's Pyramid, after Gustav Freytag, who introduced it in 1863. It depicts the main character's journey as a rising line that charts the increasing tension up until the climax, which usually occurs roughly midway through the play.[25] The climax marks the main character's major decision, one that seals his or her downfall (Hamlet decides to kill his uncle, the king, but mistakenly kills Polonius instead; Macbeth decides to murder the king, and actually does it). The downward sloping line after the climax is the falling action where the tragic results of the protagonist's decision are depicted. Rhetorically, the placement of the climax near the midpoint makes the tragic structure perfect for cautionary tales. Audiences are allowed to

FIGS. 5.64 AND 5.65. Incorporation of local flora: following Posada, Orozco, and very possibly the photography of Tina Modotti and Edward Weston, Eisenstein used the maguey plant as a key visual element in ¡*Que viva México!*, and titled one of the sections of the film after it. In that segment, he used the maguey to frame the death of a peon during a shoot-out with *hacendados*. De Fuentes staged the death of one of Los Leones similarly in ¡*Vámonos con Pancho Villa!*.

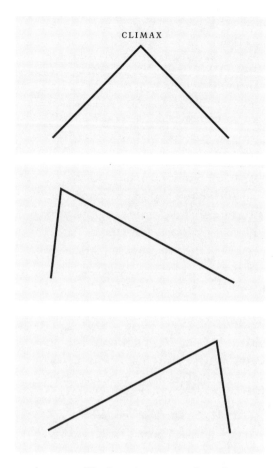

CLIMAX

TOP | FIG. 5.66. The dramatic structure of tragedy, described by Gustav Freytag in 1863. At the midpoint climax, the protagonist makes a fateful decision. Examples include *Hamlet* and *Macbeth*, as well as the Revolutionary Trilogy films.

MIDDLE | FIG. 5.67. The tragic structure of *King Lear*, de Fuentes's *El prisionero 13*, and, as we'll see, *¡Vámonos con Pancho Villa!*.

BOTTOM | FIG. 5.68. The censored version of *El prisionero 13* had this structure, identical to Hollywood's happy-ending movies, with the climax moved to the film's final minutes. In a Hollywood climax, the protagonist makes a *good* decision and triumphs.

consider the consequences of a character's bad action for some time and in some depth.

A good example from the trilogy is *El compadre Mendoza*. Mendoza betrays Gen. Nieto at minute 69 of an 81-minute film by arranging the meeting where his compadre will be murdered. Though it has a later-than-usual climax, *El compadre Mendoza* is still tragic, marking the downfall of its protagonist.

But as this film illustrates, the climax's center placement is not a hard-and-fast rule. Even in Shakespeare's tragedies its position could vary quite a lot. While *Hamlet* has a perfectly symmetrical pyramidal structure, *Macbeth*'s murder of the king occurs earlier than the midpoint. And in *King Lear* the climax is earlier still, in the play's second scene. There, Lear announces that he will divide his kingdom into three parts and give one to each of his three daughters. Fatefully, however, he decides to base the size of the endowed parcel on how much they love him. *King Lear*'s dramatic structure looks like fig. 5.67.

This is identical to *El prisionero 13*'s dramatic structure, at least in its original version. Early on—and decades before the revolution—Col. Carrasco makes a bad decision, drunkenly threatening to kill his wife in a fight over the custody of their son. Fed up and terrified, she leaves with their child, goes into hiding, and raises Juan by herself. By beginning during the Porfiriato, de Fuentes mounted a scathing critique of Mexican patriarchy, showing how it undermined the revolution and poisoned future generations. Juan dies because of his father's drunkenness, dishonesty, corruption, and concupiscence. Furthermore, Carrasco's behavior was abetted—and rewarded—by *machismo*, a

The Classical Mexican Cinema

patriarchal system shown to be impervious to the ideals of the revolution, perversely persisting from the Porfiriato through Madero's revolution and into Huerta's regime.

The censored version of the film, however, with its tacked-on happy ending, reversed the outcome and gutted de Fuentes's ideological criticism. To placate the Mexican government, the film's plot was reworked into a structure like that shown in fig. 5.68.

This is the dramatic structure common to most American films. In it, the protagonist makes a last-minute *good* decision and achieves his or her goal. Best suited for telling successful quest stories, it illustrates how doing the right thing is redemptive, resulting in both individual and social benefits. Placing the climax just before the end caps the film with a triumphant conclusion—and denies viewers time to question the plausibility of the ending or delve very deeply into its ideological implications. With less than five minutes left in *Star Wars IV*, for example, Luke Skywalker decides to trust The Force and destroys the Death Star. At a ceremony, he and Han Solo are given medals, and, to the accompaniment of John Williams's soaring fanfare, the film ends and the credits roll.

The climax in the censored version of *El prisionero 13* is even later than that—in the film's last thirteen seconds. Awakening from a drunken nightmare, Carrasco comes to his senses and smashes the bottle of tequila on the floor, silently vowing to turn over a new leaf. The re-edited film transforms it into a conventional Hollywood-type close-call narrative complete with a happy ending—completely invalidating de Fuentes's original critique. No matter how much of a *macho* scoundrel

Carrasco was, the government-censored film says, all will be well because he ultimately renounced his dissolute lifestyle. Moreover, the surprise ending's sudden shift back in time to the days of Porfirio Díaz's regime negates the first version's interpretation of the revolution. De Fuentes's original said that the revolution failed because the corruption and immorality of an ingrained *macho* system undermined it. In the revised film, *the revolution hasn't happened yet*. The resultant *El prisionero 13*, then, is not a critique of the revolution but an indictment of the dishonest Díaz dictatorship. (Of course, looked at more closely, the revised ending makes no sense at all. How could Carrasco's Diaz-era nightmare possibly have forecast the revolution? How could it be so historically precise and prescient as to predict the rise of General Huerta to become president some twenty years in the future?)

The first two films of the trilogy, then, were standard tragedies that effectively utilized the form to make their caustic commentary on the revolution and Mexican patriarchy. The comment made by *¡Vámonos con Pancho Villa!*, an uncommon tragedy, is bleaker still. It is an early-climax tragedy in the shape of *King Lear* and *El prisionero 13*. But it possesses one crucial difference: the misfortunes that befall the six Leones are not the result of character flaws, moral lapses, or bad choices; on the contrary, the Leones are punished for making a *good* choice. Their downfall comes from deciding, at minute 11, to do the honorable and patriotic thing, namely to get involved in the revolution, join Villa, and try to create a better Mexico (fig. 5.8).

Two interpretations of the tragic structure of *¡Vámonos con Pancho Villa!* come to mind, both troubling. One is that Mexicans are cursed, doomed to fail due to some external factor—God, the fates, history, bad luck. A second, darker, explanation is that there is an internal factor, something inherently wrong with Mexicans that prevents them from achieving success—almost as if they possessed some malformed DNA. Either way, ¡Vámonos con Pancho Villa! is a searing portrayal of the revolution, Mexico, and Mexicans, yet one that was consciously made by de Fuentes. Recall his justification of the tragic ending of El compadre Mendoza that I quoted in chapter 1. He could have given it a Hollywood happy ending, he told a reporter at the time. But, he continued, in what could stand as a succinct expression of CMC filmmaking, "Mexican cinema ought to be a faithful reflection of our way of being, bleak and tragic, if what we are attempting is to present truthful profiles of ourselves, rather than making a poor imitation of what we are given by Hollywood."[26]

De Fuentes's unswerving dedication to giving "a faithful reflection" of the Mexican experience probably explains why ¡Vámonos con Pancho Villa! fared so poorly at the box office and also why it is so critically respected in retrospect. Audiences shied away from the film when it was first released because it cut too close to the bone so soon after the fact. It is held in such critically high regard today for being the most honest depiction of the physical, psychological, and moral devastation of a revolution that occurred a century ago. To do that, the film's dramatic structure needed to replicate the revolution's tragic one: initial idealism thwarted by corruption, cruelty, and betrayal.

De Fuentes's Turning Point:
Allá en el Rancho Grande
—

Formally, except for the faces of Mexico and analog montages, de Fuentes pretty much abandoned his experimentation with visual and narrative style in *Allá en el Rancho Grande*. Instead he settled for an entertaining crowd-pleaser that gave Mexico's recent history a conventional happy ending. Thematically and ideologically, *Allá en el Rancho Grande* withdrew from the daring analysis that characterized the trilogy. And though it touched on serious issues—class differences, alcoholism, sexual exploitation by the hacendados—all these social tensions were neatly resolved via a fairy-tale, triple-marriage ending.

Allá en el Rancho Grande begins in post-revolutionary Mexico, 1922, and then jumps forward to the present, but takes place in a sort of Mexican never-never land where the revolution didn't happen. Everyone knows his or her social station and is comfortable with it; benign aristocratic *patróns* treat their contented peons like children, and they, in turn, are happy just to work and live on the Big Ranch. It represented, as García Riera put it, the flight from the violent reality of the revolution to the bucolic myth of the happy hacienda.[27]

It was also the movie Mexicans wanted to see. (And the Mexico that international audiences wanted to see, too.) Part romantic melodrama, part comedy, part musical, it originated the *comedia ranchera*, a uniquely hybrid genre that became a staple of Mexican cinema for decades. It is probably the most celebrated, best known, and most seen Mexican film of all time; everyone knows and can sing the lyrics of its title song. Its profits gave Mexican filmmaking a sturdy financial footing and ushered in the Golden Age. It solidified de Fuentes's place as the premier director in Mexico.

But in going from the Revolution Trilogy to *Allá en el Rancho Grande*, de Fuentes left classical filmmaking for the mainstream. He would never return. Though he would continue to be acclaimed a preeminent director for the rest of his life, he would no longer be considered the leader of Mexico's cinematic vanguard. That spot would be taken over first by Fernández and Figueroa, and then Luis Buñuel. In hindsight, de Fuentes's artistic career had the same tragic *King Lear* structure as the original *El prisionero 13* and *¡Vámonos con Pancho Villa!*. His groundbreaking CMC experimentation arrived at its apex early, with the Revolution Trilogy. But with *Allá en el Rancho Grande* it gave way to an increasingly bland MMC style that was commercially successful but cinematically, thematically, and ideologically conformist.

CHAPTER 6

The Cinematic
Invention of Mexico

THE POETICS AND POLITICS OF
THE FERNÁNDEZ UNIT STYLE

—

HE FILMS THAT Emilio "El Indio" Fernández (1904–1986) directed between 1943 and 1950 are the most explicit disavowal of Hollywood during the Golden Age and Mexican cinema's purest, most successfully sustained realization of an authentically native film form. They perfectly exemplify the Classical Mexican Cinema. His primary collaborator in developing the distinctive nationalistic poetics exhibited in these films was the talented, like-minded Gabriel Figueroa (1907–1997), regarded during his lifetime as one of the world's greatest cinematographers. Their inimitable combination of visual style and cultural criticism evolved over the course of a long and productive partnership that began with the tragic revolutionary-era romance *Flor silvestre* (1943) and gained international recognition when their next film, *María Candelaria* (1943), won the Golden Palm Award at the first Cannes Film Festival in 1946. All told, Fernández and Figueroa worked together for fifteen years on twenty-four films, but the ones they made in the first seven years, from 1943 to 1950, are where their CMC style is most clearly in evidence, and, I would argue, most successfully employed.[1] Beginning in 1950, and certainly after 1951, for a number of reasons—personal, economic, artistic, industrial, and global—Fernández struggled to maintain the bold signature style that was fused so effortlessly to his critique of racism, classism, and *machismo* in his earlier films.

While Fernández's collaborations with Figueroa have drawn considerable historical and critical attention,[2] there have been only a few neoformalist analyses of the distinctive style they developed—though the number is slowly increasing. An essay that I published first in 1992 and in a revised form in 1994[3] has been joined by Lieberman and Hegarty's comparison of Figueroa's cinematography with that of his Hollywood mentor, Gregg Toland,[4] Patrick Keating's study of Figueroa's work with Fernández and Buñuel,[5] and Dolores Tierney's occasional breakdown of Fernández's style in performing her textual analysis.[6] More recently, specific studies of Figueroa's cinematographic style appeared in a volume of the journal *Luna Córnea* that was dedicated to his career; especially insightful are the essays by José Antonio Rodríguez and Ceri Higgins.[7]

The most detailed formal study by far has been filmmaker and author Ceri Higgins's book-length investigation of Figueroa's body of work, *Gabriel Figueroa: Nuevas perspectivas*.[8] As Higgins puts it, her objective in focusing on Figueroa's work is "to examine the reasons why he and his images became the central icons of Latin American cinema."[9] Masterfully researched, closely argued, and carefully written, it is a perceptive investigation of the entirety of Figueroa's film work, not just his partnership with Fernández. On the subject of their collaboration—the focus of this chapter and my previously published essays—Higgins takes me to task for, among other things, giving Fernández most of the credit for the imagery in the films they made together. Guilty as charged. When I first conceived this book, I thought that this chapter would be little more than a slightly updated version of that original essay of mine. As I began working on it, however, I saw that my earlier analysis was flawed, incomplete, and needed revising. I'm glad I have the chance to set the record straight here. Revisiting the Fernández-Figueroa films took me far beyond a simple rewrite of my previous work—it was a major overhaul. I rethought, reconceptualized, and recast the framework of my original essays, and what I present here is a completely new chapter.

In my defense I can say that when I wrote those essays more than two decades ago, tracking down copies of the Fernandez-Figueroa films was extremely difficult, so I was forced to work with only the few that I could get my hands on. Fortunately, most of their films have become available since then, making it possible for me to gain a more comprehensive understanding of their body of work. And one of the things I discovered is that Fernández's 1940s films resulted from the director's collaboration not just with Figueroa, but with two other associates whose contributions were crucial: screenwriter Mauricio Magdaleno and editor Gloria Schoemann. I now consider the Fernández films I analyze here as the product of a four-filmmaker team, the Fernández film unit. Delving into their work from this new perspective revealed that despite Higgins's valuable contribution, there is still analytical work to be done on the remarkable run of films the Fernández unit made from 1943 to 1950. Accordingly, this chapter provides a detailed examination of the poetics of those films, describing their style, tracing their artistic and cinematic influences, and interpreting their thematic and ideological implications.

These films are the bedrock of the Classical Mexican Cinema and among the most revered landmarks of Mexico's cinema. They thrust Fernández, Figueroa, and Mexican film into the international spotlight. At a time when few directors were known, much less thought of as artists, Fernández was celebrated the world over as Mexico's finest filmmaker. Critics both in Mexico and abroad admired his films, which made the rounds at major film festivals. At home, audiences flocked to them, and the industry recognized their quality. Between 1945 and 1949, his films won thirty Ariel Awards (the Mexican equivalent of the Academy Awards, issued yearly by the Mexican Academy of Cinematographic Arts and Sciences) in all the major categories (best film, direction, acting, cinematography, script, musical score, costume design, and editing). Fernández won four Ariels for best direction. Figueroa won five, and was also awarded international prizes at festivals at Cannes, Venice, Locarno, and the Golden Globes in Hollywood.[10]

Since then, Fernández's cinematic legacy has grown and endures to this day. One measure is his films' effect on Mexican art and artists, which may have had an impact as profound as Posada's half a century earlier. In his book on Fernández, published the year of the director's death, 1986, journalist and cultural critic Paco Ignacio Taibo acknowledged the lasting and "powerful influence" that one of his best-known films, *Río Escondido* (1947), had on all manner of artists.[11] Furthermore, many of the films from the first decade of his career are permanent fixtures in the Mexican cinematic canon, as evidenced by the 1994 *Somos* magazine poll of the top one hundred films I referred to previously. A sign of the

preeminent position he holds in Mexican cinema history is the fact that he placed ten films in the poll, the most of any director:

#11—*Enamorada* (*A Woman in Love*, 1946)
#12—*Pueblerina* (*The Woman of the Pueblo*, 1948)
#20—*Víctimas del pecado* (*Victims of Sin*, 1950)
#23—*Río Escondido* (1947)
#28—*Salón México* (1948)
#30—*Flor silvestre* (*Wildflower*, 1943)
#37—*María Candelaria* (1944)
#80—*La perla* (*The Pearl*, 1947)
#92—*La malquerida* (*The Unloved Woman*, 1949)
#93—*Las abandonadas* (*The Abandoned Women*, 1944)

These films defined Mexico on theater screens around the world. As Mexican film historian Emilio García Riera put it, in the eyes of international critics and audiences, the Fernández-Figueroa films "did not simply represent Mexican cinema, they were Mexican cinema."[12]

They are the epitome of the Classical Mexican Cinema in the 1940s. With them, Fernández realized his filmmaking ambition of creating uniquely Mexican films that broke away from what he considered to be Mexico's imitative cinema of the 1930s and 1940s, movies he disdained for being highly derivative, "copied from theatre, from *zarzuela* [Spanish musical comedy], or from the United States."[13] Fernández's nationalistic cinematic goals were formed early, in the mid-1930s, when he was struggling to make the transition from actor and novice screenwriter to director. "I understood that it was possible," he said later, "to create a Mexican cinema with our own actors and our own stories, without having to photograph *gringos* or *gringas* or tell stories that had nothing to do with our people."[14]

Fernández began his directing career in 1942 with this revisionist mind-set, aiming to forge a uniquely Mexican style to tell Mexican stories, about Mexicans, for Mexicans—a perfect eight-word description of the Classical Mexican Cinema. His pursuit of a native film aesthetic received a big boost when he began collaborating with Figueroa on *Flor silvestre* in 1943. The cinematographer was on the same aesthetic quest, and together they began developing their style, drawing inspiration from Mexican artists who were or had been involved in redefining Mexican expressive forms. Particularly important, according to Figueroa, were "Diego Rivera, Rodríguez Lozano, and—above all—José Guadalupe Posada."[15] They were so successful in devising a distinctive national style that Fernández would later boast—and with good reason—"There only exists one Mexico: the one I invented."[16]

Despite his authorial swagger, however, Fernández did not create these CMC films alone. He was lucky to find the ideal collaborator in Figueroa, a man with a background in art, photography, and film who shared the same cinematic goals and possessed the technical expertise to realize them. And he had the additional good fortune of partnering with two other filmmaking colleagues who made important contributions to Fernández-Figueroa's canonical CMC films.

The Fernández Filmmaking Unit

One of the more interesting aspects of the ten Fernández films on the *Somos* list is the consistent presence of a team of fellow filmmakers working with him. Figueroa shot all ten, Gloria Schoemann edited eight, and all but two were coscripted by Fernández with novelist-playwright-journalist-screenwriter-and-sometime-director Mauricio Magdaleno. In light of this, it seems advisable for the critic and historian to consider the ten best-known, most esteemed films as the product of an efficient, closely knit filmmaking group—the Fernández film unit—rather than crediting them solely to Fernández, as is the usual practice, or, occasionally, to the team of Fernández and Figueroa. Such an approach helps explain why the two films Fernández directed before he began working with the team in 1943 lacked the self-assured flair so characteristic of the unit-made films. And, as we will see, the dissolution of the unit is one of the factors that led to the decline evident in the films he directed after 1950. Working without one or more members of his team, his films lacked the style and panache of those made during the peak seven-year period. Significantly, no films made after 1950 appear on the *Somos* list.

In the unit-made films, however, the elements of what is now regarded as the Fernández style appear confidently, naturally, and harmoniously. No doubt Fernández was the guiding hand, but I am hypothesizing that when he worked with these three colleagues—who, like the director, were just launching their film careers at the most exhilarating time in the nation's film history—there was a shared excitement that sparked a special creative chemistry in all of them. The joy of experimentation and discovery coupled with the thrill of blazing new trails alongside trusted, gifted associates were key reasons why the films are distinctive and unlike any other cinema made in Mexico or the world. The four were artistic kindred spirits who shared a common goal, and their talents were complementary; they likely spurred one another to do their best work.

This collaboration resulted in a series of films in which the whole was greater than the sum of its parts—and the parts were considerable. Of them, Figueroa's contribution is easiest to credit; clearly, as Magdaleno said, "without Gabriel, 'Indio' would not have been able to do what he did."[17] But the input of the two lesser-known unit members was critical, too, if more difficult to pin down, as is regrettably too often the case for screenwriters and editors in film history. Nevertheless, from interviews and from the internal evidence of the films themselves I will attempt to piece together the nature of their input and their working relationship with Fernández, who, after all, tied all the creative strands together.

THE DIRECTOR

Though he is the best known of the group, the details of Emilio Fernández's life are the most obscure. Biographers have tried for decades to verify various claims he made—that he taught Rudolph Valentino to dance the tango, for instance (doubtful), or that he was the model for the Oscar statuette (possible, though some dates don't jibe). What emerges from all of this historical detective work is a portrait of an inveterate storyteller who viewed everything—including his life story—as malleable raw material to be shaped into its most captivating narrative form. As we will see when we touch on his screenwriting method, Fernández recounted his past in the same way that he constructed film stories—events, situations, and conversations were freely created, deleted, borrowed, or modified in the service of fashioning a compelling yarn. Thus, though many particulars of his biography need to be taken with more than a grain of salt, the rough shape of it goes like this.

His father was an army officer and his mother was a Kikapú Indian. He attended military school as a young teenager and served in the army shortly thereafter. Fighting on the side of the presidential hopeful Adolfo de la Huerta, who opposed the Alvaro Obregón government in 1923, Fernández was captured and sent to prison. Somehow, he escaped to the U.S.[18]

He ended up in Hollywood, probably in 1926, where he worked odd jobs and then became a movie extra (which paid $7.50 per day),[19] falling in with a colony of other Mexicans and Latin Americans who had migrated there to try their luck in the movies (fig. 6.1). Some, like Dolores del Río, her cousin Ramón Novarro, and Gilbert Roland, had become silent film stars. Some, like Lupe Vélez and Raquel Torres, were on the verge of stardom (Vélez was about to co-star with Douglas Fairbanks in *The Gaucho* [1927]; Torres would star in MGM's first all-talkie feature, *White Shadows in the South Seas* [1928] and later with the Marx Brothers in *Duck Soup* [1933]). Some, like Margo (María Margarita Bolado)

TOP | FIG. 6.1. In one of his jobs as a Hollywood extra, Fernández appeared in "The Carioca" musical number in *Flying Down to Rio* (1933).

BOTTOM | FIG. 6.2. Fernández dancing the *jarabe tapatío* in Fernando de Fuentes's *Allá en el Rancho Grande*.

and Lupita Tovar, were awaiting their big break. (For Margo, a child dancer in her uncle Xavier Cugat's band, it was Frank Capra's *Lost Horizon* [1937]; for Tovar, it was the female lead in the Spanish version of *Dracula* [1931] filmed at Universal.) For some, it never came. Emma Roldán, for example, failed in Hollywood but returned to Mexico and became one of the most successful character actresses of the Golden Age, working steadily until her death in 1978. Like Fernández, several would later become directors back in Mexico: Carlos Navarro (who worked at MGM as production head), Tito Davidson (from Chile), Roberto Gavaldón, Chano Urueta, Gilberto Martínez Solares, and the Cuban René Cardona.[20]

Fernández said he became obsessed with film when he saw fragments of Eisenstein's *¡Que viva México!* in a small editing room in Los Angeles, probably in 1933.[21] "Eisenstein was a revelation for me," he said later. The Soviet director made Fernández realize that "film was the most splendid of all the forms of expression."[22] With his roommate, Chano Urueta, another future director, he began learning how to make movies, and together they made a short experimental film, shooting on weekends with a borrowed camera.[23] By the time he went home to Mexico in 1933 or 1934, he had dedicated himself to a career in movies. Initially, he played small supporting roles (for example, in de Fuentes's *Cruz Diablo* [1934] and *Allá en el Rancho Grande* [1936] (fig. 6.2), and in Urueta's adaptation of the acclaimed novel of the revolution, *Los de abajo* [1940]), and then landed the lead in Carlos Navarro's *Janitzio* (1935). At the same time, he was trying his hand at scriptwriting (*Los muertos hablan* [*The Dead Speak*, 1935], *Cielito lindo* [*Beautiful Sky*, 1936], *Adiós Nicanor* [Goodbye, Nicanor, 1937].[24]

But directing was always the goal, and he got his chance with *La isla de la Pasión* (*Passion Island*, 1942), based on a script he had written and shopped around Mexico City for years.[25] Shot in part on location in Acapulco, the film was a modest commercial and critical success. At the same time, he became fixated on developing an authentic Mexican cinematic aesthetic. As he told one interviewer, his hope was that *La isla de la Pasión* would serve as "a path toward what many of us desire in regards to Mexican cinema. A way to express the spirit of Mexico, and to destroy the false and always pernicious [stereo]typing [of ourselves]." In his opinion, Mexico's cinema was in deplorable shape, due to Mexican filmmakers' "dangerous practice" of making films based on "themes that aren't ours."[26] He had finally directed his first film, one that was well received, but he would not rest until he discovered a way to capture *lo mexicano* on film. Fernández would direct one more film, *Soy puro mexicano* (1942), a rather odd comedy-drama about Nazi spies operating out of a hacienda thwarted by a good-hearted bandit (Pedro Armendáriz), before joining the band of collaborators and finally beginning to make films that expressed "the spirit of Mexico."

THE EDITOR

During a career that spanned four decades, Gloria Schoemann (1910–2006) was one of Mexico's most accomplished, proficient, and prolific editors. A monumental figure in Mexican cinema, she edited 221 films between 1942 and 1983. In the process, she was nominated for eleven best editing Ariels and won three; she also garnered two lifetime achievement awards: the Salvador Toscano Medal from the Cineteca Nacional (1993) and a special Golden Ariel (2004). To give a sense of Schoemann's importance in Mexican film production, it would be fair to say that the place she occupied during the Golden Age was roughly equivalent to Dede Allen's in Hollywood from the late 1950s to 2008. Just as Allen left her imprint on New Hollywood films in the second half of the twentieth century with her editing of films as varied as *Bonnie and Clyde* (1967), *Dog Day Afternoon* (1975), *The Breakfast Club* (1985), and *Wonder Boys* (2000), so too did Schoemann impact four decades of Mexican film, from the Golden Age to Mexico's "Nuevo Cine" (New Cinema) in the 1970s and 1980s.

Born in Mexico City, like many Mexican compatriots in the 1920s and 1930s Schoemann went to Los Angeles as a young woman to work in the movies, finding a few jobs as an extra in several productions. Returning to Mexico, she had a small role in *Hombres del mar* (*Men of the Sea*, 1938, directed by Chano Urueta), and then turned to film editing in 1942. Besides Fernández, during her long career she worked with top Golden Age directors such as Luis Buñuel, Julio Bracho, Miguel M. Delgado, Gilberto Martínez Solares, Roberto Gavaldón, Norman Foster, and Alejandro Galindo.[27]

The Mexican film production system was unlike Hollywood's in that editors were not studio employees, but independent contractors who worked film to film. At the start of her career, she edited at Films Mundiales, the production company that produced Fernández's breakthrough movies. The company was managed by Agustín J. Fink. There, projects were organized by director-teams, as she put it. "When I began at Films Mundiales," she recalled, "I was lucky to be made part of a team; well, I call it that because I always worked on the films of Julio Bracho and Emilio Fernández, all of them in general with Gabriel Figueroa as cinematographer."[28] Here is how Schoemann described the operation of Fernández's "team":

> In those days, the custom was to gather the cinematographer, the screenwriter, the director, and the editor for a script reading; we would then begin to comment on the continuity, the dialogue, and so forth. From the beginning we visualized what was necessary; in addition, the editor had the obligation to indicate which things

[scenes, sequences] didn't add to the whole . . . or would slow down the film's rhythm.[29]

Though Fernández was known to be volatile and temperamental, Schoemann found him extremely easy to work with. "'Indio' heard all the comments," she recalled, and "was very accessible, a joy to work with." Most importantly, a healthy creative atmosphere was fostered in which "everyone respected each individual's specific talent."[30] Magdaleno also noted the unit's upbeat esprit de corps, and credited the amicable and respectful working environment to Fink. "He was a very cultured man," Magdaleno said, "a true creator of film who knew how to treat a team and keep them united."[31]

To get a fuller appreciation of the job Schoemann did, it is important to keep in mind key differences between Mexican filmmaking and the Hollywood and European systems. To begin with, as Schoemann told one interviewer, there was the fairly low standing of editors in Mexico. "In the U.S. and Europe, editors have professional status and are highly respected." In those systems, moreover, "the editor is often present during the shooting, and if she asks for an extra scene or a close-up . . . it is done." In Mexican filmmaking, the editor worked at her editing bench and never visited the set. If a Hollywood editor realized she needed extra shots during the editing process, retakes were routinely scheduled. In Mexico, on the other hand, "retakes or additional scenes never happen, so the editor has to figure out how to solve problems the best she can."[32] This put a lot of pressure on the other members of the unit: Fernández and Magdaleno must have had to write as complete, polished, and

precise a script as possible, and Fernández and Figueroa had to be sure to shoot all the necessary coverage during the filming. As the final link in the creative chain, Schoemann had to assemble a coherent film with whatever footage was delivered to her, whether or not there were missing shots, omitted patches of exposition, breaks in continuity, or holes in the story's logic. Regrettably, because all we see is the final film, we will never know just how creative Schoemann's editing truly was.

THE SCREENWRITER

Mauricio Magdaleno's (1906–86) resumé is as impressive as Schoemann's. From 1933 to 1962, he wrote or cowrote fifty-five produced scripts, working alongside many major directors of the Golden Age cinema. As a young man in Mexico City, he was active in theater companies, wrote plays, and worked as a newspaper reporter. He broke into the movie business with his original story for de Fuentes's *El compadre Mendoza* in 1933, for which he was paid 65 pesos.[33] His next produced script was his first for Fernández— an adaptation of Fernando Robles's novel, *Sucedio ayer* (*It Happened Yesterday*), for the director's breakthrough film, *Flor silvestre*. In between those first two film projects, the prolific Magdaleno was busy writing plays, novels (*El resplandor*, which some consider his best novel, was published in 1937),[34] teaching literature courses, and producing radio programs for the Ministry of Education.

My best guess about Magdaleno's creative role is that he contributed to scripting Fernández's films the way Alfred Hitchcock's screenwriters did for him, that is, by sculpting a narrative out of a catalogue of favorite set pieces that the director had in mind. ("I don't bother about plot," Hitchcock once said, which he regarded "a necessary evil.")[35] Thus, screenwriter Ernest Lehman recalled that the inception of *North by Northwest* (1959) was Hitchcock mentioning to him that he had "always wanted to do a chase across the faces of Mt. Rushmore."[36] Likewise, according to Magdaleno, his general working process with Fernández amounted to this: "Emilio would give me ideas—there were many—and I would select from them."[37]

What another of Hitchcock's scriptwriters, Samuel Taylor, who scripted *Vertigo*, said about him would probably have applied to Fernández as well:

> He was the master of the situation, the master of the vignette, the master of the small moment. He always knew what he wanted to do with those.
>
> . . . So for him, it was like a mosaic, and when he finally got the entire mosaic put together you saw the story. Now, if he didn't have a good writer, there were going to be pieces missing in that mosaic.[38]

Roughly the same dynamic—fashioning a comprehensible narrative "mosaic" from the director's situation inventory—typified the Fernández-Magdaleno collaborative process. Apparently, Fernández, like Hitchcock, thought in movie moments, scenes, and situations, not words. Although extremely articulate in film language, he was not a literary man. "Indio didn't read," Magdaleno recounts, "but he did watch an incredible number of films; he didn't read anything— what did he care about reading?—but when it came to movies, he knew them backwards and forwards."[39]

According to Magdaleno, their working method on *Las abandonadas* (*The Abandoned Women*, 1944) was typical of how they worked on many of Fernández's films. As we will see and as Magdaleno recalled, the "original" story that Fernández came up with was a stitched-together narrative quilt made from bits and pieces of other movies. Evidently this was typical—most of the ideas Fernández routinely rattled off to Magdaleno were characters and plotlines lifted from movies he had seen. When someone would tell him that such and such an element had already been used in this or that film, he responded, "So much the better! It's been proven to be good."[40] Because many were Hollywood films, no doubt a big part of Magdaleno's contribution was to transpose these movie scraps from their American context to a Mexican one. Again, referring to the writing of *Las abandonadas* and Fernández's story for it, Magdaleno recalled: "The truth is that he combined memories of films he had seen in the U.S. He took a little from each one. He would say, 'I saw this and we can use it.' He would also borrow from Mexican history. And from Mexican cinema."[41] Not surprisingly, then, *Las abandonadas* is an amalgam of cinematic and historic elements. Its basic plot was lifted from the Helen Hayes tearjerker *The Sin of Madelon Caudet* (1931), to which was grafted the ending of *Madame X* (1929, 1937) and the infamous case of the *automóvil gris* bandits and Enrique Rosas's *El automóvil gris*.

Constructing a coherent whole from these borrowed snippets must have taken up a lot of Magdaleno's and Fernández's scriptwriting time. In contrast to Hitchcock, Fernández possessed a firm grasp of story and plot, at least in broad strokes. "I am magnificent at dramatic construction," he bragged. "More than a writer, I am a dramatic architect, a dramatist. . . . I have a very keen dramatic imagination in story construction."[42] But Magdaleno must have had a knack for plot structure too. Reflecting on their partnership and the workings of the unit, Figueroa concurred with Fernández's self-assessment, at the same time acknowledging Magdaleno's substantial organizational contribution:

> Mauricio Magdaleno, who worked on all his [Fernández's] films . . . was an excellent writer. Emilio would sketch out the story and ask Magdaleno to develop it further. Magdaleno was very familiar with Mexican history, and knew the particulars of the Mexican Revolution very well. He had even been Sub-secretary of Education. I am sure he introduced changes and invented a great deal.[43]

Magdaleno's job, then, appears to have been fashioning a final script from, first, the ideas the director gave him, and then the plot outline that he and Fernández developed. Going from outline to finished script, Magdaleno must have fleshed out the narrative, filled in the connective tissue, and provided the necessary details—transitions, characterization, and dialogue.[44] As Figueroa suggests, no doubt Magdaleno added and subtracted things during the drafting process, as Fernández must have, too, with the director having the deciding vote.

And it was Fernández who also specified who got screen credit. In Mexican films of the time, the writing credit was split into two parts: *argumento* (original story) and *adaptación* (screenplay). Magdaleno suggests that Fernández designated credit to suit himself, and in most of the eight films we're considering that they wrote together, he usually gave himself story credit and shared the scriptwriting credit with Magdaleno—regardless of the actual division of writing labor. In one interview, however, Magdaleno claimed that he alone wrote the story for *Río Escondido*. When asked why Fernández received original story screen credit for it, he replied: "Well, that's the way Emilio is. Sometimes he'd put my name down as storywriter, sometimes as screenwriter. We never discussed that. But for certain that story is totally mine."[45] And Magdaleno was even more adamant in claiming sole story credit for *Salón México*, too, though on screen he shared both story and scriptwriting credit with Fernández. "*Salón México* is my film," he said. To such a degree, he went on, that "you could say that the only thing I didn't do was direct it."[46]

The obvious irony in Fernández's borrowing from American movies, of course, was that he was simultaneously promoting himself as the anti-Hollywood, thoroughly authentic Mexican filmmaker. I will return to this seeming conundrum later in the chapter, when I do a close reading of *Las abandonadas* and examine some of his swiping from Hollywood in that and other of his films. But for now let me propose that even though he did copy bits from Hollywood cinema, he transformed them in his films, made them his own, had them say what he wanted to say, and, paradoxically, remained true to his goal of developing a genuine Mexican cinema.

The Classical Mexican Cinema

As a boy, Gabriel Figueroa learned painting at the Academy of San Carlos, the school of the arts in Mexico City, which he credits with teaching him the basics of composition, perspective, and light. He also studied the violin at the National Conservatory of Music, but was forced to cut short his formal training when his family could no longer afford the tuition. Interested in the arts, but needing to support himself with something practical, he took up photography, doing passport pictures and odd jobs for a professional photographer, José Guadalupe Velasco, where he began to learn studio lighting.[47] Figueroa worked freelance for a time after that, and then became a still photographer on various film productions from 1932 to 1934, among them Arcady Boytler's *La mujer del puerto* (1934). Once on the film shoots, his interest gradually shifted to cinematography.[48]

He became part of the camera crew, working his way up from lighting assistant to camera operator on *¡Vámonos con Pancho Villa!*.[49] Though he had befriended two of the leading directors of photography in Mexico, the Hollywood transplants Alex Phillips and Jack Draper, he felt he needed formal technical training. At the founding of CLASA studios, he was asked to sign on as one of its first employees. Instead, he proposed a deal. If they would send him to study cinematography in Hollywood, when he returned he would work for CLASA. To his surprise, they accepted and in 1935 he left for a four-month scholarship to study in Hollywood.[50]

Once there, he tracked down a former associate of Phillips's, Gregg Toland, one of Hollywood's leading cinematographers. By that time Toland had nearly a decade's worth of filmmaking experience to his credit and was about to embark on a chapter of his career during which he would shoot some of the most stunningly photographed films of the studio era, among them William Wyler's *Wuthering Heights* (1939), *The Little Foxes* (1941), and *The Best Years of Our Lives* (1946); John Ford's *The Grapes of Wrath* (1940) and *The Long Voyage Home* (1940); and Orson Welles's *Citizen Kane* (1941). Toland agreed to mentor Figueroa and they became lifelong friends.

Returning to Mexico, Figueroa signed with CLASA and was lighting assistant and operator for Draper on *María Elena* (1936); he then shared director of photography credit with him on three more films, all directed by de Fuentes (*¡Vámonos con Pancho Villa!* [1936], *Cielito lindo* [1936], and *Las mujeres mandan* [1937]). As luck would have it, his first solo credit as director of photography was on de Fuentes's *Allá en el Rancho Grande*, which, as we have seen, was a foundational film for Mexico's Cine de Oro; it also brought him international recognition when he won the award for best cinematography at the 1938 Venice Film Festival.[51]

Having established himself as a top director of photography, he embarked on a search for a visual style that would faithfully record the national experience. Like his friend Diego Rivera and other painters and muralists such as José Clemente Orozco and David Alfaro Siqueiros, Figueroa "looked to realize a Mexican cinematography." He was driven, he said, by a desire "to succeed in gaining recognition for the Mexican landscape throughout the world. That was the expression that the great artists, the painters, the writers . . . were searching for. I was part of that movement of artists who expressed—or better said, sought to find—the Mexican style."[52] A few years later he would meet Fernández, who was also struggling to develop a nationalistic cinematic form, and together they created the most distinctive style in Mexican film history.

In 1941, Figueroa and a group of fellow filmmakers, among them director Chano Urueta and actor Arturo de Córdova, formed a new production company, Films Mundiales, with businessman Agustín J. Fink brought in as company president.[53] It was a cooperative venture in which, according to Figueroa, "All of us contributed 50 percent of our salaries in exchange for a partnership" in the company.[54] (Later I will discuss the fate of this joint venture.) One of Films Mundiales's upcoming projects was *Flor silvestre*. Fernando de Fuentes was Fink's first choice to direct, but he was already committed to make *Doña Barbara* (1943) with María Félix. De Fuentes recommended Fernández, and Fink hired him along with Magdaleno as his cowriter, and Figueroa as director of photography.

"It was with Fernández," Figueroa recalled, "that I really began to develop my own style." In Fernández, Figueroa had found a cinematic dynamo whose pursuit of an authentic Mexican cinema perfectly aligned with his own search for "Mexican cinematography." "We spoke the same language," Figueroa said. "We thought in images."[55] Their working relationship was based on a mutual trust that was established early. "He liked my work from the very first camera placement," Figueroa said, describing their first job together on *Flor silvestre*.[56]

The usual practice was for Fernández to explain the general objective of the shot and then leave the details of framing, lighting, and composition to Figueroa. As Figueroa recalled:

He [Fernández] allowed me to compose a scene anyway I wanted. He would describe the setup initially, explain what he wanted to convey, and then say something like, "There, now set up the lights and put the camera wherever you wish." So I would place the camera, choose the angle, and illuminate a scene, always looking for the desired effect.[57]

With all the unit members in place, just one more thing needs to be discussed before I begin the analysis of the Fernández unit style—the state of Mexico's film industry. This is important to understand because, as luck would have it, at the exact time that Fernández rose to prominence, Mexico became the world's dominant Spanish-language film producer.

Mexican Film Culture during World War II

The coincident boom in Mexican filmmaking that occurred from 1940 to 1947 was a major factor in Fernández's becoming *the* Mexican auteur. In large measure, it was attributable to the U.S.'s World War II–era Good Neighbor Policy and the resulting Mexico-USA pact. Under the terms of the agreement, Mexico gave the U.S. "military co-operation, inexpensive labor and guaranteed sales of raw materials." In exchange, "Mexico received numerous loans and technological aid to invigorate its shaky economy to reposition itself in the Latin American, European and even

US markets." As part of the arrangement, Hollywood provided Mexico's cinema industry with technical support, raw materials, film stock, "and, on several occasions, made direct production investments."[58]

This led to the production of films with greater budgets and better production values than had previously been seen in Mexico. That in turn resulted in Mexico becoming the leading Spanish-language film industry, eclipsing Argentina and Spain (neither of which received Hollywood support, for political reasons). Table 6.1 shows annual film production during the Golden Age.[59] We'll look at the postwar years later, but for now notice how the Mexican film industry flourished during wartime, particularly the jump in production from 1940 to 1945.

One of the greatest beneficiaries of the industry's unprecedented economic prosperity was Fernández. After directing two hits in 1943, *Flor silvestre* and *María Candelaria*, he enjoyed big budgets and the freedom to make the films he wanted to make. Higher budgets generally ensured longer shooting schedules, allowing him and Figueroa to work at their optimum, more measured, creative pace. Table 6.2 lists all of Fernández's Golden Age films along with, where available, the films' costs. The budgets for his films made between 1944 and 1948 were high, with several over 1 million pesos. Comparing that with the 100,000-peso budget for his first film, *La isla de la Pasión*, in 1942, which was closer to the cost of a typical film at the time, gives a sense of his privileged status.

Producers were willing to bankroll him as long as his films were popular. Determining exactly how well they performed at the box office, however, is difficult if not impossible

TABLE 6.1.
Annual film production during the Golden Age

Year	Number of films produced
1938	57
1939	37
1940	29
1941	37
1942	47
1943	70
1944	75
1945	81
1946	71
1947	58
1948	81
1949	108
1950	122
1951	101
1952	98
1953	77
1954	112
1955	83
1956	90
1957	94
1958	104

Source: Emilio García Riera, *Historia documental del cine mexicano (1959–1960)*, vol. 10 (Guadalajara, Mexico: University of Guadalajara Press, 1994), 13–14.

TABLE 6.2.
Budget and length of first run for Fernández's Golden Age films

Film	Year	Budget (in pesos)	Length of first run	Film	Year	Budget (in pesos)	Length of first run
La isla de la Pasión	1942	100,000	2 weeks	Islas Marías	1951	—	1 week
Soy puro mexicano	1942	—	1 week	Siempre tuya	1952	—	1 week
Flor silvestre	1943	—	4 weeks	La bien amada	1951	600,000	1 week
María Candelaria	1944	—	4 weeks	Acapulco	1952	—	2 weeks
Las abandonadas	1945	1,200,000	6 weeks	El mar y tú	1952	—	2 weeks
Bugambilia	1945	1,300,000	4 weeks	Cuando levanta la niebla	1952	—	4 weeks
Pepita Jiménez	1946	—	3 weeks	La red	1953	—	2 weeks
La perla	1947	2,500,000	5 weeks	Reportaje	1953	—	4 weeks
Enamorada	1946	—[a]	7 weeks	El rapto	1954	—	3 weeks
Río Escondido	1948	1,025,000	4 weeks	Rosa blanca[c]	1954	—	1 week
Maclovia	1948	Approx. 1,000,000	9 weeks	La rebelión de los colgados[b]	1954	—	3 weeks
Salón México	1949	600,000	3 weeks	Nosotros dos[c]	1955	—	1 week
Pueblerina	1949	400,000	3 weeks	La Tierra de Fuego se apaga[c]	1955	—	Not exhibited in Mexico
La malquerida	1949	600,000	4 weeks				
Duelo en las montañas	1950	500,000	1 week	Una cita de amor	1958	—	3 weeks
The Torch	1950	—	1 week	El impostor	1960	—	1 week
Un día de vida	1950	—	1 week				
Víctimas del pecado	1951	—	2 weeks				

SOURCES: Various volumes of Emilio García Riera's *Historia documental del cine mexicano* (Guadalajara, Mexico: University of Guadalajara Press, 1994) and García Riera's *Emilio Fernández, 1904–1986* (Guadalajara: University of Guadalajara Press, 1987).

NOTES: 1. After 1950, the budgets of most films are difficult to determine. 2. *La rebelión de los colgados* was begun by Fernández, who quit over a dispute with the producer and was replaced by Alfredo B. Crevenna. 3. After 1956, Fernández would not direct again until 1961, after the Cine de Oro era was over. 4. The films are listed in the order in which they were completed, not released; the dates given are the Mexico City release dates.

[a] The budget for *Enamorada* is not known, but it must have been an expensive film. According to Benito Alazraki, the film's producer, María Félix's salary alone was 300,000 pesos.

[b] Fernández was replaced as director.

[c] Films made outside of Mexico: *Rosa blanca* in Cuba, *Nosotros dos* in Spain, *La Tierra de Fuego se apaga* in Argentina.

to know. No financial records of ticket sales exist for this period, and therefore the metric I used to measure commercial success is the length of a film's first run in Mexico City. By this standard, table 6.2 illustrates that the dozen films from *Flor silvestre* to *La malquerida* did very well indeed.[60]

Until 1950, then, Fernández had it all: a supportive creative team, optimal working conditions, generous budgets, box office success, industry recognition, and festival awards. During that time, the Fernández unit created an impressive body of work unlike anything ever filmed, exquisite films that perfectly exemplified the Classical Mexican Cinema.

The Poetics of the Fernández Unit Style
—

The Fernández unit style was created by borrowing and synthesizing from numerous artistic and cinematic sources. So as I work my way down this list and describe the films' poetics, I will at the same time be discussing their influences, sources, and inspirations. Sometimes, if one of the unit members explicitly refers to it, as Magdaleno did in the case of *Las abandonadas*, the connection is clear. At other times, the evidence is circumstantial. In these instances, I will make the case for my informed guesses based on evidence in the films compared to the work of an artist or similar elements (a scene, a situation) present in another film.

Until I arrive at the section on narrative structure and thematics, much of what follows focuses on the films' visual style. Therefore, I will necessarily be addressing the contribution and collaboration of Fernández and Figueroa. This is not to say that Magdaleno and Schoemann did not

contribute to the look of the films. Though it appears unlikely as a general rule, from time to time Magdaleno might well have specified the visual particulars for a shot or scene in the script. And Schoemann, responsible for organizing the images given her into the film's coherent final form, unquestionably affected the films' visuals as well as, to a degree at least, their sound design. But, as I have said, their efforts are much more difficult to credit. Furthermore, since neither Magdaleno nor Schoemann were present on the set, it was primarily Fernández and Figueroa's job to create and capture the images that would ultimately become the film.

Finally, let me be clear about what I am claiming here. Except in a few instances, such as the inventive way Figueroa's filtering system captured the clouds and his innovative rendering of extreme blacks in *Río Escondido*, I am not saying that these formal characteristics were discovered or used exclusively by the Fernández unit. Other filmmakers, in Mexico and beyond, utilized them; many had been in use since the days of silent cinema. Fernando de Fuentes's *¡Vámonos con Pancho Villa!* used foreground objects and the maguey plant as framing devices, but such compositions gradually disappeared from his work after that film and *Allá en el Rancho Grande*. (Tellingly, Gabriel Figueroa was the assistant director of photography on the first and the cinematographer on the second.) The use of the native agave plant somewhat in the manner of Eisenstein-Tisse could also be found in a film like *Enemigos* (1934), directed by Chano Urueta.

In the U.S., numerous films noir used darkness and shadow to portray a treacherous worldview. Around the same time as the

Fernández unit was producing its best work, several Hollywood filmmakers, including John Ford, Orson Welles, William Wyler, and Anthony Mann, were making extensive use of the extreme foregrounding of characters, low-key lighting, and low camera angles (once again, all were practices dating back to silent cinema). Other international directors, such as Kenji Mizoguchi and Jean Renoir, had used extreme foregrounded elements to expand the depth of field in the frame.[61] What I do maintain in this chapter, however, is that no Mexican or Hollywood filmmaker combined *all* of the formal elements listed here, or used them as insistently and consistently as the Fernández unit did during its extraordinary seven-year run. And, as we will see, very few filmmakers did it as well either. By combining the following formal elements—most of them known and used internationally, a few specifically developed by Figueroa—the Fernández unit created the most distinctive and memorable cinematic vision of Mexico.

NATIVE MOTIFS AS NATIONAL ICONS

Once again, as we saw with de Fuentes, a prominent artistic influence was Posada, whose work heavily inspired future generations of Mexican artists. As Diego Rivera said, the artists of his time fed "subconsciously on the life and work of Posada,"[62] and Rivera, José Clemente Orozco, and David Alfaro Siqueiros proudly promoted his native aesthetic in their murals. Posada's influence on Fernández-Figueroa came directly from his vast body of work, as well as being filtered through the work of contemporary Mexican artists, and, naturally, Eisenstein's *¡Que viva México!*

One thing surely not lost on Fernández and Figueroa was the fact that Posada's art emerged from a popular medium that was easily accessible to a mass audience. That his turn-of-the-century etchings had first appeared in the penny press, had been seen by countless Mexicans, and were now regarded as great art must have served as a vindication of their own cinematic endeavors. In their own way, Fernández and Figueroa were attempting the same thing: the utilization of movies—a sort of moving image penny press of their times—as a medium for transmitting their vision of Mexico. Bringing art to the masses, of course, was one of the core tenets of postrevolutionary Mexican art in general, and the impetus for muralists painting on the walls of public buildings. Arguably, Fernández and Figueroa's films went even further. Figueroa was close friends with the muralists, and he recounted several times that they "said that my films were murals in movement; greater murals, because mine traveled and theirs did not."[63]

Another lesson derived from Posada and Eisenstein was to employ overlooked, taken-for-granted, and seemingly unimportant quotidian details of Mexican life—the devotion to the Virgin of Guadalupe, the celebration of the Days of the Dead and the ubiquitous *calaveras* (skeleton figures), the countless maguey and cactus plants dotting the countryside—and use them as part of a national visual grammar. Crucially, then, Posada provided Fernández-Figueroa with a plastic model for promoting the autochthonous over the European (in style and content), the rural and folkloric over the urban and cosmopolitan, and the popular over the elitist. Let me illustrate by focusing on one element, the maguey

The Classical Mexican Cinema

FIG. 6.3. José Guadalupe Posada, *Sorprendente Milagro. Segunda Aparición de Nuestra Señora la Virgen Santísima de Guadalupe, entra la Hacienda de la Lechería y San Martín* (*Amazing Miracle. Second Apparition of Our Lady the Most Blessed Virgin of Guadalupe, between the Hacienda of the Dairy and San Martin*), 1893. Posada's combining the patroness of Mexico and a common feature of the country's landscape economically proclaimed that this could only be Mexico.

FIGS. 6.4 AND 6.5. Two lithographs by José Clemente Orozco. *Top, Dos magueyes and dos mujeres* (*Two Magueys and Two Women*, 1929). The maguey helps separate the various planes of the composition: foreground (the maguey), mid-ground (the two women), and background (the dark mountain structure behind them). *Bottom, Magueyes, nopal, y figuras* (*Magueys, Cactus, and Figures*, 1929); note that the foregrounding here occurs on both sides of the frame, with a maguey in the left center and the cactus on the right edge. (Courtesy the José Clemente Orozco Foundation)

plant, which has been said to be a symbol for the Mexican people.[64] I have used the same Posada engraving in fig. 6.3 that I used in chapter 2 (fig. 2.1) to trace an aesthetic lineage that stretches from Posada to Orozco to Eisenstein's *¡Que viva México!* and finally to Fernández-Figueroa, who made the maguey one of their central visual motifs in their CMC films. I will trace the chain of influence in the next section.

FOREGROUNDING

A favorite compositional technique of Figueroa's was placing an element in the near foreground, usually in one of the bottom corners, as a kind of anchor for the rest of the frame. It immediately added depth by presenting tension between foreground and background. Following the trail of the artistic employment of the maguey, we note that Figueroa might well have borrowed this motif from José Clemente Orozco (he borrowed at least one other, as we will see), who quite possibly also influenced Eisenstein (figs. 6.4–6.7).

As seen in figs. 6.8–6.11, Figueroa's foregrounding went beyond magueys and cactuses to include all sorts of objects and/or

FIG. 6.6. Eisenstein's *¡Que viva México!* Cinematographer Eduard Tisse combined low angles, deep focus, and the dramatic placement of the maguey in the extreme foreground corners of the frame.

FIG. 6.7. *Flor silvestre* (1943).

FIGS. 6.8 AND 6.9. *Top*, in *La perla* (1947), villagers await the return of the fishermen. (These shots are somewhat similar to those in a scene in Luchino Visconti's *La terra trema*, released the following year.) *Bottom*, women of the village on their way to the town square in *Rio Escondido* (1947).

FIGS. 6.10 AND 6.11. *Top*, from the beginning sequence of *Pueblerina* (1949), with a reclining fellow prisoner as the foreground element at the bottom of the frame. The use of the image of the Virgin of Guadalupe on the far wall locates this prison cell and identifies the nationality of the prisoners. *Bottom*, María Félix as a struggling teacher sent to a remote village in *Río Escondido* (1948).

characters placed close to the camera, creating a near-far tension and enhancing the frame's composition-in-depth.

Another type of Figueroa's foregrounding made the near element a frame for the action in the mid- or background, a variation of the frame-within-the-frame technique (figs. 6.12–6.14).

A PREPONDERANCE OF LOW-ANGLE SHOTS

Like Orozco, whose human subjects were often viewed from below eye level, and like Eisenstein and Tisse, for whom the low-angle shot was practically the default perspective (fig. 6.6), Fernández-Figueroa's compositions typically looked up at their subjects. This gave their Mexican characters power and dominance in the frame and was consistent with the aims of their artistic nationalism, namely

to proclaim the importance of Mexico and the dignity of its people (figs. 6.15–6.19).[65]

Figueroa was probably influenced by the work of his mentor, Gregg Toland, who favored low angles, and Fernández was definitely inspired by the films of John Ford, who also sought to imbue his characters with nobility. Eisenstein and Ford, Fernández said, were his film teachers. He admired the former, but aspired to the latter. "The greatest poet of the cinema is John Ford," Fernández said. "In his conception of landscape . . . he was a poet, a painter."[66] You see the use of low angles over and over again in Ford's work, particularly in the best known of the two films Toland shot for him, *The Grapes of Wrath* (1940), where the director used low camera angles to give the migrant workers a measure of respect (fig. 6.20).

LEFT | FIGS. 6.12 AND 6.13. *Top,* one of the town's elites arrested by the conquering rebel general is forced to the ground and photographed between the general's legs in *Enamorada* (1946). *Bottom,* rebel troops around a campfire in *Las abandonadas* (1944).

ABOVE | FIG. 6.14. The husband in *Pueblerina* (1948), on his way to compete in the local rodeo.

THE POETICS AND POLITICS OF THE FERNÁNDEZ UNIT STYLE

FIGS. 6.15 AND 6.16. *La perla. Top,* Quino (Pedro Armendáriz) surveys the sea. *Bottom,* his wife, Juana (María Elena Marqués), holding a stone, comes to Quino's rescue when thieves attack him.

FIGS. 6.17 AND 6.18. *Top, María Candelaria* (1944). Low-angle shots of the humble *indios* (Pedro Armendáriz and Dolores del Río) underscore Fernández's ideological project of honoring indigenous Mexicans. *Bottom, Flor silvestre* (1943). A low-angle shot gives Esperanza (Dolores del Río), the daughter of a campesino, dignity and stature in this scene in which she is spurned by her lover's upper-class parents.

FIG. 6.19. *Río Escondido.* Rosaura (María Félix) shaking hands with the president of Mexico, who has personally asked her to reopen a school in a remote village. The president is obviously powerful, but by filming Rosaura from a low angle Fernández-Figueroa accentuates her status as a teacher and, by extension, the importance of education in a new, modern Mexico.

FIG. 6.20. Tom Joad (Henry Fonda, *right center*) and other migrant workers head off to pick crops in John Ford's *The Grapes of Wrath* (1940, with cinematography by Gregg Toland).

Parenthetically, Ford-Toland may have influenced Fernández-Figueroa in other ways as well. For instance, the fact that the Hollywood filmmakers had the artistic courage to take an extreme long shot from as far away from the subject as the one that occurs near the end of *The Grapes of Wrath* (fig. 6.21) may well have encouraged Fernández-Figueroa to capture a shot like the one found in *Río Escondido*, in which the doctor (Fernando Fernández) accompanies the teacher (María Félix) to the remote village (fig. 6.22).

In *Enamorada*, Fernández-Figueroa play an interesting variation on the usual meaning of low angles. For one sequence they used the low-angle shot ironically, as Orson Welles and Gregg Toland did in *Citizen Kane* (1941), to indicate that a character's power and dominance is limited. In the scene the morning after Kane loses the gubernatorial election, Welles and Toland dug a hole in the studio floor so they could shoot from as low an angle as possible. The resulting shots show Charles Foster Kane spatially confined by

FIGS. 6.21 AND 6.22. *Top*, a remarkable Ford-Toland composition in *The Grapes of Wrath* (1940)—an extreme long shot (ELS) so distant that the figure of Tom Joad can barely be seen—which is why shots like this were rare in the Hollywood system, and why Toland and Ford were so gutsy to even try it. *Left*, a similar use of extreme long shot by Fernández-Figueroa in *Río Escondido* (1948). An ELS like this was as unusual in Mexican cinema as Ford-Toland's were in Hollywood.

FIGS. 6.23 AND 6.24. The ironic use of low-angle shots. *Top*, the morning-after shot in *Citizen Kane* (1941) shows the audience what Charles Foster Kane (Orson Welles) can't see—that his great wealth has morally constrained him. *Bottom*, in *Enamorada* (1946), the powerful Gen. Reyes (Pedro Armendáriz) realizes the extent of—and limits to—his authority when he visits a church.

enemies of the revolution as he sees fit. Now he's come to the church to find an old friend, the parish priest. Walking down the center aisle, while the priest and altar boys sing "Ave Maria" in the choir loft, he is confronted with symbols—to believers anyway—of a higher power. In the film, Gen. Reyes's character arc is a conversion narrative that takes him from ruthlessness, required to win the revolution, to compassion, required to be fully human. That journey begins with this scene, in which he is reminded of his place in the grander scheme of things—a scheme, it is just occurring to him, that might include a divine dimension.

A side effect of their low-angle shooting in exterior shots was the lowering of the horizon line in the frame, and sometimes eliminating it altogether. In so doing, Fernández-Figueroa shifted the balance of the composition skyward, toward what would become recognized the world over as "Figueroa's skies" (figs. 6.25 and 6.26).

"FIGUEROA'S SKIES"

the ceiling above him, and caught in a trap of his own making. It's a visual depiction of his power undermined by his hubris, his morality compromised by arrogance. Kane's moral unawareness, his failure to comprehend the consequences of his marital infidelity, has ensnared him (figs. 6.23 and 6.24).

Fernández-Figueroa's use of the ironic low-angle shot in *Enamorada*, however, is different; it marks the dawning of a character's awareness. Rebel General Reyes (Pedro Armendáriz) is the absolute authority in the town he has just captured. In the film's first act, we see him wield his power swiftly and mercilessly, imprisoning and executing

Another key inspiration for Fernández-Figueroa was the prolific Mexican artist Gerardo Murillo, better known by his pseudonym, Doctor Atl (1875–1964). Acknowledged as the founder of the nationalist art movement in Mexico and as the nation's "first contemporary landscape painter,"[67] he created, in the words of one Mexican art critic, "an aesthetic geography of the mountains and valleys of Mexico."[68] Born in Xochimilco, he traveled and studied painting in Europe, and upon his return to Mexico he became a leading figure in a Mexican artistic renaissance that rebelled against the primacy of European art and aesthetics in the Americas.[69]

The Classical Mexican Cinema

His rejection of Eurocentric artistic traditions led to the exploration of Mexican themes, and he developed a bold new Mexican aesthetic to convey them. At its core was his determination to capture what he deemed *lo mexicano* in a rough and unadorned fashion. In "inventing" Mexican painting, he deconstructed established Western aesthetic techniques and then recombined them to suit the Mexican experience. This affected every aspect of his work—the subjects he painted, the materials he used, the colors he chose— even including the formulation of a "new perspective," which I will discuss in the next section. For now, let's focus on Fernández-Figueroa's achieving the distinctive look for the skies in their films.

One of the key features in many of Dr. Atl's landscapes was the way the clouds dominated the sky and the land. To accurately depict Mexico and truly grasp its significance, Dr. Atl's landscapes declared, one needed to understand that the heavens were as important as the topography.

Figueroa is justifiably famous for developing a technique for capturing clouds, known as "Figueroa's skies." But achieving the sort of three-dimensionality found in Dr. Atl's paintings in film was very difficult. Simply photographing the sky renders clouds as an undifferentiated flat and milky mess, lacking contours or definition. Seeking a solution, Figueroa studied Renaissance painters. "I started thinking," he said, "about what got between my camera and the landscape, and I began to experiment with black and white filters to counteract that layer of air I disliked so much."[70] Using an infrared filter to remove atmospheric haze produced a much clearer image.

They used this filter during the war to photograph at night, and it occurred to me to use it in the daytime. . . . I later bought a set of Wratten filters and combined greens with slightly lighter reds so I could obtain the infra-red [*sic*] effect in varying intensities. We had to paint the actors' lips brown so that they wouldn't appear white; otherwise, we didn't have any problems.[71]

The combination of low-angle shooting, the resultant lower horizon line, and skies with rounded, three-dimensional clouds gave Fernández-Figueroa's films their unique-looking exterior shots. He created in film what Dr. Atl had accomplished with paint, a combination of unique landscapes and "skyscapes" identified solely with *lo mexicano* (fig. 6.27).

FIGS. 6.25 AND 6.26. Figueroa's skies and the lowered or absent horizon line. *Top*, Pedro Armendáriz in *Flor silvestre* (1943). *Bottom*, María Félix in *Río Escondido* (1948).

Of course, other filmmakers had attempted and were continuing to attempt to find the best way to capture Mexican landscapes in their photography. Eisenstein and Tisse conveyed the distinctive look of the Mexican skyline in ¡Que viva México! (fig. 6.6). So, to an extent, did Paul Strand, the celebrated American still photographer and director of photography of the Mexican government–produced narrative film Redes (The Wave, 1934).[72] However, whereas Strand composed shots like the one shown in fig. 6.28 only intermittently in Redes, Figueroa's skies were a regular feature of exterior scenes in the Fernández unit films. Moreover, due to his filtering system, Figueroa was able to capture clouds with much more detail and texture than other filmmakers, successfully producing a look that was unmistakably his— and unmistakably Mexico.

To create his native art, Dr. Atl took components of Western artistic traditions and recombined them to convey lo mexicano. His idea for a new Mexican perspective was to combine linear perspective (the frontal system of pictorial design that relies on parallel lines converging at a central vanishing point, so dominant in Western artistic tradition) with "curvilinear perspective," a representational scheme that stresses spherical shapes in nature. According to Dr. Atl, this perspective more realistically approximates the act of seeing by the human eye, and has the added advantage of "establishing more ample possibilities for a new interpretation of nature." To Dr. Atl, curvilinear perspective is more complex and thus more complete, dedicated as it is to filling in all planes of a painting—foreground, middle ground, and background. This was something that, in Dr. Atl's estimation, classical Western painting ignored, being so preoccupied with foreground figures. "It always seemed to me," Dr. Atl said, "that the representation of vast spaces was incomplete, even in the works of the most eminent landscape artists, ancient or modern."[73]

TOP | FIG. 6.27. Figueroa's skies: Las abandonadas (1944). Margarita (Dolores del Río) makes her way from her village to the city. See other examples in figs. 6.7, 6.9, 6.11, 6.15, 6.17, 6.18, 6.22, 6.30, 6.31.

BOTTOM | FIG. 6.28. In the Paul Strand–photographed Redes (1934), there were occasional shots featuring the clouds above the Mexican landscape, but they did not appear with the insistent regularity of Figueroa's "skyscape" compositions in the Fernández unit films.

Following Dr. Atl, Figueroa adopted curvilinear perspective, but used it in all types of shots, not just landscapes. Influenced by Dr. Atl and others, Figueroa used his modified curvilinear perspective to frame all sorts of compositions. As Figueroa put it, in addition to Dr. Atl, he

> was also inspired by the perspectival experiments of Orson Welles and Gregg Toland, and before them by the Spanish painter, Diego Velásquez. His *Las Meninas* is without any doubt one of the best renderings of perspective in the world, curvilinear as well as rectilinear. I used both perspectives when framing a scene—the latter more than the former, of course.[74]

In order to appreciate what Figueroa's saying here, let's first understand what is meant by curvilinear perspective. It describes a perspective system that attempts to give two-dimensional objects a three-dimensional look. Objects look slightly distorted, making them appear to bow toward (barrel distortion) or away from (pincushion distortion) the viewer. Instead of being drawn to a single point, as is the case with the vanishing point in rectilinear perspective, in curvilinear perspective the viewer's eye travels along the curving line, and is torn between looking left or right.

Looking carefully at Velásquez's *Las Meninas* (is there any other way to look at it?) you get a sense of what Figueroa was likely referring to when he said the painting exhibited both perspectival systems, rectilinear and curvilinear (fig. 6.29). Its rectilinear perspective resolves itself at the vanishing point of the outstretched hand of the man holding

the door in the rear. But there is curvilinear perspective present, too, enhancing the curves of the dresses (no doubt "inflated" by interior dress hoops) worn by the girls in the foreground, especially the ivory-and-gold-accented dress worn by the Infanta Margarita in the center foreground, and her nearest attendant, to the left, between the Infanta and the painter. Both of those dresses bow slightly, but without noticeable distortion, toward the viewer, giving their outfits volume and roundedness.

In combining both perspectival systems in one composition, then, Figueroa did the same thing as Velásquez, creating a distinctive visual dialectic unlike the frames of most other Mexican films and most other films of any nationality, then or now. Once again, Figueroa was well aware of what he was doing:

> The principle of rectilinear perspective is to guide the gaze to a particular point centered in the frame. Curvilinear perspective, on the other hand, works to split the eye between two distinct perspectival points of entry, joined by means of lines travelling along a curved plane within the frame. This increases the illusion of depth. In addition, the technical development of wide-angle lenses made it possible to add even more depth and content to a particular frame or scene.[75]

A shot from *Pueblerina* illustrates what he means (fig. 6.30). Dominating the frame is Paloma (Columba Domínguez), the woman from the pueblo of the title, who is busily preparing a meal for her wedding reception. The rounded shape of the huge bowl fills the foreground of the frame, side to side and to

FIG. 6.29. *Las Meninas* (1656), by Diego Velásquez. The curve of the girls' dresses, especially of the Infanta Margarita in the ivory-and-gold-accented dress in the center foreground, and of the girl between her and the painter, are the key curvilinear elements. The rectilinear vanishing point is the raised hand of the man in the doorway at the rear of the painting. Thus, as Figueroa said, Velásquez's painting contained both rectilinear and curvilinear perspectives.

the bottom edge, creating the curved plane and increasing the illusion of depth, just as Figueroa explained. In the middle ground behind her stretches the yard, bounded by a fence, where the fiesta is planned to take place. Further in the background is the distant horizon with its vanishing point. Figueroa created a richly complex composition here. To begin with, there is the tension between near and far, an expected property of a deep-focus composition like this. In addition there is the added dynamism of the two perspective systems simultaneously at

play, each with its competing focal points. The rectilinear perspective vanishing point is at the horizon midpoint, behind Paloma's shoulder in the center background. But the curvilinear perspective in the foreground draws the viewer's eye along the curving edge of the large bowl and around its oval lip, from the center to either rim, then back again.

Rather than being a rare occurrence in Fernández-Figueroa films, dual-perspective systems appeared often. This was because Mexican culture provided Figueroa with a nearly ubiquitous circular object, especially

FIG. 6.30. Curvilinear and rectilinear perspectives combined in *Pueblerina*.

FIGS. 6.31 AND 6.32. *Top*, the stepdaughter (Columba Domínguez) retreats from her stepfather (Pedro Armendáriz) in *La malquerida*. *Bottom*, an example of both perspective systems present in an interior shot from *Pueblerina*. The engaged couple (Columba Domínguez and Roberto Cañedo), with her son (Ismael Pérez), appear before the town constable (Manuel Dondé).

in rural Mexico, where many of the films take place—the sombrero. Not every shot containing a sombrero automatically exhibited both perspectives, of course. It depended on the depth of field in the composition, since the most effective presence of both systems required deep focus, as we saw in Velásquez's *Las Meninas*. As Figueroa says, he always used rectilinear perspective, but when possible he would add curvilinear perspective if the focus was deep enough to allow him to achieve sharp focus on the turned-up brim of the hat, usually one positioned in the foreground, and keep the background in focus, or nearly so (figs. 6.31 and 6.32). The result was an extremely intricate and dynamic composition that does indeed operate the way Figueroa claimed, and created a look unique in film history.

EXPRESSIONISTIC LIGHTING

Looking at the dramatic structure of the ten films we're considering, rarely do we find a happy ending. Nine of them end tragically, or, at the very least, have qualified happy endings. In this, Fernández resembles Ford—and for that matter Orson Welles, too—in that all three were tragic artists who favored low-key

lighting so much it was their default pictorial choice. Superb visual artist that he was, Figueroa was happy to oblige, using light and its absence to paint many of his compositions with moody half-lights and shadows. "Lighting," Figueroa once said, "is the privilege of the cinematographer. He is the owner of the light."[76]

Of course, international film language, which was fairly standardized by the 1940s, had established the convention of using low-key lighting for moments of character distress—deaths, grieving, despair, confusion, separation, loss. But Fernández, like Ford, was predisposed to relating tragic stories, and his cinematographer conveyed those unhappy tales with darker-than-usual—and in one case even darker than absolutely necessary—lighting.

One example will show one of Figueroa's influences and also serve to illustrate how he made the composition darker than his source material. As we have seen, Figueroa learned from and was inspired by Mexican artists, but he only cites one direct borrowing in his interviews—using Orozco's *Requiem* as the basis for a shot in *Flor silvestre* (figs. 6.33 and 6.34).[77] Besides modeling the shot after Orozco's lithograph—and honoring the artist in the process—what's interesting is how much darker Figueroa's version is. In terms

of costuming, two of Orozco's figures wear white, offset by the pitch-black darkness inside the doorway and the ground beneath the mourners. Overall, gray tones dominate Orozco's picture. In Figueroa's shot, on the other hand, there is only one tiny triangle of white, a bandana covering the back of the neck on the character at the extreme right, and much of the rest of the composition is shades of charcoal gray running to black. Orozco's lithograph is dark, but Fernández-Figueroa's version—and *vision*—is darker still.

The images shown in figs. 6.35 and 6.36, from *María Candelaria* and *Enamorada*, respectively, are but two more of the many examples of low-key lighting in the Fernández

FIGS. 6.33 AND 6.34. From Mexican art to Mexican cinema. *Top*, José Clemente Orozco's *Requiem* (1928), acknowledged by Figueroa to be the source for this shot, *bottom*, from *Flor silvestre* (1943) of mourners gathered at the doorway of a villager stricken by influenza. (*Requiem* courtesy the José Clemente Orozco Foundation)

FIGS. 6.35 AND 6.36. *Top*, *María Candelaria* (1943). Low-key lighting is used to accentuate sadness: María's lover, Lorenzo (Pedro Armendáriz), in jail. *Bottom*, expressionistic lighting underscores the key climactic moments in *Enamorada*: in the shadowy foreground the rebel general (Pedro Armendáriz) realizes, with the help of the priest (Fernando Fernández), that he must change and become more flexible and humane.

The Classical Mexican Cinema

FIGS. 6.37–6.40. "The most beautiful blacks you've ever seen": Figueroa specially processed the film to push the black tones to an extreme in *Río Escondido* (1947).

unit films. But in *Río Escondido* Figueroa took it to an extreme. To produce the most intense use of darkness in his career, Figueroa specially processed the film to render the darkest blacks as dark as possible. "I was always experimenting," Figueroa later told a writer for *American Cinematographer*:

> Toland had put this in my head. On *Río Escondido* I changed the lab's tonal range down toward the black hues. It's as if *Aida*'s aria had been written in the key of G and I had it transposed into the key of C and had it sung by a bass. It's the same thing. The range was 6.5 and I changed it to 4. I had to illuminate the white shirts with sun reflectors to keep them from turning milky, but I got the most beautiful blacks you've ever seen.[78]

This is one area where Figueroa took the Fernández unit films not just beyond what any Mexican films had done, but also beyond what any filmmakers at the time were doing. The only thing comparable, I believe, was a film I'll analyze in chapter 8, *Distinto amanecer*, which Figueroa also shot (figs. 6.37–6.40).

DIAGONAL COMPOSITIONS

The Diagonal in Two Dimensions

A favorite compositional design motif frequently employed by Fernández-Figueroa is the diagonal line. Since it was also a favorite motif of Sergei Eisenstein's, they were very likely influenced by its repeated use in *¡Que viva México!* (fig. 6.41), for instance in a composition such as the one from one of the dance numbers in *La perla* (fig. 6.42). As it was for Fernando de Fuentes, the diagonal for

FIGS. 6.41 AND 6.42. *Top*, compositions like this renowned Eisenstein-Tisse image from *¡Que viva México!* are likely antecedents to and influences on Fernández-Figueroa, as seen in the shot of the harp player (*bottom*), from the fiesta sequence in *La perla*.

Figueroa-Fernández was used in two dimensions as well as three. As a two-dimensional element, the diagonal appeared as a line, an edge, or a triangular shape that transected the frame, dramatically adding dynamism by slicing the composition at an angle (figs. 6.43–6.47).

The Z-Axis, the Mise-en-Scène Diagonal

Again, just as de Fuentes did in his Revolution Trilogy, Fernández-Figueroa used the diagonal in three dimensions by extending action into an obliquely angled z-axis. This method of emphasizing composition-in-depth became an integral part of their films' mise-en-scène. One common technique they followed was staging the action along a diagonal line away from or toward the camera, stressing the depth of focus in the frame from foreground to background (figs. 6.48 and 6.49).

Another favorite Fernández-Figueroa compositional device was a blocking scheme whereby Fernández-Figueroa "stacked" similarly costumed characters from foreground to background (figs. 6.50–6.52). For the viewer scanning the figures and faces as they fanned out in the frame from near to far, the resulting repeated pattern created a natural receding diagonal. Once again, there was likely an Eisenstein-Tisse influence, since there were numerous shots like this in *¡Que viva México!*.

FIGS. 6.43 AND 6.44. Expressionistic diagonals, using skewed angles in nature to indicate characters caught in a world out of balance. *Top*, the teacher (María Félix) in *Río Escondido*, alone and suffering from a heart condition, makes her way to her remote school. *Bottom*, an image that perfectly depicts Quino's (Pedro Armendáriz) physical and emotional state in *La perla* after thieves try to kill him, his wife, and his baby to steal his priceless pearl.

The Classical Mexican Cinema

FIGS. 6.48 AND 6.49. Action on the z-axis away from the camera in *Enamorada* (1946). *Top*, Beatriz (María Félix) walks down a long colonnade pursued by the rebel general she has just met—and slapped in the face. *Bottom*, Beatriz leaves the church after speaking to the priest.

FIGS. 6.45–6.47. *Enamorada* (1946). One of the most iconic shots in all of Mexican cinema and one of cinematographer Gabriel Figueroa's most inspired compositions. In the extreme close-up of Beatriz (María Félix) awakening to a serenade, her nose and the imaginary line connecting her eyes form intersecting diagonal lines. Meanwhile, on the street below the conjunto sings, "What beautiful eyes you have, beneath those eyebrows."

Fernández-Figueroa's framings, however, are generally closer to the subjects, shot from a low angle, and produce compositions with a steeper, more pronounced "z-axis angle." Besides creating arresting and compelling compositions, in exterior daylight shots these z-axis diagonals also highlighted the considerable deep focus Figueroa was able to achieve. In interiors, however, especially nighttime or low-light situations, it is obvious that he was unable to attain the extreme pan (or so-called "universal") focus that his friend Toland was realizing with Welles and Wyler. This was not an aesthetic choice but a financial one. After the tremendous deep focus accomplished in *Citizen Kane*, Toland

TOP | FIG. 6.50. Diagonal staging in *¡Que viva México!*.

RIGHT | FIGS. 6.51 AND 6.52. "Stacked" characters arranged along the angled z-axis create a three-dimensional diagonal in *Río Escondido*.

encouraged Figueroa to try the same pan focus system in his films. But that, Figueroa recounted later, would have been "very expensive for Mexican cinema." Pan focus was "easy to achieve outdoors, but you need a strong light to close the aperture indoors, and that's where the problems start."[79] As can be seen in fig. 6.52, he was not able to maintain sharp focus all the way down the line of faces. Thus Figueroa's focus was as deep as he could afford to make it. But, except for daytime shots, for example, figs. 6.48 and 6.49, it was not the sort of universal focus that Toland was able to pull off working in Hollywood with Welles and Wyler.

SONG AND DANCE

Beyond the typical musical sound track that accompanied every Mexican film of the time, Fernández nearly always included additional music in the form of singing and dancing scenes in his films. This ran the gamut from full-fledged production numbers to serenades, dancehall tunes, and ballads. A talented dancer (remember, he began his acting career by dancing in *Flying Down to Rio* and *Allá en el Rancho Grande*), Fernández appreciated the production and entertainment value that musical spectacle brought to his films. In addition, the musical numbers helped stamp the films as Mexican by memorializing the community rituals he was recording. Here, he was likely influenced by both Mexican and Hollywood filmmaking. In Mexico, after *Allá en el Rancho Grande* made the song and dance a movie staple, musical performances became a de rigueur convention of Golden Age cinema regardless of genre. The other model must have been the films of John Ford. It is almost as if Fernández thought to himself, "Well, if John Ford can inject singing and dancing in his films, so can I."

The Classical Mexican Cinema

As it did for Ford, the songs and dances served multiple functions. First, of course, it was a way of celebrating his marginalized characters and their communities. Ford used these musical interludes to rejoice along with his working-class communities (*How Green Was My Valley*, *The Grapes of Wrath*), his ethnic pioneers in numerous Westerns, and his Irish characters throughout his body of work. Fernández did the same for his indigenous protagonists, humble campesinos, and the prostitutes in his two *cabaretera* genre films.

Music, dancing, and fiestas were also utilized to define character, just as Ford did. In both Ford and Fernández's films, characters that do not attend dances or, worse, try to prevent or disrupt them are marked as villains. In *La perla*, though the entire village has turned out for a fiesta to celebrate Quino's good fortune in finding the large pearl, the greedy villains—the doctor, the pearl dealer, Quino's village "friends"—do not partake in the festivities. And in *Pueblerina*, after the campesino lovers, Paloma and Aurelio, are married, the rich and powerful González brothers threaten the villagers to keep them from attending the wedding reception.

A third function of music and song in Fernández's films is helping to set the dramatic tone. If for no other reason than because they serve as a respite from the usually intense melodrama, the musical intervals generally lighten the mood. Indeed, the absence of music in Fernández's universe is ominous, preventing a break away from the protagonist's dramatic distress—for either the character or the audience. Accordingly, the three films with little or no communal music, *María Candelaria*, *Río Escondido*, and *La malquerida*, are his bleakest tragedies. And it is

the very lack of music and dance that becomes a crucial plot point in *Pueblerina*, leading to its most memorable scene. The González brothers successfully scare away the villagers and nobody shows up for Paloma and Aurelio's wedding fiesta. After hours of waiting, they finally realize what has happened. But the couple work their way through their humiliation and disappointment, and early the next morning decide to make their own music. In one of the more lushly romantic sequences in the Cine de Oro, they first dance together, and then they sing a duet, "Tú, solo tú" ("You, Only You"), which has become a standard can't-live-without-you love song that is still performed and recorded and whose lyrics are part of the national cultural memory. Using music as a narrative device, Fernández showed the lovers overcoming heartbreak through their mutual devotion.

A fourth use of music and song served another narrative purpose—to provide a kind of Greek chorus commentary on plot developments that have just happened or are happening as the song is being sung. It was a fairly common Fernández "touch" and it appeared in the first of the unit-made films, *Flor silvestre*. One that occurs thirty-five minutes into the film marks the beginning of act 2. The night after he has been banished by his wealthy father for marrying Esperanza, a commoner (Dolores del Río), José Luis (Pedro Armendáriz) rides back to his father's hacienda to try to mend the relationship. Accompanying him are Esperanza's grandfather and three musicians (played by El Trio Calaveras) singing the ballad "Flor silvestre," which recaps the narrative in terms of José Luis's emotional stakes. Twenty-five minutes later, at the conclusion of act 2, there is a similar scene, when José Luis returns to the hacienda and finds his father murdered by renegade rebel bandits. The three musicians are found drunk and on the floor, singing "El hijo desobediente" ("The Disobedient Son"). The song, a sorrowful Mexican standard, tells a tale of a rift between father and son. Though these lyrics are not exactly a narrative summary, they do capture the emotional and psychological mood—of a disobedient son who leaves his home and must deal with the unintended consequences. These songs cast a pall over the rest of the film, preparing audiences for the deeper tragedy about to unfold in act 3.

García Riera criticized Fernández for allowing the music to intrude upon the diegesis in this way. Such over-the-top—and on-the-nose—melodramatic effects were beneath the director, he believed, since they were characteristics of the run-of-the-mill Mexican films (called "*churros*," the name of an inexpensive, popular, and nutrition-free pastry sold by street vendors). It is an interesting point. If Fernández was so critical of the Mainstream Mexican Cinema, why imitate those films? I can think of two reasons. One, his love of music overruled any reservations he may have had about this formulaic MMC convention. Two, Mexican ballads were authentically *mexicano* and therefore belonged in his native aesthetic—one more element that set his films apart from Hollywood and other national cinemas.

NARRATIVE: STEALING FROM HOLLYWOOD, EXPRESSING *LO MEXICANO*

Fernández was an inveterate movie thief. Fellow filmmakers called him on it and Magdaleno admitted it. His contemporary, director Julio Bracho, accused him of plagiarizing F. W. Murnau for both *María Candelaria* and *La perla*. (Historian Paco Ignacio Taibo I speculates that Bracho was referring to the experimental film project Murnau undertook with documentarian Robert Flaherty, *Tabu: A Story of the South Seas* [1931], though I don't see many similarities between it and *María Candelaria* or *La perla*.)[80] According to another Mexican film director, Alberto Isaac, Leni Riefenstahl complained to him that *María Candelaria* was based on her film *The Blue Light* (1932). (In this case there are some similarities, most notably the character of the young woman who is shunned and hated by the villagers.) And both Isaac and García Riera claim that it was well known that the ending of *Enamorada* was poached from Josef von Sternberg's *Morocco* (1930).[81] That is probably true, but that's not all Fernández pilfered from Hollywood for *Enamorada*. He ripped off the three main characters from MGM's *San Francisco* (1936)—the confident male lead, his best friend the priest, and the strong-willed woman (Clark Gable, Spencer Tracy, and Jeanette MacDonald in the American film; Pedro Armendáriz, Fernando Fernández, and María Félix in Fernández's rendition)—as well as the scene of the priest leading a children's chorus in a church choir loft. And I am about to discuss perhaps his most egregious cinematic larceny, his lifting of plot elements from *The Sin of Madelon Claudet*, *Madame X*, and *El automóvil gris* for *Las abandonadas*.

But first, what are we to make of Fernández's cinematic kleptomania, his consistent practice of ransacking movies, especially Hollywood ones, for their plots, characters, scenes, and moments? Doesn't that automatically compromise his professed anti-Hollywood stance and undermine his efforts to create an authentic Mexican film aesthetic? It depends on what he did with the pilfered material. I would argue that with Magdaleno's help Fernández altered the original to such an extent that it became less a copy and more a new work. They transformed the source, placed it in the Mexican context, made crucial modifications and additions, and somehow managed to stay true to Fernández's goal of making a uniquely Mexican cinema. Paradoxically, then—and nearly inconceivably—Fernández used Hollywood films against Hollywood filmmaking, and succeeded in making films for, by, and about Mexicans that denounced racism, sexism, and classism in Mexico.

Las abandonadas is an instructive example. In it, Fernández borrowed from two Hollywood movies and a Mexican one to make a pointed, protofeminist critique of *machismo*. Most of *Las abandonadas* is a reworking of *The Sin of Madelon Claudet* (1931), a melodrama about the sacrifices a single mother makes so that her son can become a doctor. It was Helen Hayes's first film, and for her performance of a desperate mother who turns to prostitution to support her son she won a best actress Academy Award. Besides obviously moving the action to Mexico, Magdaleno and Fernández made three critical alterations to *The Sin of Madelon Claudet*.

The first is immediately situating *Las abandonadas*, in the film's opening eight

minutes, squarely within the *cabaretera* genre, a seduced-and-abandoned narrative that was becoming popular with Mexican audiences. Many viewers would have seen the film that originated the genre, the nation's first "talkie," *Santa* (1932), and would have been aware of the film that solidified the *cabaretera* formula, *La mujer del puerto* (1934). In both of these, as in *Las abandonadas*, a woman from a small town or village is impregnated by a man who deserts her. Her family spurns her. In *Las abandonadas*, Margarita (Dolores del Río) is banished by her father for being a "*perdida*" (lost woman). She leaves her community in disgrace, ends up in the city, and turns to prostitution as a last-resort means of supporting the baby boy she's given birth to. Placing the story of *The Sin of Madelon Claudet* within the *cabaretera* genre instantly made it part of Mexico's movie vernacular, a familiar story in a local context. Moreover, as a *cabaretera* film, it shared the genre's ideological raison d'être: namely, to criticize *machismo*'s exploitation of women. *Las abandonadas*, like so many other *cabaretera* films, argues that patriarchy made her a prostitute.

The second important change made to *The Sin of Madelon Claudet* for *Las abandonadas* is a minor but significant addition made to the film's central love story, which takes up the second act. It relates the romance between Margarita, who has become a high-class call girl (fig. 6.53), and Gen. Juan Gómez (Pedro Armendáriz). It's a subplot lifted nearly whole from *The Sin of Madelon Claudet*, where Madelon becomes the kept woman of an aristocrat who is later revealed to be an imposter. In *Las abandonadas*, Magdaleno and Fernández conclude the Margarita-Gómez affair when he is exposed as the leader of the *automóvil gris* gang. He is killed in a shootout and, though innocent, Margarita is imprisoned for being an accomplice, and her son is remanded to an orphanage. This addition not only braids the story tightly to Mexican history but also illustrates more ways patriarchy failed Margarita: she is betrayed by another male, by the legal system that unjustly incarcerates her, and, ultimately, by the revolution, which, for all of its grand ideals, never made things better for abandoned women like her.

The third way *Las abandonadas* differs from *The Sin of Madelon Claudet* is its ending, which is a revised climax borrowed from another Hollywood melodrama, *Madame X*. In a sudden, unexpected, deus-ex-machina plot development in *Las abandonadas*'s final seven minutes and thirty-five seconds, an unknown woman is accused of murder. The details of the killing are never explained, but Margarita's grown son, Margarito (Victor Junco), a young and inexperienced lawyer, is appointed

to defend her. Margarita, now old beyond her years, attends the trial, proudly watching her son with the crowd in the balcony. Margarito has been told his mother is dead and is unaware that she prostituted herself to send him to law school.

The reason Magdaleno and Fernández switched to the *Madame X* ending was to be able to hammer home the film's message, an indictment of *machismo* made explicit in Margarito's final argument to the jury. "That mother," he says, indicating his client, "that abandoned one . . . has not committed any crime other than to act against the man who deceived her." Here Schoemann cuts to a close-up of Margarita (fig. 6.54), another innocent abandoned woman. Margarito then concludes by declaring the sanctity of women and motherhood. "Where there is a woman," he says, "you will find all the purity of life. But where there is a mother, there is God." (There is another cut to a close-up of Margarita here.) The audience in the packed courtroom cheers and applauds, and, without adjourning, the jury summarily finds the woman defendant not guilty.

Magdaleno and Fernández started with *The Sin of Madelon Claudet* and *Madame X*, stirred in *El automóvil gris*, and produced *Las abandonadas*, a film that fit comfortably into a Mexican film genre, referenced the nation's revolutionary history, and critiqued *machismo*, too.

FIGS. 6.53 AND 6.54. *Las abandonadas*: a woman crushed by *machismo*. The two extremes of Margarita's (Dolores del Río) life. *Top*, at the pinnacle of her career as a prostitute, at the moment that Gen. Gómez first sees and falls in love with her. *Bottom*, near the end of the film, after she has sacrificed everything for her son, from the courtroom balcony she watches him defend a woman accused of murder.

The Classical Mexican Cinema

Once you begin looking for them, quotes from American movies crop up all over Fernández's filmography, but, as in *Las abandonadas*, they are adapted, "Mexicanized," and enlisted into ideological service against *machismo* and the discriminatory treatment of *indios*, women, the working class, and the poor.

Several surprising borrowings from Hollywood in *Río Escondido* and their eventual transformation should suffice to illustrate the director's method. *Río Escondido*'s opening is lifted from, of all things, *Yankee Doodle Dandy* (1942), a show biz biopic of songwriter, director, producer, and theater star George M. Cohan, played by James Cagney. That film begins—somewhat improbably—with an elderly Cohan being summoned to the White House by the president, a framing device for the film's recounting of Cohan's life from childhood to superstardom. *Río Escondido* begins the same way—and even more improbably—with Rosaura (María Félix), a country school teacher, entering the presidential palace and, in a private meeting, being asked by the president to go to the small town of Río Escondido. Her charge is to reopen the school that had been closed by a tyrannical cacique (rural boss).

Once again, Fernández finds a way to make the action wholly Mexican. The opening was shot on location in the presidential palace, and before ascending the staircase, Rosaura pauses to take in the historical site she is about to enter. On the sound track, a choir sets the reverential tone and several voice-over narrators give the history of the building—and of Mexico itself. She pauses before a huge Diego Rivera mural as the narrator gives its significance: "This is the history of your nation, the history of the nation

FIGS. 6.55 AND 6.56. *Top, Yankee Doodle Dandy*, the inspiration. George M. Cohan (James Cagney) enters the White House and is escorted up the stairs to the president's office. *Bottom*, the Fernández version in *Río Escondido*, shot on location in the presidential palace: Rosaura (María Félix), a schoolteacher, walks up the stairs past the Diego Rivera murals illustrating Mexican history.

of Mexico." Then, using images from the mural, *Río Escondido* relates Mexican history from the Conquest to the present. Where the Hollywood film used portraits on the wall as art decoration, Fernández makes the presidential palace and Rivera's mural a history lesson (figs. 6.55 and 6.56).

Later, Fernández steals the startling opening of William Wyler's *The Letter* (1940), where Leslie (Bette Davis) shoots a man to death on the front stairs of her home. In *Río Escondido*, however, the shooting is the climax: when the evil cacique (Carlos López Moctezuma) visits Rosaura's house in the middle of the night and tries to rape her, she shoots and kills him, ending his reign of terror. The beginning of *The Letter* is so unexpected and arresting it is understandable how Fernández would be captivated by it. But by changing the context, the director makes it his. In Wyler's original film, based on W. Somerset Maugham's play, the protagonist, Leslie, is an unfaithful wife who murders a lover who wants to leave her, and then tries to cover it up. In *Río Escondido*, Rosaura is the only one in the town who stands up to the villainous local boss, even after he has his former mistress killed, shuts off the villagers' water supply, and then murders a small boy who, in desperation, had tried to steal water from the well. Leslie is a liar and a cheat; Rosaura is a fierce and fearless force for good (figs. 6.57 and 6.58).

These elements, then, comprised the Fernández unit style, one that characterized the group's contribution to the Classic Mexican Cinema and successfully created a cinematic Mexico. Like other film movements—Italian neorealism, for instance, or the French New Wave—its tenure was short, lasting only seven years, though its influence lingered for decades, even into the present. The next part of the story—its demise over the next decade—is one of changing times, evolving business practices, strained relationships, and human fallibility.

The Decline of the Fernández Unit Style
—

After 1950, the streak of Fernández movies that merged nationalistic fervor, formal innovation, and ideological critique ended. He continued making films, but none achieved the commercial and artistic success that Fernández enjoyed from 1943 to 1950. Gone were the seemingly automatic raft of awards given to Fernández at the yearly Ariel ceremonies. Gone, too, was the global acclaim that had once greeted his films at international film festivals. What happened to the "Fernández touch?" Three factors, I believe, undermined his abilities as a director and artist: changes in the Mexican film industry, the gradual dissolution of the Fernández unit, and problems in his personal life. Cumulatively, they caused a career downturn from which Fernández never recovered.

FIGS. 6.57 AND 6.58. *Top*, in the opening scene of *The Letter* (1940, directed by William Wyler), Leslie (Bette Davis) kills her lover. *Bottom*, at the climax of *Río Escondido* Rosaura (María Félix) shoots and kills the vicious cacique (Carlos López Moctezuma) after he tries to rape her.

The Classical Mexican Cinema

When the war ended, so did the U.S.'s Good Neighbor Policy and the economic protectionism Mexico had enjoyed because of it. With that, Hollywood's technical and financial involvement in Mexican filmmaking dwindled. Meanwhile, Spain and Argentina began producing more films, eating away at Mexico's film superiority in the Spanish-language market. In addition, Mexican filmgoers began attending Hollywood films in greater and greater numbers, favoring them over domestic fare. As table 6.1 shows, the first evidence of these postwar business changes was the dramatic dip in Mexican film production in 1947. After four straight years of releasing more than seventy films per year, the number dropped below sixty. And while subsequent annual numbers might make it appear that the industry quickly rebounded, those figures are deceptive, reflecting Mexico's new—and ultimately disastrous—film production strategy. Attempting to maintain the healthy profit margins they had grown accustomed to during the boom war years, producers proceeded to make more films with smaller budgets and on shorter schedules. They were pressed to do so by William Jenkins, the American head of the monopoly that controlled 80 percent of Mexico's exhibition, because his theaters sorely needed domestic product. In the long run, that only made things worse. The inexpensive Mexican films looked shoddy and inferior in comparison with Hollywood movies, and gave Mexican filmgoers a reason to avoid them.[82]

The new practice of turning out cheaper "quickies" hit Fernández especially hard. The kind of filmmaking he was used to, making films with big budgets and longer shooting schedules, was over. Table 6.2 reveals how his budgets began shrinking at the end of the 1940s, and though figures for most of the 1950s films are not available, it was becoming clear that the days of million-peso and higher budgets were over. Furthermore, beginning in 1950 he had to accept typical shooting schedules of three weeks or less,[83] forcing him to work at a more accelerated pace than he was accustomed to. On top of everything else, like the rest of Mexican cinema, he was losing his audience.[84]

The downward tipping point is *Víctimas del pecado* (1951). A *cabaretera* vehicle for the popular Cuban dancer-singer Ninón Sevilla, *Víctimas del pecado* was made to capitalize on the success of her previous prostitute genre melodrama, *Aventurera* (1950). *Víctimas del pecado* pales in comparison with Fernández's own *Salón México*, though, and is essentially a series of eight song and/or dance numbers stitched together with tired *cabaretera* clichés. It does benefit from Figueroa's striking cinematography, but otherwise it lacks Fernández's usual flair and substance.

And he suffered a blow to his reputation within Mexico's film community when he was fired from *La rebelión de los colgados* (1954), apparently for working too slowly. Whether or not that was true, his dismissal had to have hurt his pride, damaged his professional standing, and probably made it harder for him to find work. This led to the bitter irony of the director who created Mexico on movie screens around the world having to leave the country to make films. Three of the '50s films were shot outside of Mexico—*Rosa blanca* in Cuba, *Nosotros dos* in Spain, and *La Tierra de Fuego se apaga* in Argentina.

While there appear to be at least a couple of commercial successes in the 1950s, several of them may have succeeded for reasons other than the return of the "Fernández touch." *Reportaje* (1953), for example, played four weeks, but it touted an all-star cast, a ploy used by nervous producers hoping to recapture the audience that was abandoning Mexican movies in favor of Hollywood productions. *El rapto* (1953) enjoyed a three-week first run, but it was superstar Jorge Negrete's final film, released four months after his death, and his many fans attended it to catch a last glimpse of him on screen. *La rebelión de los colgados* (1954) also played three weeks, but since Fernández was replaced by the producer it's difficult to know what exactly his contribution was and to what degree it was considered his film.[85] The nadir is the third-to-last film on the list, *La Tierra de Fuego se apaga*. Shot in Argentina, it was deemed so bad that it was never released. And his directorial productivity was actually less than it appears on the list. *El impostor*, the last film he directed in the 1950s, was completed in 1956 but not released until 1960. This means that he actually made no films for six years, from 1956 to 1962, when he released *Pueblito*. Clearly, then, after 1950 the luster associated with the Indio Fernández name brand was gone.

THE BREAKDOWN OF THE FERNÁNDEZ UNIT

Gradually, his filmmaking team broke up. Of the ten films Fernández directed from 1952 to 1956, only one, *Una cita de amor* (1956), had the full participation of all the members of the old unit. To a degree, Magdaleno did continue to collaborate with him throughout the 1950s, but Schoemann's presence was more erratic, most likely due to other commitments rather than anything personal between her and the director. Figueroa, too, began skipping productions, and his presence was sorely missed, since no other cinematographer was able to capture the Mexican landscape the way he could.

When asked about the dissolution of the Fernández-Figueroa partnership, Figueroa noted a change in the director's attitude and behavior. "He began to act arrogantly," he recalled, "and began using his scripts or rewriting the scripts of others, sometimes at the last minute. And, speaking frankly, that was not El Indio's strength." The director's gift, Figueroa explained, "was visual expression, forceful imagery, the dramatic tension between characters on the edge."[86] Figueroa was his director of photography for the ill-fated *La Tierra de Fuego se apaga*, and was well aware of the weaknesses of the script, which Fernández was writing with an Argentinian writer. Before the shooting started, Figueroa warned Fernández about the screenplay's problems, and the director promised that all would be fixed in time. The result was an unreleasable film—a professional humiliation for all concerned.[87]

To make matters even worse, it seemed to Figueroa that Fernández was beginning to plagiarize himself. "After about the twentieth film we did together," said Figueroa, "I began to notice that he was beginning to repeat himself, to repeat things I did not like at all. Without saying anything explicitly, I slowly began to withdraw, eventually refusing to work with him altogether."[88] Always in demand, Figueroa busied himself with other projects, especially those with another director beginning to make a name for himself in the industry, Luis Buñuel, and photographed all of his Mexican films in the 1950s.

TROUBLES IN FERNÁNDEZ'S PERSONAL LIFE

Despite Schoemann's account of her harmonious working relationship with Fernández, it wasn't so with everybody. He was a mercurial personality with an awful temper. Figueroa understood this and was very crafty about how he maintained their collaboration on an even keel. "I got along with him very well," Figueroa said. "We never fought because I always made sure to leave after the second drink, so there was no opportunity to fight. Besides, our collaboration worked greatly to his advantage; he knew better than to get into a fight with me."[89] Regrettably, sometimes Fernández did not know better with others.

Early in 1956, when his career had turned sour, he made public anti-Semitic statements against "bad Jews" in the periodical *Esto*. His target was certain Jewish film producers who, according to him, only sought profits rather than making quality cinema. He actually went on to name them—Gregorio Walerstein, Alfredo Ripstein Jr., Simón Wishnack, and Sergio Kogan. They had formed a group that controlled the film industry and, he claimed, they had "turned Mexican cinema into an embarrassment." Moreover, he accused them of considering Mexicans to be a "fourth-class race," which is why they brought in foreign directors.[90] (Alberto B. Crevenna, who replaced him on *La rebelión de los colgados*, was German.) The real embarrassment, tragically, was the public unraveling—via self-inflicted wounds—of a filmmaking giant.

Sadly, his behavior would get worse—much worse.

To end a decade that had been professionally and personally calamitous, there was yet another disaster. In the early morning hours of May 26, 1959, after an all-day drinking party with three journalists and a photographer at the director's home, there was an argument that turned violent. One of the journalists evidently hit Fernández in the jaw. The director went to his room, retrieved a pistol, and chased the fleeing party. He caught up with one of them and shot him point blank, killing him.[91] No charges were filed, but that moral transgression would haunt Fernández for the rest of his life. He would continue to make films, sporadically directing eight more before he died in 1986, but they were no longer central to the nation's film culture the way they had been in the 1940s. In a way, he had become like an ostracized protagonist from one of his films—only, unlike María Candelaria, Margarita in *Las abandonadas*, and Paloma and Aurelio in *Pueblerina*, his mark of Cain was well deserved. Appallingly, Fernández would be involved in another killing. In 1976, while scouting locations for a film in the state of Coahuila, he killed a twenty-six-year-old farmer. For that killing he served six months in prison.[92]

It would be fitting, I think, to let Figueroa have the last word. In an interview, he recounted seeing Fernández for the last time, visiting him on his deathbed. Upon leaving and thinking back on their collaboration, he remembered Fernández's "unique personality" and reflected on "that fierce and intuitive artist, who was so faithful to what he believed, which was *lo mexicano*."[93]

Ironically, the industrial changes that affected Fernández so catastrophically had a salubrious effect on another up-and-coming director who was to be the next master of the Classic Mexican Cinema, Luis Buñuel.

The prosperity of the 1940s gave the Spanish surrealist, famous for the avant-garde shorts he made in France, the chance to finally direct—at age forty-seven—his first feature-length narrative film. To contend with the meager budgets and tight schedules he was assigned, he prepared assiduously and scored some modest early commercial successes. Because of that, his producer allowed him to make a film for himself—*Los olvidados* (1950), photographed by Gabriel Figueroa. As luck would have it, *Los olvidados* won Buñuel the best director award at the 1951 Cannes Film Festival. Though no one knew it at the time, certainly neither Fernández nor Buñuel, that prize marked the passing of Mexico's cinematic torch. The Classical Mexican Cinema was about to take on a decidedly surrealist flavor.

CHAPTER 7

Luis Buñuel in Mexico

—

HE LAST FILMS of the Classical Mexican Cinema were directed by Luis Buñuel (1900–1983) during the 1950s and early 1960s. Interestingly, however, though the literature on Buñuel and his films is extensive, his Mexican motion pictures have received relatively little attention or recognition. An even more mystifying gap in the Buñuel literature is the lack of neoformalist analysis of either his Mexican or his European films. Let me elaborate on this situation and how this chapter seeks to rectify it.

Luis Buñuel's directing career can be divided into three discrete stages: the early avant-garde experiments, 1929–1933; the

Mexican films, 1946–1965; and his mature European phase, 1964–1977. For decades many historians and critics overlooked Luis Buñuel's Mexican films, focusing instead on the better-known European works that bookended his cinematic career. They concentrated on his two pioneering surrealist masterpieces, *Un chien andalou* (*The Andalusian Dog*, 1929) and *L'age d'or* (*The Golden Age*, 1930), which introduced him to the world as cinema's leading avant-garde provocateur, and perhaps the short documentary he made shortly afterward, *Las Hurdes: Tierra sin pan* (*Las Hurdes: Land without Bread*, 1933). Or they skipped ahead to the seven highly esteemed surrealist films of his second European period, which began with *Le journal d'une femme de chamber* (*Diary of a Chamber-maid*, 1964) and included *Belle de jour* (1967), *Le voie lactée* (*The Milky Way*, 1969), *Tristana* (1970), *Le charme discret de la bourgeoisie* (*The Discreet Charm of the Bourgeoisie*, 1972), *Le fantôme de la liberté* (*The Phantom of Liberty*, 1974), and *Cet obscure objet de désir* (*That Obscure Object of Desire*, 1977). When his Mexican films were mentioned at all, it was usually to acknowledge *Los olvidados* (1950), which won Buñuel a best director award at Cannes and returned him to the first rank of international auteurs, and possibly *Viridiana* (1962), a Mexican-Spanish coproduction that won a Cannes Palme d'Or and is popularly understood as the springboard to his late European masterworks.

This selective focus on the pictures made in Europe disregards the fact that the majority of the films that Buñuel directed, twenty-three out of thirty-two, were made from 1946 to 1965, a time when he lived and worked in Mexico and became a Mexican citizen. It ignores two decades' worth of work that was crucial to Buñuel's development as a director and that formed the link between his early surrealist shorts and his later critically acclaimed films. It discounts the fact that he learned how to make feature-length films by working within the bustling Mexican studio system. As Buñuel himself said of his years as a director in Mexico when interviewed in 1963, "Until I came here, I made a film the way a writer makes a book, and on my friends' money at that. Here in Mexico I have become a professional in the film world."[1]

And, finally, it overlooks the many splendid films he made in Mexico, which, except for two made outside the country (*Le journal d'une femme de chamber* and *Cela*

s'appelle l'aurore [*That Is the Dawn*], 1956), are exemplary of the Classical Mexican Cinema. Several of them are considered among the best Mexican films ever produced. Indeed, seven of Buñuel's films appeared on the *Somos* survey of Mexico's one hundred greatest films, three of them placing in the top ten:

#2—*Los olvidados* (1950)
#6—*Nazarín* (1959)
#7—*Él* (*This Strange Passion*, 1953)
#16—*El angel exterminador* (*Exterminating Angel*, 1962)
#46—*Susana* (1951)
#47—*Ensayo de un crimen* (*The Criminal Life of Archibaldo de la Cruz*, 1955)
#95—*La ilusión viaja en tranvía* (*Illusion Travels by Streetcar*, 1954)[2]

Outside of Mexico, the recognition of Buñuel's Mexican films is just starting. For instance, in 2003 UNESCO added *Los olvidados* to its Memory of the World Program Registry, a worldwide initiative to preserve cherished archival holdings. And three of the six Buñuel films that appeared on the 2012 *Sight and Sound* critics' poll of the 250 greatest films of all time were from his Mexican period: *Los olvidados*, *Viridiana*, and *El angel exterminador* (the other three were *Un chien andalou*, *L'age d'or*, and *The Discreet Charm of the Bourgeoisie*).

But if the tide is slowly beginning to turn, the question remains—why were Buñuel's twenty-one Mexican films critically neglected for so long? Partly, film studies' Eurocentrism was to blame. Buñuel's career is in fact a perfect example of it in action—the European films are admired modernist classics; the Mexican films largely unknown.

Another factor working against the Mexican films is that Buñuel's European works are his most surreal and thus perfect specimens for structuralist, poststructuralist, and especially psychoanalytic analysis, in vogue around the time he was releasing those films. And to be fair, part of it had to do with the difficulty in accessing the Mexican films.

Another factor contributing to the lack of attention to his Mexican films also explains the lack of work on his poetics, namely the fact that historians and critics were fixated on Buñuel the surrealist at the expense of Buñuel the filmmaker. Thus the study of his Mexican period films was largely a matter of spotting the "Buñuelian" touches to see how they might be related to his early and later surrealist works. This is certainly understandable. How could film critics and historians *not* come under the spell of such odd, unforgettable imagery, such bewildering situations, and such curious character behavior? So in a way Buñuel brought it on himself. But he couldn't help it. He was a committed surrealist who—as we will see—snuck a dreamlike detail or two even into some of his "straight" films. That imagery was startling and indelible, while, in comparison, some of his Mexican movies' formulaic plots were often forgettable and his unobtrusive style "invisible" because it didn't call attention to itself. It's perfectly reasonable that the initial critical response to his Mexican films was—and probably still is— to pick through them for their "Buñuelisms" rather than appreciate them as a whole and on their own merits.

Over the years, there have been a few critics who gave Buñuel's Mexican films a fair hearing. Mexican historian Emilio García Riera's commentaries on Buñuel's films provided an early, even-handed model of appreciation, carefully locating the director's work within a national and industrial context while keeping in mind his surrealist roots.[3] There was also the early study of his Mexican body of work by Eduardo Lizalde, *Luis Buñuel: Odisea del demoledor* (*Luis Buñuel: Odyssey of a Demolisher*, 1962).[4] Beyond Mexican critics, Freddy Buache's *The Cinema of Luis Buñuel* (1973),[5] Raymond Durgnat's *Luis Buñuel* (1967, revised in 1977),[6] and Francisco Aranda's *Luis Buñuel: A Critical Biography* (1985)[7] all took Buñuel's Mexican films into account, as did John Baxter in his breezy but informative biography (1998).[8] In addition, a sort of critical reclamation project has begun to correct the critical discourse on Buñuel's Mexican period. Victor Fuentes's *Buñuel en Mexico* (1993) and Iván Humberto Ávila Dueñas's *El cine mexicano de Luis Buñuel* (1994) focused exclusively on his Mexican films.[9] In terms of correcting the lack of attention paid to Buñuel's Mexican films, Ernesto R. Acevedo-Muñoz's *Buñuel and Mexico: The Crisis of National Cinema* (2003) is a landmark study, indispensible for anyone looking to grasp the import of the director's work during the nearly two decades he worked there. Acevedo-Muñoz addresses the political, industrial, and cultural context of Buñuel's filmmaking in his Mexican period, and also astutely analyzes many of the films with a keen and perceptive eye (though he omitted six that I will include because their content was, in his opinion, "particularly non-Mexican" and therefore not germane to his research).[10]

Still, while the critical and historical imbalance concerning Buñuel's Mexican filmmaking is being righted, there is plenty of work remaining to be done—the continued recognition of the importance of the Mexican films as well as an analysis of his cinematic poetics. Concerning the examination of Buñuel's formal techniques, to date we only have some passing commentary here and there by, for example, Durgnat,[11] David Thomson,[12] and Kristin Thompson and David Bordwell.[13] But no one has yet undertaken a systematic investigation of the poetics of Buñuel's Mexican films, which is what I intend to do here.

Indeed, to many, there was no Buñuel style to examine. As one film critic who participated in the *Somos* poll put it, "His filmmaking style was plain and economical, almost unnoticeable."[14] Others have been similarly unimpressed. "Buñuel is not and never has been a stylist of the first rank," wrote Andrew Sarris in 1962. "To Buñuel, the cinema is just a vehicle for his ideas. Once these ideas have taken the appropriate plastic form, he shoots very quickly, and any additional values are either incidental or accidental."[15] For critics engrossed in identifying surrealistic qualities, such reactions are not surprising because, as I have said, those signature moments are so stunning and arresting it is easy to miss the subtleties of Buñuel's overarching style, which was impressive for being just the opposite: restrained and inconspicuous, fluid and economical, but also unique and idiosyncratic.

What I want to do in this chapter, therefore, is to focus on Buñuel's poetics in his Mexican phase. Highlighting his style is crucial for at least three reasons. First, it's the best way to appreciate Buñuel's substantial contribution to the Classical Mexican Cinema. Just as my close readings of the poetics of the de Fuentes trilogy and the Fernández unit films revealed how those directors used cinematic style to depict *mexicanidad*, so too a careful examination of Buñuel's filmmaking techniques will bring to light his commentary on *lo mexicano*. His distinctively graceful, self-effacing style camouflaged his withering critique of the Mexican status quo, and the subversive way he deployed that style made him the premier CMC filmmaker of the 1950s and the first years of the 1960s. In fact, because of the decline of Emilio Fernández, after 1950 Buñuel became the lone—and the last—CMC filmmaker.

A second reason to concentrate on Buñuel's style is that ignoring it minimizes him as a filmmaker. As I will show, some of the technical virtuosity Buñuel displayed compares favorably to the work done by eminent stylists such as Jean Renoir, Orson Welles, and Alfred Hitchcock. This level of proficiency is all the more impressive when you consider the industrial and economic constraints he was working under. Thus, in the debate over his technique, I side with David Thomson's assessment:

There has always been a temptation to view Buñuel as one of the few towering artists who have condescended to adopt film as their means of expression. According to that approach, we may assess him as a Spaniard, as a surrealist, and as a lifelong antagonist of the bourgeoisie. All those strains persisted in Buñuel's films and they repay close attention. But it seems to me an error to think that Buñuel—often working quickly—was casual about the medium. On the contrary, I believe that he is one of the greatest of directors simply because of the expressive mastery of his films.[16]

Due to our tunnel vision, we've lost sight of Buñuel the experienced, talented, professional filmmaker. He became that in Mexico.

A third reason to focus on Buñuel's Mexican period style is because those films are the link between his early avant-garde shorts and the feature-length European masterworks he made three and four decades later. Through it all, he managed to continue inserting his surrealistic elements, even though, as a commercial Mexican director, he understood that the primary industrial imperative was to "tell a story"[17] and, of course, make money for his producers. Asked by *Cahiers du Cinema* if his Mexican producer, Óscar Dancigers, obliged him "to make melodramas of very facile subjects," Buñuel's reply was simple and candid. "Yes," he said, "and I always agreed."[18] Thus he dutifully employed traditional narratives and appeared to adhere to standard Hollywood-MMC storytelling practice. But beginning with *Los olvidados* in 1950, his films were Trojan horses—plain-looking vehicles for his surrealistic bombshells. At the same time, he was developing his unique cinematic style. He adapted creatively to the budgetary and scheduling constraints he was forced to work under, and eventually those adaptations became his style, which he carried into the late European films. Analyzing the poetics of Buñuel's Mexican films helps us understand how he arrived at the sophisticated surreal stylishness of his later films—how, that is, he went from *Un chien andalou* to *That Obscure Object of Desire*.

My goal in this chapter, then, is to describe the subdued but individualistic cinematic style Buñuel developed during his Mexican period, to show how it looked like the Mainstream Mexican Cinema but actually subverted it, and to demonstrate how his films came to exemplify the last phase of the Classical Mexican Cinema, from 1950 to 1962. I will base my analysis of his cinematic poetics on the following twenty-one films made over an eighteen-year period—his made-in-Mexico films plus the Mexican coproductions:

Gran casino (1947)
El gran calavera (*The Great Carouser*, 1949)
Los olvidados (*The Young and the Damned*; *The Forgotten Ones*, 1950)
Susana (1951)
La hija del engaño (*Daughter of Deceit*, 1951)
Subida al cielo (*Mexican Bus Ride*, 1952)
Una mujer sin amor (*A Woman without Love*, 1952)
El bruto (*The Brute*, 1953)
Él (*This Strange Passion*, 1953)
Abismos de pasión (*Wuthering Heights*, 1954)
La ilusión viaja in tranvía (*Illusion Travels by Streetcar*, 1954)
Robinson Crusoe (1954)
El río y la muerte (*The River and Death*, 1954)
Ensayo de un crimen (*The Criminal Life of Archibaldo de la Cruz*, 1955)
La muerte en este jardín (*La mort en ce jardin*; *Death in the Garden*, 1956)
Nazarín (1959)
La fièvre monte à el pao (*Los ambiciosos*; *Fever Rises at El Pao*, 1960)
La joven (*The Young One*, 1960)
Viridiana (1961)
El ángel exterminador (*Exterminating Angel*, 1962)
Simón del disierto (*Simon of the Desert*, 1965)

How Luis Buñuel Came to Mexico

—

Buñuel spent the time between making *Las Hurdes* in 1932 and his first Mexican assignment in 1946 taking a series of cinematic odd jobs as he tried to get in a position to direct. (Although he claimed in his memoir that in the mid-1930s "somehow I never really thought about making another movie,"[19] his activities during his cinematic exile belie that statement.) He accepted a six-month position at MGM in 1930 to study filmmaking in Hollywood, but was disappointed by how little creative control directors had in the system. Upon returning to Europe, he worked in the Paris office of Paramount Pictures in the dubbing division, and then took a similar job for Warner Brothers in Madrid. There, he was approached to executive-produce feature-length sound films for Filmófono, which he did from 1935 to 1936. There is some evidence that he had a hand in directing the films he produced, but it is unclear if he did and if so to what degree, and he rarely mentioned this filmmaking chapter of his life in any detail later on.[20] Whatever the case, the experience of making genre films within a commercial system—by his account he was executive producer of eighteen of them[21]—served him well ten years later when he got his chance to direct *Gran casino* in Mexico, and helps explain how he achieved a technically challenging shot in it that I will discuss later.

When civil war broke out in Spain in 1936, Buñuel's loyalties were with the republic and against Francisco Franco's fascists. As things worsened for the republicans, he left for the U.S. in 1938 and returned to Hollywood, hopeful of finding work and ultimately making films there. When no film work materialized in California, he found work at the Museum of Modern Art in New York editing propaganda films until 1943. Back in Hollywood, he took a short-lived dubbing job at Warner Brothers, and by 1946 was unemployed.

That same year, Buñuel agreed to accompany an old friend, film producer Denise Tual, to Mexico City. She hoped to interest a Mexican producer in making a film of Federico García Lorca's play, *The House of Bernarda Alba*, with Buñuel attached as director. They met with Dancigers, who passed on the García Lorca project but offered Buñuel a job directing a musical-melodrama, *Gran casino*.[22] By this time he had a wife and two sons to support, and was desperate to direct; he accepted the offer.

Did he abandon his surrealist principles by agreeing to direct low-budget genre films in Mexico? This was a crucial question for Buñuel because, unlike some others in the surrealist movement, he was a true believer. Surrealism was more than an artistic fad for Buñuel; it was a way of life, a value system, and a moral code. "For me," he said, "surrealism was not an aesthetic, just another avant-garde movement; it was something to which I committed myself in a spiritual and moral way."[23] Because adhering to surrealist principles was a matter of personal integrity, he was careful to keep the faith. For him, it was vitally important to be able to say that he "never made a single scene that compromised my convictions or my personal morality"[24] in his Mexican filmmaking.

TABLE 7.1.

Annual film production during the Golden Age,
correlated with the number of directors who made
the films and the number of new directors making
their first films

Year	Films produced	Directors	Average number of films per director	Director debuts per year
1938	57	40	1.42	18
1939	37	25	1.48	8
1940	29	20	1.45	4
1941	37	26	1.42	5
1942	47	36	1.31	10
1943	70	44	1.59	10
1944	75	50	1.50	14
1945	81	43	1.88	1
1946	71	39	1.82	1
1947	58	33	1.76	1
1948	81	39	2.08	1
1949	108	47	2.30	—
1950	122	49	2.49	3
1951	101	43	2.35	—
1952	98	41	2.39	3
1953	77	36	2.14	1
1954	112	43	2.60	1
1955	83	34	2.44	2
1956	90	35	2.57	2
1957	94	36	2.61	1
1958	104	34	2.97	—

SOURCE: Emilio García Riera, *Historia documental del cine
Mexicano (1959–1960)*, vol. 10 (Guadalajara: University
of Guadalajara Press, 1994), 13–14.

When Buñuel arrived in Mexico in 1946, the
movie business was thriving and would continue to do so for several more years. As we
saw at the end of the previous chapter, production was booming and profits were high,
but amidst the prosperity serious problems
were emerging. Evidence of this can be seen
in table 7.1, which cross-indexes the number
of films produced from the 1930s into the
1950s with the number of directors making
them along with the number of directorial
debuts. Though yearly film production figures rose steadily, that growth masked some
troubling filmmaking policies that undermined creativity. When Emilio García Riera,
who compiled this data, compared annual
film production to the number of directors who made those films and the number
of new directors allowed to break into the
business, the statistics reveal a major flaw in
the system. At the beginning of the Golden
Age, from 1938 to 1944, García Riera notes,
seventy-nine new directors made their first
films. In the next fourteen years, however,
only seventeen directors made their debuts.
The number is actually twelve because five of
the seventeen were, like Buñuel, experienced
filmmakers transplanted from other countries. Note that there were seven years when
only one new director broke into the business, and in three, 1949, 1951, and 1958, there
were no directorial debuts at all. The pioneering directors of the 1930s and early '40s
were aging, but younger talent was denied the
chance to replace them.

One reason for this, argues García Riera,
was the filmmakers' union, the Sindicato de

Trabajadores de la Producción Cinematográfica Mexicana, which was formed in 1945. It consisted of six sections—directors, actors, writers, composers, musicians, and technicians—and each section made its own rules on membership. Aspiring filmmakers were blocked from joining the union in order to protect established directors. The extremely low number of first-time directors in the years following 1945 coupled with the high average number of films per director in the same period exposes the inherent weakness of this policy. In order to arrive at an average of between two and three per director, many of the thirty or so directors made significantly more films than the average. Thus we have the case of Rafael Baledón, who directed nine films in 1958, and Miguel M. Delgado, who directed seven. Churning out that many pictures per year could hardly have enhanced those pictures' quality.[25]

As we saw in chapter 6, the falloff in quality would eventually be crippling, but it resulted from the way films were financed and produced in Mexico during the Golden Age. The Mexican film industry was producer driven, not studio driven. Anyone with enough money could become a producer and make a film by signing the stars, contracting the unionized workers and creative personnel, and booking time at one of the studios. By the early 1940s the demand for space was so great at the three main studios, CLASA, Azteca, and Mexico-Films, that a fourth, Tepeyac, was refurbished, and a new one, Churubusco Studios, was built by an American businessman and co-owned by RKO studios.

Producers and production companies typically financed their films with loans from the government-run Banco Nacional Cinematográfico. As Acevedo-Muñoz points out, the bank was where the film production power really lay, not with the studios, which merely housed the productions. Box office success and returning a profit were the primary goals for the producers, of course, as with any business, but doubly so because they had to repay the bank's loan with interest to keep themselves in good standing for the next film loan. Moreover, the national film bank tended to fund projects with high profitability potential. This perpetuated a producing culture whereby producers who made popular films had the best chance of receiving loans.[26] With profitability prized over creativity, the primary incentive was for inexpensive, quickly made, paint-by-number genre films.

How did classical Mexican films ever get made in a system of motion picture financing that practically mandated the production of MMC films? Usually as a reward for profitability. Once a director proved his commercial viability it was easier to find a producer to back a more personal project. Fernando de Fuentes parlayed the success of some of his early films to leverage the making of the movies that became the Revolution Trilogy. Similarly, the Fernández films of the late 1940s and, as we will see in the next chapter, Julio Bracho's *Distinto amanecer*, were funded by producers who were betting on filmmakers who had just released box office hits. Likewise, Buñuel got the chance to make *Los olvidados* "with almost total artistic freedom" as a sort of dividend from Dancigers for having delivered a profitable picture in *El gran calavera*.[27] And once his more personal films began to catch on, his projects—despite their increasing strangeness—found producers willing to back them

The Classical Mexican Cinema

because they had an audience. The one CMC anomaly, as we will see in the next chapter, is Adolfo Best Maugard's *La mancha de sangre*, which was made outside of—and in spite of—the existing financial-industrial framework.

To return to the status of the industry when Buñuel broke into the business, the conclusion of World War II appeared to signal good times but was in fact the beginning of the end of the Golden Age. I outlined the postwar situation in the last chapter, but let me sketch in a few more details of the downturn in Mexico's movie business because they relate to Buñuel's career there. A resurgence of filmmaking in Spain and Argentina threatened the Mexican film industry, but Mexico somehow managed to maintain its dominance as Spanish-language film producer in the 1950s. The Mexican film industry was, however, completely overwhelmed by movies from the United States and Europe. Three-quarters of the films exhibited in Mexico during the 1950s were American or European.[28] And because the majority of them were generally of better quality, with superior production values, Mexican audiences gradually began favoring them over the slapdash domestically produced films. Clearly, making cheaper films for a shrinking audience was unsustainable, and reality finally caught up with Mexican moviemaking in the 1960s. By 1961, Mexican film production dropped to its lowest levels since 1947, and both Spain and Argentina were competing as never before for screen time in Spanish-language markets. This eventually led to *la crisis*, the collapse of the Mexican film industry in the 1960s.[29]

Interestingly, though this boom-to-bust trajectory was the backdrop to Buñuel's nineteen years as a Mexican director, for the most part it didn't adversely affect his career. He got in just under the wire, beginning his directing when Mexico's filmmaking was peaking. Through discipline and preparation, he became skilled at turning out low-budget genre films on short schedules and snuck in bits of surrealism in the process, getting bolder and bolder as he went. Ironically, those bizarre touches made his films stand out from the other Mexican films in a crowded field, and he created his own inimitable niche brand. Even Spain's rise and Mexico's corresponding fall in the Spanish-speaking market was beneficial for him. One of his best-known films of the Mexican era, the 1961 Cannes Palme d'Or winner *Viridiana*, was a Mexico-Spain coproduction made possible by the backing of two newly formed Spanish production companies.[30] It caused a scandal, was condemned by the Vatican, and made a fortune. With the notoriety, Buñuel became a celebrity and *Viridiana*'s box office success allowed him to make *El ángel exterminador*, his final feature-length Mexican film.[31]

Buñuel and Surrealism
—

Surrealism's aim was to expand the idea of reality by recognizing the importance of dreams. In *The Surrealist Manifesto* (*Le manifeste du surréalisme*, 1924), its founder, André Breton (1896–1966), wondered why the accepted idea of reality was limited to waking life. Why were dreams and dreaming, which consume so much of our lives, excluded? Why do we lend "so much more credence . . . to waking events than to those occurring in dreams"?[32] Breton proposed redefining reality to include dreams and christened this comprehensive super-reality "surrealism."

Beyond making way for dream imagery, as a movement surrealism sought to destroy traditional concepts of establishment art. And it went further still, aiming to take down the entire social structure. As Buñuel once put it, "The real purpose of surrealism was not to create a new literary, artistic, or even philosophical movement, but to explode the social order, to transform life itself."[33] The surrealists' principal weapon in this campaign was scandal, meant to shock the system out of its complacency and turn it in a new direction.

It was a movement practiced in all the arts, but one of the most famous, notorious, and purest examples of surrealism in any art form was Buñuel's first film, *Un chien andalou* (*The Andalusian Dog*, 1929). Cowritten by him and another young Spaniard living in Paris, the painter Salvador Dalí, the sixteen-minute film was financed by Buñuel's mother. Their script was fashioned from their dream images, and their filmmaking method, as Buñuel later described it, was very simple. "No idea or image that might lend itself to a rational explanation of any kind would be accepted," Buñuel said. "We had to open all doors to the irrational and keep only those images that surprised us, without trying to explain why."[34] *Un chien andalou* caused quite a stir, but *L'age d'or*, the next film Buñuel directed from a script by him and Dalí, was even more controversial and incited a riot. During one screening, members of the "League of Patriots" and the "Anti-Semitic League" launched stink bombs, physically attacked members of the audience, splattered ink on the screen, and destroyed artwork by some of the leading surrealist artists on display in the lobby. The police responded by banning the film. Except for viewings at small cine clubs, *L'age d'or* was largely unseen for nearly fifty years.

Obviously those first experimental shorts accomplished exactly what Buñuel intended—to upset audiences with a steady stream of shocking images. Eventually, though, Buñuel came to realize that *Un chien andalou* and *L'age d'or* were "unrepeatable experiments" and that he couldn't continue "putting sliced eyes and hands with ants in all my films."[35] Furthermore, working in the studio system in Mexico and obligated to "tell a story," he had to devise a different filmmaking strategy to deliver his anti-bourgeois critique. Out of necessity, he conceived a shrewd way to continue unsettling viewers, one different from what he had used in the early avant-garde experiments, and one he would employ for the rest of his life.

Rather than make films comprised of a relentless chain of provocative imagery, he would utilize standard Hollywood-MMC filmmaking techniques, hoping to lull audiences into letting their guard down. In most of his Mexican films, especially in his early ones, he cued viewers to anticipate typical MMC fare via formulaic plots and seemingly traditional character development and unambiguous happy endings. With this recognizable narrative baseline established, his subversive surrealist insurgency would begin. Unexpected bursts of violence, irrational behaviors, and unmotivated camera placements suddenly surfaced. Suppressed sexual desires, manias, and fetishes—his and his characters'—were unleashed. Ironic, implausible endings sabotaged the standard three-act, happy-ending structure. Characters were denied agency, rendering them helpless rather than heroic.

Instead of rejecting plot and Hollywood-style continuity, as he had done with *Un chien andalou* and *L'age d'or*, he embraced them. What he discovered was that an unexpected surreal element suddenly appearing within a realistic context heightened the mystifying effect he was after. "Not everything," he realized, "had to be Surrealist in a painting by a Surrealist painter, only one small detail that logically shouldn't be there."[36]

The Poetics of Luis Buñuel's Mexican Films

—

Buñuel combined several repeated techniques into a consistent, recognizable style. In the following analysis, I want to focus primarily on his cinematic style, but since it was developed to transmit his surrealistic content, it is impossible to separate the two. So as I describe his cinematic poetics, I will necessarily be showing how his style conveyed his surrealism, and how together they articulated his criticism of the Mexican bourgeois status quo.

The following are among the most salient features of Buñuel's poetics.

IRRATIONAL SPARKS

Buñuel's surrealism drove his filmmaking style. So as a beginning director in Mexico, his first challenge was how to incorporate it into his films. His initial strategy was to slip small samples of the raw, unformed, and unfiltered images that spontaneously emerged from his unconscious—"irrational sparks," he once called them[37]—into otherwise coherent realist narratives. As Buñuel wrote in his memoir about writing the script for *Los olvidados*, "I wanted to insert a few bizarre images which would flash onto the screen just for an instant, just long enough for the audience to wonder if it had really seen them or not."[38] These additions might not have functioned logically or rationally, but they succeeded metaphorically.

A fairly straightforward example is a scene in his first Mexican film, *Gran casino*, where the protagonist, Gerardo (Jorge Negrete), kills the evil henchman El Rayado (Alfonso Bedoya), who is hiding behind a curtain to assassinate him. When Gerardo delivers the fatal blow, Buñuel superimposes breaking glass over the gun striking the curtain. The superimposition is not realistic—obviously there was no pane of glass there—but it does work metaphorically, emotionally, and, curiously, narratively. Something is being shattered, a life is being taken, and the cracked glass marks a tonal shift in the movie as it veers from light musical romance to gangster melodrama (fig. 7.1).

And it wasn't just imagery that Buñuel utilized to produce surreal sparks. At the climax of *Nazarín*, Buñuel used sound as the incongruous and extra-diegetic irrational element (figs. 7.73–7.75, below). It is the drums of Calanda, music from Buñuel's hometown traditionally performed in the streets for twenty-four hours on Good Friday. (He used the same drumming music in *L'age d'or* and in

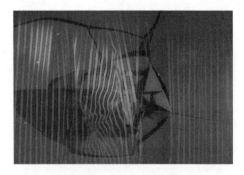

FIG. 7.1. An irrational spark in *Gran casino*. When the hero strikes and kills the villain hiding behind the curtain, Buñuel superimposes an extra-diegetic image of shattering glass. It doesn't make logical sense—there's no glass there—but instead functions metaphorically.

Simon of the Desert.) He added this music from his childhood, unheard in the rest of the film and likely unfamiliar to most viewers, over Nazarín's crisis of doubt. Once again, Buñuel's irrational spark worked, resulting in an emotionally satisfying and dramatically fulfilling ending that escapes rational explanation. At their best, Buñuel's surrealist touches are, like any good metaphor, aesthetically effective but ultimately ineffable.

He snuck in the broken glass "irrational spark" in *Gran Casino* because it was a brief and unobtrusive addition. However, given much more leeway with *Los olvidados*, his third Mexican film, Buñuel was able to include more—and wilder—"sparks." "I wanted to introduce crazy, completely mad elements into the most realistic scenes," he said of his filming of the film.[39] These "sparks" were also stylistically different. Unlike the introduction of the extra-diegetic shattered glass in *Gran casino*, the objects that formed the "sparks" in *Los olvidados* were common features of the story world, though combined in strange, disquieting ways.

A prime example occurs in the scene where Jaibo's gang assaults Don Carmelo, the blind man (Miguel Inclán). After beating him, they leave him sprawling on the ground. As he crawls about in the dirt, out of nowhere a black rooster appears next to his bloody face (fig. 7.2). Toward the end of the film Buñuel rhymed that image by having a white chicken step over Pedro's (Alfonso Mejía) dead body (fig. 7.3). Continuing the film's bird fetish, Don Carmelo, a sort of *curandero* (medicine man) for the neighborhood, uses a dove as a folk remedy to treat a sick woman, rubbing it over her exposed back to transfer her illness to the bird (fig. 7.4). More roosters appear in the film: Pedro's mother kills one with a broom, one appears in Pedro's nightmare, and he kills two more in a rage at the reformatory.

FIGS. 7.2–7.4. Surrealist sparks from odd juxtapositions and repetitions in *Los olvidados*. A black rooster appears in the face of the assaulted blind man, Don Carmelo. A white chicken walks across Pedro's dead body. Don Carmelo, a part-time *curandero*, rubs a dove over the exposed back of a sick woman.

The Classical Mexican Cinema

SURREALIST SEQUENCES

Besides these short "irrational sparks," Buñuel included two longer surrealist sequences in *Los olvidados*. They are iconic passages in CMC filmmaking, unforgettable moments not just in Mexican film, but in all of cinema history. Moreover, they are watershed moments in Buñuel's filmmaking career, the first incorporations of extended surreal elements into seemingly realistic narratives.

The first, Pedro's nightmare, is one of the best representations of the dream state in cinema, and set a dream-depiction standard. To create it, Buñuel put together a series of violations of traditional movie continuity, and his delight in flouting standard Hollywood-MMC practice is palpable. The sequence begins traditionally, with a double exposure of Pedro, which by 1950 was a conventional movie trope to announce the beginning of a dream and to distinguish the dreamer from the dream (one of the better-known examples was in Buster Keaton's *Sherlock Jr.* [1924]). After employing that cliché, however, Buñuel goes on a continuity violation spree. Among the conventions he tramples on to create Pedro's nightmare are the use of slow motion for the entire sequence, sound out of synchronization with characters' lip movements (in some cases they speak without moving their lips at all), continuity inconsistencies (Pedro's mother walks away from him holding nothing, then turns back and returns holding a piece of raw meat; at first the boy under his bed is Julian, later it's Jaibo), and a jump cut of Julian's side-to-side head movement (figs. 7.5 and 7.6).

The second surrealist sequence, Jaibo's (Roberto Cobo) death near the end of the film, is not a dream, but a journey inside

FIGS. 7.5 AND 7.6. The first surrealist sequence in *Los olvidados*: Pedro's nightmare. It begins with the "dream Pedro" separating from the dreaming Pedro. He finds Julian, the boy Jaibo killed that day, laughing under his bed. At one point, there is a jump cut in Julian's side-to-side head movement. Later in the dream, there is a continuity break when Jaibo replaces Julian under the bed.

Jaibo's last moments. A chilling scene, it positively exalts the irrational. Over a MCU of Jaibo writhing in agony after he has been shot and lies dying, Buñuel again uses a superimposition—a dog running on a wet street toward the camera. On the sound track he adds haunting, whispered voice-overs, coming first from Jaibo, and then from others. Jaibo begins by speaking not his final words, but his final thoughts.

Jaibo: "You're in for it now, Jaibo. You've been shot in the forehead."

Another voice, possibly Pedro's: "Watch out, Jaibo! The mangy dog, look, it's coming."

Jaibo: "No. No. I'm falling into a black hole. I'm alone. Alone."

A woman's voice (Buñuel said it was Jaibo imagining the mother he never knew or only faintly remembers speaking to him):[40] "As always, my son, as always. Go to sleep, my son, and stop thinking."

The superimposition ends, Jaibo dies, and his passing is marked in a special—and for 1950, an extraordinarily uncommon—cinematic manner: with a freeze frame. The end of motion is the end of his life. It's yet another filmmaking violation, and, according to Aranda, the first use of the freeze frame, a technique that he claims influenced François Truffaut so much that he copied it in the famous ending shot of *Les quatre cents coups* (*The 400 Blows*, 1959).[41]

The visual and sonic elements combine poetically, not logically, to humanize Jaibo at the moment of his death. With this sympathetic farewell to Jaibo, Buñuel humanizes the most troubled, violent, and dangerous of the film's street kids (figs. 7.7 and 7.8).

One final note about Buñuel's surrealist sparks. Not all of them saw the light of day—at least not in *Los olvidados*. Evidently Dancigers found some of them too crazy, too expensive, or both, and he vetoed them. In an interview with André Bazin, for example, Buñuel mentioned a rejected "spark" he had hoped to include in one of the murder scenes:

> When Jaibo goes to beat up and kill the other boy, the camera pans across a huge eleven-storey building in process of construction in the background; and I would have liked to put a hundred-piece orchestra into it. It would have only been glimpses, vaguely and fleetingly. I wanted to include lots of elements of this kind, but I was absolutely forbidden.[42]

BRECHTIAN TOUCHES

To a great extent, Buñuel's surrealism provoked viewers by flaunting the unexpected, as he did with his "irrational sparks" images and juxtapositions. With Pedro's nightmare and Jaibo's death, he added filmmaking violations. But as strikingly memorable as those scenes were, in a way they were less

FIGS. 7.7 AND 7.8. The second surrealist sequence in *Los olvidados*: the death of Jaibo. *Top*, the superimposition of a dog with no connection to the dying boy operates metaphorically—Jaibo was just another stray dog ignored by Mexican society. *Bottom*, he dies with his eyes open in a freeze frame.

The Classical Mexican Cinema

surprising because their strangeness was narratively motivated. Both depicted special circumstances of suspended or diminished rationality and consciousness—Pedro dreaming, Jaibo dying—and that gave Buñuel the storytelling license to break filmmaking rules in order to represent them. But there are two other excellent, more extreme examples of his rule breaking in *Los olvidados* that were nar ratively at least—completely unmotivated and astonishing as a result. In them, his surrealism was so disruptive it was Brechtian.

In the most brazen case, Buñuel deliberately breaks a fundamental provision of the Hollywood-MMC filmmaker-viewer pact: the invisible fourth wall. In the movies, characters go about their business, never acknowledging the audience watching them. Buñuel's major Brechtian transgression occurs in a scene after Pedro is sent to reform school. Unhappy with his fate, angry with his mother who turned him in, and in a rebellious mood, Pedro looks directly at the camera, ignoring the law against direct address, and returns our gaze.[43] (Buñuel would do it again the following year in the last shot of *La hija del engaño*, when the protagonist looks into the camera and says, "You see, nothing turns out right for me!" But, as a closing wink at the audience from a long-suffering character, it was more acceptable narratively.) Buñuel compounds that offense by having Pedro throw a raw egg right at the lens, where it smashes into a gooey mess. (Actually, it doesn't hit the lens itself—I doubt Gabriel Figueroa would have allowed that—but appears to break on a sheet of glass placed in front of it that was then pulled away) (figs. 7.9 and 7.10).

After that eruption, the film reverts to the standard movie invisible-fourth-wall

FIGS. 7.9 AND 7.10. Direct address in *Los olvidados*. This one's for you! In an angry and rebellious mood at the reform school, Pedro returns our gaze and then throws an egg at us, where it smashes right in front of our face.

objectivity Buñuel had employed up to that point. When the egg hits the glass, though, Buñuel destabilizes the viewers' position, complicating their relationship to the poverty and hardship they are watching. Like Brecht, Buñuel hopes to pull viewers closer to the suffering, and prod them to go from watching social problems to questioning the system that tolerates them. Through his rule breaking, Buñuel's critique becomes personal, involving viewers in general and Mexican ones in particular. Yes, the system's to blame, but aren't you part of the system?

Another very subtle and culture-specific instance of breaking the fourth wall in *Los olvidados* has a similar effect of uncomfortably drawing the viewer into the action. Because it requires fluency in the language, it directly targets Spanish-speaking viewers. The scene in question is the one in which Jaibo and his gang assault a double amputee. The man is feisty and he refuses to be intimidated, so they drag him out of his makeshift wagon, which Jaibo pushes down the street, leaving him thrashing about on the sidewalk without a means of transportation. It's a hard scene to watch, not just because of its depiction of the young boys' heartless cruelty, but also because Buñuel cast an actor who was actually an amputee (fig. 7.11).

An additional small detail makes it even more difficult for viewers, especially, I would argue, Mexican ones. On the amputee's cart is printed the phrase, "Me Mirabas." Emblematic of the man's pride and defiance, it roughly translates to "You looking at *me?*" The message is part of the story world, but it's also available for Spanish-speaking viewers to read. And like the signs used in Brechtian theater, it's meant to interrupt the narrative flow and throw audience members who

stare at him and read the words on his cart off balance. It's saying, "Why are you staring at me?" and "Don't feel sorry for me—I don't want your pity." and "Are you capable of seeing me as a human being?" Endlessly complicating the viewing experience, Buñuel refused to make it easy for his audience.

FRAMES WITHIN THE FRAME

The Figure in the Window

In general, Buñuel used the frame-within-the-frame technique as it was used by others, especially Fernando de Fuentes, namely to direct our eye toward certain details. But he also used it to isolate and accentuate a striking, haunting image. He was still a surrealist, still the same man who directed *Un chien andalou* and *L'age d'or*, but realized in Mexico that the best way to introduce surrealism was by the careful selection and arrangement of particular images in a precise sequence. As much as any of the great filmmakers and major stylists, as much as, say, Hitchcock, Murnau, and Eisenstein, Buñuel sought the perfect image to put his ideas across. In the main, he used conventional means—usually just a CU—to draw attention to his familiar catalogue of personal fetishes: women's thighs, feet, roosters, insects, and the like. And to do this he employed LSs, MSs, CUs, and conventional MMC continuity. But to emphasize an especially compelling image of the human face, he frequently placed a frame around it, often a windowpane. In Buñuel's body of work, the figure in the window had an impressive lineage, making its first appearance in *Un chien andalou*, and can be seen in a number of his Mexican films (figs. 7.12–7.18).

FIG. 7.11. Buñuel uses another Brechtian device, a sign, that once again calls the invisible fourth wall convention into question and destabilizes the standard viewer-film objectivity pact.

TOP LEFT | FIG. 7.12. The figure in the window in Buñuel's first film, *Un chien andalou* (1929).

BOTTOM LEFT | FIG. 7.13. The figure in the window in *Susana*. In the middle of a thunderstorm, Susana (Rosita Quintana) appears at the window of a wealthy family's hacienda.

ABOVE | FIG. 7.14. The figure in the window in *Los olvidados* (1950). Pedro seeks shelter near the end of the film.

TOP | FIG. 7.15. The figure in the window in *Subida al cielo*. The face of the dead girl seen through the coffin window.

BOTTOM | FIG. 7.16. The figure in the window in *Él*. Pathologically jealous and delusional, a frantic Francisco (Arturo de Córdova) searches for his wife near the end of Buñuel's indictment of *machismo*.

TOP | FIG. 7.17. The figure in the window in *The Young One*. Evvie (Kay Meersman) looks out into the night, listening to the music played by an African American visitor. As shot and framed by Buñuel, however, it's another disconcerting instance of direct address.

BOTTOM | FIG. 7.18. The figure in the window in *Viridiana*. Rita (Teresa Rabal), the maid's young daughter, watches as Don Jaime makes love to his drugged niece.

The Unheard Conversation

When the frame-within-the-frame was a two-shot, Buñuel would sometimes show the characters talking, but mischievously deny us the ability to hear what they were saying. On one level, he's frustrating viewers, placing them in the same position as many of his characters, who were continually thwarted in attempting to achieve their goals. On another, he's subverting traditional film practice, in this case the Hollywood-MMC filmmaking convention of omniscient narration whereby all information is available to viewers. With the unheard conversation, Buñuel forced his viewers to use their imaginations to fill in some narrative blanks, which was actually easy to do. But by having them imagine what characters were saying, Buñuel worked his way into their heads, which is right where he wanted to be, tinkering with their imaginations (figs. 7.19 and 7.20).

The Mise-en-Scène Proscenium

Sometimes Buñuel would take advantage of the frame-within-the-frame and use it as a mini-proscenium for the characters, a small stage where they perform. It was one of the ways Buñuel spotlighted the action by bringing it closer to us, as he does in the window scene in *The Young One* (fig. 7.20), the scene of the women passengers delivering a baby in *Subida al cielo* (fig. 7.21), or, in the case of the attempted murder at the bell tower in *Él*, marking its gruesome importance (figs. 7.22–7.23).

The Impossible or Improbable Vantage Point

A variation on the mise-en-scène frame is an unrealistic but visually compelling shot Buñuel used occasionally: a reverse angle shot from a physically impossible or improbable vantage point. Customarily, the shot/reverse shot pattern moves the camera back and forth within unencumbered space. But in these cases, Buñuel placed the camera in dubious locations. In one scene in *Susana*, for example, Susana flirts with Alberto, the son

TOP | FIG. 7.19. The unheard conversation in *Él*. When Francisco (Arturo de Córdova) finally gets the opportunity to speak to Gloria (Delia Garcés), a woman he has become infatuated with, Buñuel stages their brief conversation behind the patio window. Frustratingly—but realistically—we can't hear what they are saying. Viewers must fill in the narrative ellipsis.

BOTTOM | FIG. 7.20. The unheard conversation in *The Young One*. Orphaned now that her grandfather has died, Evvie, a child just blossoming into womanhood, has to contend with the advances of Miller (Zachary Scott), the game warden and the only other person on the island where they live. The shot is also a good example of another variant of the frame-within-the-frame technique, Buñuel's creation of a mise-en-scène proscenium.

TOP | FIG. 7.21. The mise-en-scène proscenium in *Subida al cielo*. When a pregnant woman passenger goes into labor, three women quickly gather at the back of the bus to deliver her baby.

MIDDLE | FIG. 7.22. The mise-en-scène proscenium in *Él*. Infatuated with Gloria, Francisco follows her to a restaurant, where she meets her fiancé.

BOTTOM | FIG. 7.23. The mise-en-scène proscenium in *Él*. As he becomes more paranoid, jealous, and unhinged, Francisco tries to kill Gloria by pushing her from a church bell tower.

FIG. 7.24 The impossible vantage point in *Susana*. After establishing the characters in the room and the bookshelf against a wall, Buñuel shoots the reverse angle shot from behind the bookshelf. The bookshelf is a ready-made mise-en-scène frame, allowing the camera closer proximity to the characters.

of the *hacendado*, as he arranges his scientific books on his bookshelf. In an earlier shot it is established that the bookshelf is against a wall, but for their first intimate contact, Buñuel places the camera behind the bookcase, framing them with a shelf in the foreground and drawing our eyes to the small proscenium he has created for their romantic encounter (fig. 7.24).

An extraordinary example of the impossible vantage point is also one of Buñuel's most ingenious transitions. It comes in *La hija del engaño*, a melodrama about a man, Quintín (Fernando Soler), who leaves his unfaithful wife and takes their infant girl, Marta, with him. Brokenhearted, not knowing what to do with Marta, and having been told by his wife that the child isn't his, he leaves the baby on the doorstep of a rural house, and over the years sends the family money to help raise her. Buñuel uses an improbable vantage point in a transitional scene where the story jumps forward roughly twenty years, taking up the plot when Marta, and the couple's

own daughter, Jovita, are both grown women. Beyond moving the film ahead in time, the scene also reveals that, as luck would have it, Marta's stepfather is an abusive alcoholic (figs. 7.25–7.32).

LONG TAKES AND THE ONE-TAKE SCENE

Most of Buñuel's Mexican films were made on extremely short schedules, many shot in three or four weeks and edited in a day or two.[44] "In Mexico," he wrote in his memoir, "I never had a shooting schedule longer than twenty-four days (except for *Robinson Crusoe*)."[45] *Los olvidados*, *El bruto*, and *Él* each had eighteen-day shooting schedules, *Susana*, *La hija del engaño*, and *Una mujer sin amor* were shot in twenty days; the latter was edited in three.[46]

To cope with these constraints, he developed an economical filmmaking technique. Careful planning was essential, and Buñuel prepared each day's shooting in detail before

arriving on the set.[47] In addition, he minimized postproduction, especially editing. As much as possible, therefore, he eschewed Hollywood's and the MMC's analytical editing style, which required comprehensive coverage, in favor of his version of what André Bazin called the deep focus style, and which we can think of as probably derived from the earlier European tableau style popular in the 1910s (discussed in chapter 3). Buñuel did not achieve the extreme depth of field realized by Orson Welles, William Wyler, or Jean Renoir. (As we saw in chapter 6, according to Gabriel Figueroa, who photographed *Los olvidados*, *Él*, *Nazarín*, *The Young One*, and *El ángel exterminador* for Buñuel, the sort of pan focus style that Gregg Toland accomplished for Welles and Wyler, particularly in interior shots, would have been cost prohibitive in Mexico.) Nevertheless, his style did retain some characteristics of those directors' deep focus styles: long takes, a mobile camera, and a complex mise-en-scène. By means of his long take style, Buñuel effectively and efficiently recorded large chunks of narration, which found its apotheosis in, most impressively, his ability to capture entire scenes in a single take. What began as a resourceful response to scheduling and budgetary constraints became a distinctive feature of Buñuel's Mexican style.

An impressive early example of the long take appears in his very first film, *Gran casino*, in its introduction of the casino's leading entertainer, Camelia (Meche Barba). The shot lasts nearly two minutes, and in it the camera follows the singing and dancing Camelia a full 360 degrees from the stage onto the crowded nightclub floor and back (figs. 7.33–7.40).

FACING | FIGS. 7.25–7.32. The improbable vantage point in *La hija del engaño*. A remarkable combination of transition and exposition. The sequence begins shortly after Quintín has left baby Marta with the family in the country. In the middle of an argument with his wife, the husband, Lencho García (Roberto Meyer), crosses to the cupboard. The screen momentarily goes black, then we see Lencho opening the doors and realize the camera is situated inside the cupboard. The couple's arguing continues, with the wife complaining about his drinking as he takes a swig from a bottle. He shuts the doors and the screen goes black again, but this time for thirty-one seconds. The scene continues on the soundtrack, however, and we hear Lencho beating his wife. After a brief silence, another scene is heard to begin, with Lencho demanding his breakfast. A woman's voice replies that there's nothing to eat, and she opens the doors to the cupboard to show Lencho how bare it is. As the scene plays out, we realize that the story has skipped ahead about two decades. Lencho's alcoholism and abuse continue, his wife is gone, and Marta (in the foreground, played by Alicia Caro) and Lencho's daughter, Jovita (Lily Aclemar), are now grown women.

FIGS. 7.33–7.40. The long take in *Gran casino*. The big
production number from Buñuel's first feature, *Gran
casino* (1947), introduces Camelia (Meche Barba) beginning with a MCU of Barba's legs (a Buñuel fetish). She
dances from the stage to the casino floor and back again,
with a single long 360-degree take lasting 119 seconds.

Eventually, Buñuel would capture entire scenes in one long take, and at times, like his contemporaries Hitchcock and Welles, seemed to relish the challenge of pulling off a one-shot scene, especially when it involved intricate staging and camera movement. But Buñuel strove to make them organic and unnoticeable rather than bravura, show-off moments. "I detest filmmakers who seem to be saying, 'Look how clever I am,'" he once said.[48] Buñuel's virtuosity was more modest than Hitchcock's and Welles's, and as much as possible smoothly integrated into the movie's narration. Of his working method, he said: "Once I'm on the set, I indicate the movements of the actors and camera. I manage to see that the framing is functional and doesn't call attention to itself. When I watch films in which they've wanted to *épater* with the camera, I get up and leave the theater. Technical feats leave me cold."[49] The grandest of movie fetishizers refused to fetishize cinematic technique.

One aspect of Buñuel's filmmaking style that facilitated the achievement of the one-shot scene was his narrative economy. His extremely efficient narration is evident in several ways. First, his films were short. The longest Mexican film is *La muerte en este jardín*, which runs ninety-nine minutes, but most run around ninety minutes, and some considerably less than that. Working with meager budgets and short schedules mandated brief running times, of course, but even so, it's remarkable how short some of his best known, critically praised, and narratively and emotionally complex films are. For all its rich and memorable depiction of the urban underclass, *Los olvidados* is a trim eighty minutes. *La ilusión viaja in tranvía* and *Subida*

al cielo, two cross sections of Mexican society, run eighty-two and seventy-four minutes, respectively. *Él* is eighty-eight minutes long, and *Susana* eighty-six. And the short running times persist throughout his Mexican period, even toward the end of it, when he had more time and money: *Nazarín* runs ninety-four minutes, *The Young One* ninety-five, *Viridiana* ninety-one, and *El ángel exterminador* is ninety-three minutes long.

Second, he was a concise visual storyteller who allowed images, rather than dialogue, to do as much of the expository work as possible. One reason the unheard conversations work so well is Buñuel's recognition that viewers don't need to hear everything. They would be able to fill in the narrational blanks, and, in any case, what the characters were saying was not so difficult to guess. And he practiced his economic visual storytelling in other ways. In *Los olvidados*, for instance, rather than provide a traditional scene where Pedro asks the orphaned Ojitos if he needs a place to spend the night, Buñuel instead plays Pedro's offer in a dark, silent LS, with the two boys surrounded by stray dogs. When the two leave with each other and are seen together later at the barn where Pedro is sleeping, viewers easily surmise what has occurred (fig. 7.41).

Still another example of his efficient visual storytelling was Buñuel's instinct for knowing what can go unsaid. Sexual desire, for example, is best revealed in a glance, not a speech. We comprehend characters' erotic longings from Buñuel's shrewd combination of their glances and the objects of their gaze, a technique that states their desire more clearly than an extended scene or added dialogue ever could (figs. 7.42–7.45).

FIG. 7.41. Narrative economy in *Los olvidados*.
Instead of employing a conventional exposition
scene, Buñuel shows Pedro's (*right*) offer to find
Ojitos a place to spend the night in a LS and with
unheard dialog. When the two head off and then
appear in the next scene together, it's clear what
happened.

A third way Buñuel practiced narrative
economy was keeping his scenes as brief as
possible. Scenes can vary greatly in length,
but when there is significant expository work
for the characters to do, most Hollywood
scenes of the time ran between two and a
half and three and a half or four minutes.[50]
In contrast, most of Buñuel's more involved
scenes ran less than two minutes. As Buñuel
told José de la Colina and Tomás Pérez Turrent about his scriptwriting practice:

> Above all, I attempt to synthesize, to
> concentrate a three-minute scene into
> two minutes. . . . In general, while already
> writing the first treatment of a story, I
> begin thinking about it in terms of visual
> efficiency. I even have the editing of the
> shots in mind, particularly when I am
> filming. I am economical and don't shoot
> cutaways.[51]

FIGS. 7.42–7.45. Sexual desire in a glance in
Susana (*top*) and *Los olvidados*. Everything we need
to know about what the *hacendado* (Fernando
Soler) in *Susana* and Jaibo (Roberto Cobo) in *Los
olvidados* are thinking is conveyed in two shots.

The Classical Mexican Cinema

His process was to distill a scene down to its dramatic essence, usually as close to two minutes as he could. Then he would capture it in a single take or in as few shots as possible. A good example of a one-shot scene occurs in *Susana*, in the scene where Doña Carmen, the wife of the *hacendado* (Matilde Palou), learns that her husband has suddenly fired his trusted foreman. This long-take scene, which runs 1:51, moves the camera 180 degrees from a servant entering the large living room and crossing to her mistress seated in a chair in the center. Doña Carmen stands and the camera follows her as she walks over to an open window, with the patio visible through it, on the opposite side of the room. Dispensing with analytical editing, Buñuel still achieves a great deal of shot variety, including LSs, two-shot MSs, and MCUs, via his careful staging and subtle camera movements. In the style he was developing, pans and tracking shots follow the characters naturally, concealing rather than trumpeting camera movement. As he later reflected on this aspect of his style, "The camera must move slowly without the viewer noticing. . . . There should be no gratuitous camera movements; it's always preferable to take advantage of a character's movement and then follow him to justify using a dolly or a tracking shot" (figs. 7.46–7.53).[52]

Los olvidados contains a remarkable example of Buñuel combining several techniques, the one-shot scene, the mise-en-scène proscenium, the improbable vantage point, and the unheard conversation. It's a scene where Pedro, wandering the streets alone at night, is propositioned by a pederast. Buñuel covers the entire scene in a single long take and the action is framed inside the mise-en-scène proscenium of a store's display window

from inside the closed store. Because Buñuel's sound design dispenses with dialogue and ambient sounds, only the sound track music is heard (figs. 7.54–7.61).

FROM ONE-SHOT TO TWO-SHOT SCENES

In his later Mexican films, Buñuel used the one-shot scene more sparingly, though he never abandoned long takes. In *The Young One*, *Nazarín*, and *Viridiana* for instance, the one-shot scene is most often replaced by two-shot scenes, with the shots typically fairly even in length. Some scenes are comprised of a long take (or two) with a patch of analytical editing (two-shots, shot/reverse shots, or over-the-shoulder shots) in the middle. In the long takes, Buñuel continued to maintain compositional variety via his inventive staging, and panning and tracking, organically creating LSs, MSs, and CUs. Since these later films are also the ones with (slightly) bigger budgets and correspondingly longer shooting schedules, one might deduce that the one-shot scene was less a stylistic choice and more a production necessity. Buñuel had six weeks to shoot both *Nazarín* and *El ángel exterminador*, and *Nazarín* had an estimated budget of 1 million pesos, not an extravagant amount, but compared to the 100,000 pesos he had for *Gran casino* and the 400,000-peso budget for *El gran calavera*, it must have seemed generous.[53] And he once claimed that *Viridiana*, his third-to-last Mexican production, shot in Spain, was one of two films where he had the most creative freedom (*L'age d'or* was the other).[54]

With a bit more time and money, what would become his later European style begins to take shape, consisting of long takes joined

FIGS. 7.46–7.53. A one-shot scene in *Susana*. Buñuel used a moving camera and complex mise-en-scène to capture the entire scene in a single take that runs 111 seconds. In it, the mistress of the hacienda, Doña Carmen (Matilde Palou), learns that her husband has fired their trusted foreman. The maid, Felisa (María Gentil Arcos), enters and the camera tracks and pans left with her as she crosses and joins Doña Carmen. Felisa informs her of the firing and that the foreman is leaving. Doña Carmen stands and the camera tracks left with her as she goes to the open window, where she calls to the foreman (Victor Manuel Mendoza), who is preparing to leave. He joins her there in a two-shot and confirms that he's been let go. He leaves, and she turns to the camera and the scene ends in a MCU as she tries to comprehend what has just transpired.

FIGS. 7.54–7.61. The one-shot scene, mise-en-scène proscenium, improbable vantage point, and unheard conversation in *Los olvidados*. One of the film's most memorable scenes begins with Pedro crossing the street and approaching the camera, situated inside a storefront display window, followed by a man. The camera tracks closer to them, framing the proposition in a two-shot. The man offers Pedro money and just as they are about to leave together, they notice something off screen. The man hesitates and Pedro runs away. The man exits frame left as the cause of his disappearance, a policeman, enters frame right, and the sixty-five-second scene ends.

with typical Hollywood-style shooting and editing of over-the-shoulder mid-shots, and the traditional shot/reverse shot pattern. He kept the long takes, with their combination of moving camera and the careful blocking of actors, and these resulted in scenes that were narratively economical yet contained the type of compositional variety usually accomplished by analytical editing. A good example of a two-shot scene in a later Mexican film is the one in *Viridiana* where the title character, a young novice, tells the Mother Superior she's leaving the convent (figs. 7.62–7.69).

BUÑUEL'S SUBVERSIVE NARRATIVE STRUCTURE

Buñuel employed common dramatic forms—the customary Hollywood-MMC three-act happy-ending or the more rare tragic structure—but with a difference. And it's that difference, particularly in the tragedies, that makes his films consistent with the Classical Mexican Cinema, most notably Fernando de Fuentes's Revolution Trilogy and Emilio Fernández's downbeat dramas such as *María Candelaria*, *Río Escondido*, and *Salón México*. Based on their narrative structure, we can divide Buñuel's Mexican films into four categories.

The Conventional Happy-Ending Film

His one purely Hollywood happy-ending film is *Robinson Crusoe*. Crusoe survives for years on a deserted island, devises his escape by trapping the pirates and rescuing the good sailors, and finally returns to his homeland with his new mate, Friday. Moreover, he returns a man transformed, a character arc that, as we will see, is typical of Buñuel's protagonists. Physically and mentally he is

stronger, much more resilient and resourceful than before. And his worldview has shifted as well—his initial master-slave relationship with Friday has gradually evolved into friendship.

The other of Buñuel's films that might be considered to have a Hollywood-like happy ending, *Gran casino*, he subverted. The hero, Gerardo, solves the mystery, kills the gangsters' main henchman, seriously wounds their boss, and winds up with the beautiful leading lady, Mercedes (Libertad Lamarque). But the resolution is atypical (which may have had something to do with the film's failure at the box office) because Gerardo is not the one who saves the day. He is captured by the bad guys at the end, and Mercedes rescues him by selling the Gran Casino nightclub and buying his freedom. Besides the fact that it's the female lead and not the macho protagonist who is the heroic savior, Buñuel further frustrates audience expectations because the two superstars never kiss.

The Ironic Happy-Ending Films

Several other of Buñuel's films appear to have happy endings, but they generally arrive at their forced resolutions ironically, unexpectedly, and unbelievably. You can almost see Buñuel winking at viewers as "*Fin*" appears on the screen. The conclusion of *Susana* is a perfect example. It's the story of Susana (Rosita Quintana), a beautiful young woman who escapes from prison and arrives at a placid hacienda in the middle of a rainstorm and in a matter of days proceeds to disrupt the entire household. Using her sexual allure, she gets Don Guadalupe, the *hacendado* (Fernando Soler), his son, and the foreman all to fall in love with her and

FIGS. 7.62–7.69. A two-shot scene in *Viridiana*. Again using moving camera, Buñuel covers the entire scene (1 minute and 59 seconds) in two long takes of 42 and 77 seconds, respectively. In the scene, Viridiana (Sylvia Pinal) tells the Mother Superior that she is not returning to the convent. Through his blocking of the actors and camera movement, Buñuel manages to obtain the shot variety one would typically get from analytical montage.

The first long take (the first four figures) begins with an initial two-shot; then the Mother Superior crosses in front of Viridiana to the other side of the room, moving into a solo MCU. The camera then travels over to Viridiana for her head-and-shoulder MCU as she announces that she's leaving the convent.

The second long take begins with the nun's MCU reaction. After she crosses back to the other side of the room, Buñuel creates an interesting two-shot with Viridiana facing the camera in the foreground. This is followed by the reverse shot, looking over the nun's shoulder. The scene ends in a MS as the Mother Superior bids Viridiana farewell and leaves.

FIGS. 7.70–7.72. The improbable ending of *Susana*. A new dawn, a happily reunited family, and the end of the film.

compete with one another for her affections. In the process Susana turns Doña Carmen, Don Guadalupe's mild-mannered wife, into a whip-wielding harpy. Just when Susana has driven the household to the brink of destruction, the police conveniently show up, arrest Susana, and return her to prison. In the film's final scene a new dawn has broken, and the family, including the expelled foreman, who has been reinstated, is reconstituted and have

all forgiven each other. With the events of the recent past conveniently forgotten, they smile and gather at the window to greet the sunrise, no doubt wondering what sort of collective spell they were under. The foreman shuts the window and—for those viewers who can believe it—the film ends "happily" (figs. 7.70–7.72).

Other examples of Buñuel's parodies of Hollywood's and the MMC's happy endings include *Ensayo de un crimen*, the story of Archibaldo (Ernesto Alonso) who wants nothing more than to murder women, only to have his grisly desire thwarted again and again. In the final sequence, he throws the music box whose tune compels him to kill into a lake, and instantly becomes "normal." In the film's final shot, Archibaldo is completely cured, walking down a park lane accompanied by one of the women he had targeted as one of his victims. Another ironic happy ending occurs in *El rio y la muerte*, about a generations-long blood feud between two families that ends abruptly when the young heirs of the gory tradition make peace and decide to cease their bloody rivalry. (When quizzed about this unlikely upbeat resolution, given the film's depiction of ruthless *macho* vengeance, Buñuel agreed that it was forced and unbelievable. "It would have been better," he commented, "to have shot everyone dead and then, instead of putting 'The End,' to put 'To Be Continued,' or 'More Deaths Next Week.'")[55] To this list could be added *Una mujer sin amor*, whose ending has a hurt and jealous son suddenly forgiving his mother for having an affair and a child out of wedlock. And a case could be made for the inclusion of *La hija del engaño*, in which a man, Don Quintín, reconciles with his long-lost daughter in the film's final 120

The Classical Mexican Cinema

seconds. This occurs despite the fact that Don Quintín—not knowing she is his daughter—nearly shoots her husband to death in the previous scene.

The Buñuelian Happy-Ending Films

For Buñuel, self-deception is the fundamental problem and his idea of a happy ending is characters disabusing themselves of their illusions. Over and over again, the climaxes of his films come at the moment when protagonists see things as they truly are, rather than how they think they are or would like them to be. As Buñuel said, his characters grapple with the difference "between an idea of the world and what the world really is." Speaking of this overarching theme in his films, and in *Viridiana* in particular, Buñuel went on to elaborate, likening this repeated narrative to a classic of Spanish literature:

> In fact, almost all my characters suffer from a disillusionment and later change, for better or worse. When all is said and done, this is the theme of *Don Quixote*. In a certain sense, Viridiana is a Quixote in skirts. Don Quixote defends the prisoners who are being taken to the galleys and they attack him. Viridiana protects the beggars and they also attack her. Viridiana returns to reality, accepts the world as it is. A crazy dream and finally the return to reason. Don Quixote also returns to reality and accepts being only Alonso Quijano.[56]

Nazarín also follows this narrative pattern, and focusing on its climax will illuminate how Buñuel develops his disillusionment theme. Set at the turn of the century, during the Porfiriato, it tells the story of Nazarín (Francisco Rabal), a priest whose devotion

to the teachings of Christ is so absolute he would rather live among the people than in a parish house. He subsists by accepting alms, and does so cheerfully, seeing no indignity in it. "Alms do not degrade the person who receives them, nor harm his dignity," he tells a well-to-do visitor who is curious about his lifestyle.

Time and time again, however, people disappoint him and take advantage of him, and his efforts to perform acts of goodness either founder or backfire. He helps a prostitute in trouble, and she burns down the tenement where he lives. In a plague-ridden village, he begs a dying woman to commit to Christ; instead she calls out for her lover. In order to eat, he volunteers for manual labor in exchange for a meal, but the other workers object, fearing that Nazarín's willingness to work for food will jeopardize them. But despite repeatedly failing to accomplish the good he intends, he remains resolute and unswerving about his faith, his beliefs, and his principles.

Until, that is, he is unjustly arrested, and a group of thuggish prisoners beat him. "For the first time in my life," he says, "it's difficult for me to forgive." He does forgive them, because it is his duty as a Christian, "but I also despise you," he tells them, nearly breaking into tears, "and I feel guilty that I cannot separate scorn from forgiveness." To make matters worse, the next day a representative of the bishop scolds him for his rebellious nature, telling him that his actions are not befitting of a priest and are offensive to the church.

The film's climax, coming just three minutes later, is one of Buñuel's most subtle endings, and his most delicate presentation of his disillusionment theme. Nazarín is led on

FIGS. 7.73–7.75. After declining the fruit vendor's charity a second time, Nazarín (Francisco Rabal) stops, accepts the offered pineapple, and is visibly shaken as he walks on.

foot by a guard along a lonely country road. They pass a fruit vendor, and the guard stops to enjoy some of her apples. Out of charity, she offers Nazarín a pineapple, but he refuses it and walks away. He stops and turns back to her, and she offers the pineapple a second time. He refuses it again, but then thinks

better of it and accepts it, thanking her. In the film's last shot, he walks off clutching the pineapple, seemingly breaking into tears.

In the course of his rejection, hesitation, and final acceptance, a small crack has appeared in Nazarín's ironclad belief system. The man who earlier had happily, almost proudly, proclaimed his willingness to accept alms, momentarily rejected a charitable offering (figs. 7.73–7.75). For Buñuel, the film is about doubt as the seed of possible transformation. "I think doubt is an extraordinary thing," he said. "It makes you grow." Doubt prompts the examination of one's principles, and for Buñuel, that is transformation enough:

> Nazarín is so pure, so holy. . . . He has such strong convictions, and in the end, he has a moment of doubt. . . . One moment of doubt is enough for me. It's like someone falling asleep in bed . . . with a cigarette. It might go out or it might burn the house down. Doubt is like that cigarette. It might be nothing, or it could destroy everything. That's all I wanted to express. Plus, I really like that guy.[57]

More instances of the Buñuelian disillusionment happy ending are Miller in *La Joven*, who adjusts his racism just enough to help an innocent black man escape. To this list we can add the wealthy family in *El gran calavera* who learn a prosaic moral—money doesn't buy happiness. And by the end of *Subida al cielo*, Oliverio, the young newlywed, discovers that the flirtatious woman he was attracted to has seduced and abandoned him, and he returns home with a fresh appreciation for his new bride. And, for viewers who accept the endings in *Una mujer sin amor*, *La*

The Classical Mexican Cinema

hija del engaño, *El rio y la muerte*, and *Ensayo de un crimen* as happy, it must be remembered that they all involve protagonist transformations that free them of their illusions, as does *Robinson Crusoe*.

The Tragedies: Life without Agency

It should come as no surprise that the man who once said that "society goes from bad to worse" and "I no longer believe in social progress"[58] was a tragic filmmaker. Like de Fuentes's Revolution Trilogy and Figueroa-Fernández's *María Candelaria*, *Río Escondido*, and *Salón México*, many of Buñuel's films were tales of doomed characters. Structurally, one of his tragedies, *El bruto*, follows the classic tragic structure, but, as we will see, most of the others are bleaker, more extreme variations of that, akin to American films noir but even darker still.

Graphically, the dramatic structure of Buñuel's *El bruto* is similar to those of de Fuentes's Revolution Trilogy, with its fateful climax occurring fairly early, at the end of act 1 (fig. 7.76). It tells the story of a simple-minded man, Pedro (Pedro Armendáriz), the enforcer for a tenement owner, whose job is intimidating residents into vacating the property. But he goes too far, and the first man he harasses dies. From that turning point on, his situation continually worsens, very much like a character in a Hollywood film noir. And, like an American film noir, this Mexican variant tells the story of a confused but basically good man who makes a series of bad choices that ultimately lead to his death. Buñuel's other tragedies are even grimmer.

In *Los olvidados*, Buñuel used the three-act structure rather than the tragic one, and undermined Hollywood's and the MMC's favorite

dramatic form in the process. To better appreciate the nature of Buñuel's subversion of the happy-ending structure in *Los olvidados* and how he did it, let me take a moment to discuss how Hollywood's three-act structure operates. I introduced its basic shape in the discussion of de Fuentes's narrative structure in chapter 5, so let's begin there (fig. 7.77).

One way to think about the three-act structure is to see it as a modification of the tragic structure that I introduced in chapter 5, with two major differences. First, in the Hollywood-MMC three-act model, the climax shifts from somewhere around the middle of the narrative to almost the end. Second, there is a crucial difference in the protagonist. Whereas the classic tragedy is the story of a good person who does a bad thing and suffers the consequences, Hollywood's three-act story is generally the narrative of a good person who does the right thing and is rewarded for it. As we saw in chapter 5, the startling revision that de Fuentes introduced in *¡Vámonos con Pancho Villa!* was in creating a tragedy of good men who were punished for making a *good* decision. In *Los olvidados*, Buñuel's revision of the Hollywood-MMC happy-ending three-act structure is just as disturbing.

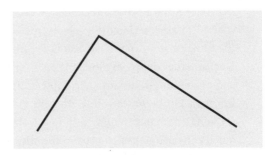

FIG. 7.76. The tragic structure of *El bruto*. The protagonist commits murder in the film's first third, at the end of act 1, and the rest of the film is the tragic falling action that culminates in his death.

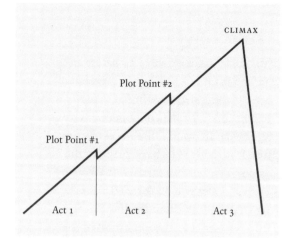

CLIMAX

Plot Point #2

Plot Point #1

Act 1   Act 2   Act 3

FIG. 7.77. Hollywood's three-act structure, adopted by the Mainstream Mexican Cinema. The graph represents the protagonist's progress on his or her quest toward a goal. Along the way, tension increases, difficulties mount, and stakes escalate. The climax, the protagonist's Big Decision, occurs just before the end (ideally, in the last five minutes or so) and is the plot's turning point, where the protagonist achieves his or her goal. The plot points are mini-climaxes, crucial protagonist decision points that end acts 1 and 2. These decisions bring the protagonist closer to achieving the goal, but also increase risk and tension. In the three-act model, the brief falling action charts the release of tension that results from the defeat of the antagonist or elimination of the problem, and the return to the status quo ante.

The three-act structure graph represents the protagonist's progress toward achieving a goal, and also the film's causal structure. The narrative is divided into three acts, marking the beginning (introduction), middle (complication), and ending (resolution) of the film. Once again, the climax is the Big Decision that the protagonist makes near the end of the film in order to accomplish his or her goal. The downward line after the climax is the hasty dénouement or falling action, the quick conclusion resulting from the climactic decision that secured the goal for the protagonist and releases tension. With four and

a half minutes to go in *Star Wars IV*, Luke Skywalker trusts the Force, turns off the computer of his X-wing Fighter, and, flying it manually, blows up the Death Star. There is a celebration, Princess Leia awards the victors medals, and the film ends.

One more important element worth noting is the plot point, a mini-climax that concludes each of the first two acts and the biggest decision made by the protagonist up to that point. Each of these mini-climaxes brings the protagonist closer to success, but simultaneously escalates the stakes, propelling the action forward by raising a question (what will be the effect[s] of this cause?) that is answered in the next act.

For most of its eighty-minute running time, *Los olvidados* hews to the three-act structure. The protagonist is Pedro, a poor kid struggling to survive in a Mexico City slum. His antagonist is Jaibo, an older troublemaker who has just escaped from jail and spoils every good deed Pedro attempts. As we will see, Buñuel's larger point is that the actual antagonist is the grinding poverty that dooms these children and from which there is no escape. Pedro helps Jaibo locate Julián, a boy he thinks betrayed him to the police. But when Jaibo beats him to death, Pedro decides to fly straight and takes a job at a knife shop (plot point #1, at 32:50). After Jaibo visits him there and steals a knife, Pedro is accused of the theft and sent to a reform school. As a kind of a test, he is given 50 pesos to run an errand for the director, but Jaibo shows up, beats Pedro, and steals the money. In retaliation, Pedro publicly denounces Jaibo as Julián's murderer (plot point #2, at 68:47). Their climactic confrontation is the film's climax (at 76:39).

If this were a conventional Hollywood

or Mainstream Mexican film, Pedro would vanquish Jaibo, either by killing him or by beating him and turning him in to the police. This victory would signal the beginning of Pedro's new and better life and provide the requisite happy ending. Instead, Buñuel's film does the unthinkable—at least from the perspective of Hollywood and Mainstream Mexican storytelling. Jaibo kills Pedro, suddenly turning *Los olvidados* into a tragedy. Buñuel violated two cardinal rules of the three-act structure—the protagonist must never die and the ending is always happy. To make matters even worse, the film ends with Pedro's body being thrown on a junk heap.

No wonder the film flopped in its first release. Attendance was so bad that producer Dancigers withdrew the film after only three days. And its problems went far beyond anemic ticket sales. To prepare audiences for the pessimistic vision of urban Mexican life they were about to see, Buñuel added a prologue that attempted to universalize the problem of poverty. Nevertheless, critics and audiences were hostile to what was perceived as the film's negative depiction of Mexico and Mexicans and its unsentimental portrayal of Mexico City's underclass. There were even calls to have Buñuel's Mexican citizenship revoked.[59] In such a climate, the brutality of the ending could not have helped things. Understanding the problem Buñuel's disturbing ending posed, Dancigers attempted to salvage the film by preparing an alternative happy ending. In it, Pedro vanquishes Jaibo (it's unclear whether he kills him or merely knocks him out), retrieves the stolen money from Jaibo's pocket, and, in the film's last shot, returns to the reformatory.[60] (How the alternate ending was made and who shot it is a bit of a mystery. According to Alfonso Mejía, Buñuel shot it, at the urging of Dancigers.)[61]

But Dancigers never had to use this ending. By a stroke of good fortune, *Los olvidados* was invited to the Cannes Film Festival, where Buñuel won the best director award. Having garnered international acclaim, the film opened again in Mexico City, where it played for six weeks and went on to win eleven of that year's eighteen Ariels, including those for best film, director, script, sound, production design, cinematography, and three acting awards (for Cobo, Mejía, and Stella Inda, who played Pedro's mother). *Los olvidados*'s commercial and critical success at home and abroad brought Buñuel back to the forefront of the world's directors. And he did it by demonstrating that twenty years after *Un chien andalou*, he could still shock audiences. In this case, he did it by using the Hollywood-MMC three-act formula, then demolishing it and replacing the happy ending with a tragic one right before viewers' eyes.

All of Buñuel's tragedies are visions of life without agency. In the case of *Él*, his stinging depiction of the insane but logical consequences of *machismo*, he creates a kind of existential horror film in which both the dashing Francisco (Arturo de Córdova) and his new wife, Gloria (Delia Garcés), are helpless. Francisco is a victim of his pathological paranoia, yet he is protected and supported by *machismo*, which, by allowing males to be absolute masters of their household, sanctions his sick behavior. Trapped within *macho* patriarchy, where the male's dominance is absolute, there's nothing a married woman like Gloria can do to protect herself from Francisco. When she reaches out to her mother and a priest, they both side with her husband.

Buñuel's other tragedies are variations on the theme of life without agency. The band of refugees in *La muerte en este jardín* become completely vulnerable once they enter the jungle. Not surprisingly, most of them die, and most die arbitrarily. Buñuel's most devastating depiction of impotence, however, is *El ángel exterminador*, a study in random victimization. Without a single character who can make a decision and impose it upon the world, it is as much an affront to Hollywood's optimistic hero quests as it is a condemnation of the bourgeoisie, the class that thinks it is all-powerful.

The pessimism evident in many of Buñuel's films, and particularly in his tragedies, where it verges on fatalism, is, I would argue, what links his cinema to the classical Mexican films treated in this book. The upper-class party guests in *El ángel exterminador* are trapped in their luxuriant lives just as surely as the poor street kids in *Los olvidados* are ensnarled by poverty. And their plight is consistent with powerless Mexican characters whose doomed struggles are featured in de Fuentes's Revolution Trilogy and in Fernández's tragedies.

Still, despite the bitter endings found in *Los olvidados*, *El bruto*, and *El ángel exterminador*, Buñuel's Mexican films are not entirely hopeless. The potential to transform indicates a hopeful possibility in at least some of Buñuel's films that lifts them a notch or two above nihilism. If, that is, characters can recognize the delusions that form the basis of their lives. That is why the climax of *Nazarín* is so significant in Buñuel's body of work. It catches Nazarín right at the instant when he might be disabused of the folly of his unquestioned and unexamined faith, a condition that more often than not makes things worse, not better. Nazarín might revise his beliefs, and that, as Buñuel said, "is enough for me." Along with similarly cautiously optimistic endings in *La joven*, *El gran calavera*, and *Subida al cielo*, it suggests that for Buñuel there is at least some possibility of things getting better.

Just as Buñuel was lucky to enter the Mexican film industry right before it spiraled into decline, so he was fortunate to find a way out when it began crumbling around him in the late 1950s and early 1960s. His savior was French producer Serge Silberman (1917–2003), who introduced Buñuel to the writer Jean-Claude Carrière (1931–). Together the three collaborated on a series of European-made art house hits with which Buñuel concluded his career: *Le journal d'une femme de chamber*, *Le voie lactée*, *Le charme discret de la bourgeoisie*, *Le fantôme de la liberté*, and *Cet obscure objet de désir* (Buñuel and Carrière also made *Belle de jour* together for producers Raymond and Robert Hakim). Buñuel's last made-in-Mexico production was *Simón del desierto* in 1965, a short (forty-five-minute) farewell to Mexican filmmaking. To borrow the title of Buñuel's memoir, it was the last sigh of the Classical Mexican Cinema, and with that the Golden Age was officially over.

Postscript: Buñuel's Style after Mexico
—

Much of the style Buñuel formulated in his Mexican films persisted into his final European phase. This can be demonstrated by examining his last film, *That Obscure Object of Desire*, where we find Buñuel still employing many of the elements we have discussed.

The Classical Mexican Cinema

SURREALIST SPARKS—A PIG IN A BLANKET

That Obscure Object of Desire is the story of a man, Mathieu (Fernando Rey), bedeviled by his infatuation with an elusive woman, Conchita, who torments him at every turn. The major surrealist touch in the film is that Conchita is played by two actresses, Carole Bouquet and Ángela Molina. But other matter-of-fact surrealist moments are scattered throughout the film. One is a recurring burlap bag gag. We see a man carry one in the street at the end of one scene. Later, at the conclusion of a conversation between Mathieu and Conchita at a park bench, he picks up a burlap bag, slings it over one shoulder, and they walk off together. And in the film's last scene, the material that a seamstress works on is unpacked from a similar burlap bag.

Another example comes in a scene in Sevilla, when two women approach Mathieu and his valet on the street. They seek alms, presumably for the baby one of them carries. When they show it to Mathieu, we see that it is a pig wrapped in swaddling clothes. Mathieu reacts as if it were a beautiful child, gives them some money, then walks off with his valet (fig. 7.78).

THE FIGURE IN THE WINDOW

Continually frustrated in consummating his relationship with Conchita, Mathieu is repeatedly driven to desperation. As he pursues the free-spirited, mercurial, and independent woman he's smitten with, Mathieu becomes a manic figure in the window (figs. 7.79–7.81).

FIG. 7.78. A surrealist spark in *That Obscure Object of Desire*: a pig in a blanket.

FIGS. 7.79–7.81. The figure in the window in *That Obscure Object of Desire*.

THE MISE-EN-SCÈNE PROSCENIUM, THE IMPROBABLE VANTAGE POINT, AND THE UNHEARD CONVERSATION

Several of the elements of Buñuel's poetics are combined in the final enigmatic scene of his final film. After Mathieu reconciles with Conchita (yet again), they walk the streets of Paris, enter an arcade, and pause at a shop window. In this mise-en-scène proscenium they watch a seamstress repair a torn piece of bloody cloth. The subsequent reverse shot harkens back to Buñuel's improbable vantage point shots, and in it Mathieu says something to Conchita we are not privy to (figs. 7.82 and 7.83).

TOP | FIG. 7.82. The mise-en-scène proscenium in *That Obscure Object of Desire*.

BOTTOM | FIG. 7.83. The improbable vantage point and the unheard conversation in *That Obscure Object of Desire*. The reverse shot is reminiscent of the pederast scene in *Los olvidados*. Buñuel frames Conchita (Carole Bouquet) and Mathieu from inside a shop window, creating a mise-en-scène proscenium, and Mathieu tells her something we can't hear.

THE LONG TAKE

To the end, Buñuel continued to rely on long takes. An excellent example occurs at the beginning of a pivotal scene in *That Obscure Object of Desire*, where Conchita taunts and humiliates Mathieu, telling him she loathes him and culminating in her making love to a boyfriend right in front of him. The long take that begins the scene runs eighty-six seconds and begins with him appearing at the gate of her house. Locked out, he watches from a wrought iron gate as Conchita greets him and then delivers a hateful monologue about how much she detests him (figs. 7.84–7.91).

NARRATIVE STRUCTURE

If there was ever a film about a protagonist without agency, *That Obscure Object of Desire* is it. Like the trapped characters in *El ángel exterminador*, Mathieu is powerless throughout the film, and never able to come to a decisive dramatic—or sexual—climax. Nor does it ever occur to him to examine whether his chauvinistic, *macho* treatment of Conchita might be adjusted to improve their relationship. (At one point, he offers to purchase Conchita from her mother, giving her money in exchange for allowing her daughter to live with him. The mother agrees, but Conchita refuses.) His desire is thwarted time and again, and the film ends with another instance of it. After they pause at the display window and Mathieu speaks to her, Conchita walks away. He follows after her and tries to take her arm, but she pushes him away—they are having yet another disagreement. In the last shot of the film, there is a sudden explosion, presumably one more terrorist attack of

The Classical Mexican Cinema

FIGS. 7.84–7.91. The long take in *That Obscure Object of Desire*. As he did in his Mexican films, Buñuel provides multiple perspectives via a long take and a moving camera. He begins this crucial scene, where Conchita (this time played by Ángela Molina) tells Mathieu how much she despises him, with an eighty-six-second take. It starts with a MS of Mathieu arriving at the gate. The camera pans and tracks back across the patio to a LS of Conchita. Panning and tracking again, the camera follows her as she crosses to the gate, where he kisses her hand. She refuses to unlock the gate and retreats back into the patio in a panning-and-tracking shot, and the perspective changes from a MS to her performing a taunting dance in LS. The camera moves to a CU as she continues to spew her rancor, and then pans and tracks with Conchita as she crosses back to the gate in a MS, arriving in a two-shot with Mathieu, where the take ends.

the kind that have occurred throughout the film. It ends without revealing whether they were wounded, killed, or escaped harm, and Buñuel concludes his filmmaking career with terrorism, the supreme example of lost agency in the modern era.

The Classical Mexican Cinema as Moral Imperative
—

Though Fernando de Fuentes, Emilio Fernández, and Luis Buñuel each developed his own individualistic style, their ideological positions were similar. Their CMC films all criticized the status quo and exposed a corrupt system; all defended the marginalized and refused to look away from social, cultural, and political problems. Essentially, their CMC films—all CMC films—were moral arguments. De Fuentes's trilogy said that once a revolution compromises its ideals, it has failed. The Fernández unit's creation of a unique Mexican cinematic style said that honest artistic expression is better for the national soul than the lazy imitation of foreign models. Buñuel's *Él* said that a marriage based on *machismo* was a relationship founded on insanity. And the tragic story of Pedro, whose dead body ends up on a junk heap at the end of *Los olvidados*, was a bitter reminder that a nation is judged by how it treats it most vulnerable citizens. This same combination of distinctive style and ethical criticism is characteristic of the three films I'll examine in the next chapter.

CHAPTER 8

Three Classical Mexican Cinema Genre Films

—

HREE MORE CMC films remain to be analyzed. Each one has its own original style and each was made by a director whose work I haven't discussed yet. Each one represents an important Mexican genre, and each revised and expanded the standard generic template in innovative ways.

The first, *Dos monjes* (*Two Monks*, 1934), directed by Juan Bustillo Oro, is an audacious piece of early sound filmmaking and one of the formative films of Mexico's horror genre. It contains the most stylized use of German expressionism in Mexican cinema, and was groundbreaking for its innovative narration. The experimentation exhibited in the second film, *La mancha de sangre* (*The Blood Stain*, 1937), derived from the Mexican avant-garde. It was a collaborative effort of the artist, theorist, and art educator Adolfo Best Maugard, the film's director, and the modernist photographer Agustín Jiménez, who was the codirector of photography (and who also shot *Dos monjes*). And despite *La mancha de sangre*'s experimental pedigree, it is best understood, I think, as a prototypical neorealist *cabaretera* film. The third, Julio Bracho's *Distinto amanecer* (*A New Dawn*, 1943), is a genre hybrid, a romantic melodrama–political thriller–*cabaretera*–film noir that captured the same sort of soul-searching found in de Fuentes's Revolution Trilogy and the Fernández unit's *Río Escondido* and *Salón México*.

Visually, it's one of the darkest of all Mexican Golden Age films, and was shot by Gabriel Figueroa, who together with Bracho produced a startlingly frank and eloquent exploration of life in postrevolutionary Mexico.

Juan Bustillo Oro's *Dos monjes*: Fated to Live with a Tragic Past
—

By the time Juan Bustillo Oro (1904–1989) directed his first sound film, *Dos monjes*, in 1934, he had already gained considerable experience as a writer and director of stage and screen. Though he studied law, film was his true passion, and during the 1920s when Mexico City's movie screens were "bursting with riches," he "got drunk on great cinema."[1] As a young movie fan, he became familiar with a wide range of European and American stars and directors, and was heavily influenced by German films, which he regarded as a counterweight to the "*cine yanqui*" that dominated movie theaters at the time.[2]

Young Bustillo Oro divided his time between filmmaking and theater, directing his first film, *Yo soy tu padre* (*I'm Your Father*, 1927) when he was only twenty-three, and founding the Now Theater (El Teatro de Ahora), an experimental theater troupe, with Mauricio Magdaleno in 1932. Busy writing and directing plays for the group, he and Magdaleno still found time to collaborate on the screenplay for *El compadre Mendoza* with Fernando de Fuentes. For a time Bustillo Oro thought he would direct *El compadre Mendoza*, but was ultimately convinced by de Fuentes, Mexico's most esteemed filmmaker at the time, to codirect the film with him. Accordingly, he helped with the selection of locations, sets, and actors (one, Antonio R. Frausto, who was cast in the pivotal role of

General Nieto, he knew from the Now Theater). But when he failed to receive a copy of the shooting script and noticed that de Fuentes's decisions were the ones the producer and crew were responding to, he realized that his codirecting title was mostly honorary.[3]

He nevertheless remained on good terms with de Fuentes, coscripting another of his films, the horror-thriller *El fantasma del convento* (*The Monastery Ghost*, 1934). Afterward, two producers asked him to adapt and direct a story written by a friend of theirs. The novice cinematographer attached to the project, the renowned still photographer Agustín Jiménez (1901–1974), had recommended Bustillo Oro to them. The existing treatment needed to be adapted into final script form, but otherwise the film was ready to be shot—the money was secured, the film crew hired, and the actors cast. Bustillo Oro jumped at the chance, but was deflated upon reading the story outline—which, by his account, was a sketchy eternal triangle plot with undeveloped characters and poorly constructed scenes.[4]

In developing it, however, Bustillo Oro had an inspiration. Given that it was the tale of two friends in love with the same woman, he would tell the story of their romance with her twice—from each man's perspective. And since one of them was sickly and at times delirious, he had a good reason to shoot the film in the moody expressionist style he admired.[5] The film he made was an unusual combination of striking visual stylistics and unconventional narrative structure. While Jiménez's dark cinematography and the stylized sets designed by Carlos Toussaint were indebted to German expressionism, its ingenious, sui generis plotting was a very early example of what I have called the "repeated event plot," a narrative told from multiple perspectives.[6] *Dos monjes* was at once a throw-back to *The Cabinet of Dr. Caligari* (1919) and a precursor of Akira Kurosawa's multiple-point-of-view mystery, *Rashomon* (1950). Set in a nineteenth-century monastery, Bustillo Oro's script is a mystery, following the prior as he investigates the case of a monk, Javier (Carlos Villatoro), who attacked a new member of the order, Juan (Víctor Urruchúa). He interviews them individually, first Javier, then Juan, and as each one relates his side of the story, events are depicted in a flashback from their respective points of view.

JAVIER'S NARRATIVE: MY BEST FRIEND BETRAYED ME

Both Javier and Juan were in love with Ana (Magda Haller). In Javier's version, he and his mother take her in when her malicious father banishes her and throws her out into the streets. Soon he and Ana fall in love and are engaged to be married when his best friend, Juan, returns from a long trip and tries to steal Ana away from him. Making matters worse for Javier is his poor health, which has sapped his strength and makes him wonder if he'll live to see his wedding day. But his doctor reassures him that it's only a passing fever brought on by fatigue. Not only will Javier live to marry Ana, but he'll enjoy many more years of good health. One evening, however, he finds Juan trying to force himself on Ana and attacks him. Drawing a pistol to defend himself, Juan shoots at Javier, but Ana steps between them and is killed instantly. Juan flees, and Javier pursues him unsuccessfully. Exhausted and brokenhearted, Javier joins the order and lives the life of a monk until Juan's unexpected appearance.

JUAN'S NARRATIVE: ANA AND I WERE IN LOVE BEFORE SHE MET JAVIER

"Everything Javier has said in his account is true," Juan tells the prior during his interview. "But," he continues,

> Brother Javier's truth is only a partial one—the truth seen solely through his eyes. Juan the sinner also has his truth, the one he lived. And if it doesn't justify his actions, it does at least explain what was for Javier something repugnant. . . . Javier never knew the drama that existed between his friend, Juan, and Ana.

As Juan relates his story, scenes are repeated from his perspective and events first seen in Javier's account take on a different meaning. According to Juan, he and Ana were in love before Javier met her, and when he left on his trip she promised to wait for him. Upon his return, he is surprised and confused to find them engaged, but keeps silent until he can speak with Ana alone. When he does, she reaffirms her love for him, explaining that she refrained from telling Javier about their relationship due to his frail health.

The garden scene, where an increasingly ill Javier wonders aloud if he'll live to see his wedding day, is a good example of the two suitors' contrasting tales (figs. 8.1–8.6).

Juan's story also introduces events unknown to Javier, such as Ana's declaring her love for him. Another is a meeting the doctor has with Juan and Ana. Just after the physician has made his optimistic diagnosis of Javier's illness, he takes Ana and Juan aside and tells them Javier's sickness is fatal and untreatable. He implores them to make his last days—or, at the most, months—pleasant

Opposing Narratives in *Dos monjes*: Javier's Illness

JAVIER'S VERSION

JAVIER'S VERSION

JUAN'S VERSION

FIG. 8.1. In failing health, Javier sits in the garden with his fiancée, Ana, and best friend, Juan. He wonders if he'll live to see his wedding day.

FIG. 8.4. The same scene from Juan's perspective. Note that in their respective versions, the narrator is dressed in white and his friend in black.

FIG. 8.2. Javier and Ana hug as he says, "Just one spring of your love, then death can come for me whenever it wants."

FIG. 8.5. Juan's version shows Ana's reaction to Javier's words, extending her hand in a silent "What can I/we do?" gesture directed at Juan.

FIG. 8.3. Ana reassures Javier. "Don't be silly," she tells him. "In my love you have an eternal spring."

FIG. 8.6. Ana says the same words, but she shakes her head to Juan as she says them, signaling that she doesn't mean it, and loves him, not Javier.

and worry free, cautioning them not to upset him in any way. Trapped into prolonging the fiction that Ana loves Javier, they have no choice but to bide their time and await the inevitable.

It never comes. Javier miraculously recovers, and they agree to do the honorable thing—Juan will leave, Ana will marry Javier, and they'll never see each other again. During their farewell—another scene Javier was unaware of—Juan attempts to kiss her one last time. Ana resists, fearing that if she kisses him she'll never be able to let him go. Javier enters in the midst of their awkward tussle, and Bustillo Oro presents a second account of Ana's death (figs. 8.7–8.18).

EXPRESSIONISM AND CULPABILITY

Juan's story presents a different version of events, but doesn't clarify things much. It does offer an alternative legal interpretation—Javier's description portrayed the killing as manslaughter (Juan fires the gun in anger after Javier strikes him), whereas Juan's frames the shooting as self-defense (Juan defends himself from his crazed friend). Ana's accidental death, however, remains unnecessary and tragic in both versions, and it's the characterization of the events leading to the shooting that is the crucial difference between accounts. In Javier's tale, Ana's death was the result of his best friend's betrayal.

Dos monjes: Ana's Accidental Shooting

JAVIER'S VERSION   JUAN'S VERSION

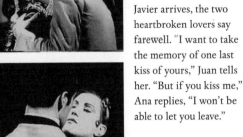

FIGS. 8.7 AND 8.8. Before Javier arrives, the two heartbroken lovers say farewell. "I want to take the memory of one last kiss of yours," Juan tells her. "But if you kiss me," Ana replies, "I won't be able to let you leave."

FIG. 8.11. A medium long shot suggests Javier's perspective when he enters.

FIGS. 8.9 AND 8.10. Javier finds Juan trying to force himself on Ana but doesn't hear what they're saying.

FIG. 8.12. Javier strikes Juan with a cane, and Juan backs away.

FIGS. 8.13 AND 8.14. Javier confronts Juan, and at first it's a standoff. Javier threatens Juan with a cane, and Juan draws a pistol to defend himself.

Dos monjes: Ana's Accidental Shooting.

JAVIER'S VERSION

JUAN'S VERSION

FIGS. 8.15 AND 8.16.
Slowly and deliberately, Juan draws a gun and the camera tilts down to the pistol in his hand as he fires it. There is no reverse shot of Javier in this version, but he is heard to cry out, "I dare you, you scoundrel." After the MCU of Juan's gun firing, the next shot is of Ana stepping in front of Javier and being hit by the bullet.

FIGS. 8.17 AND 8.18. Javier steps forward to attack Juan but there is no reverse shot of Juan firing. There is the sound of the gunshot when Juan fires in self-defense. Tragically, Ana steps in front of Javier just at that moment and is hit.

From Juan's perspective, Ana's death was the sad, ironic, and unintended consequence of their trying to do the right thing.

Nevertheless, Juan's report shifts the culpability toward Javier, for aggressively attacking him without first seeking an explanation. This shading of evidence against Javier along with the questioning of his mental stability is reinforced through the film's expressionistic low-key lighting and distorted set design. Because the film's darkness and skewed sets predominate in Javier's narrative—and all but disappear in Juan's story—it seems that Bustillo Oro was imitating the pictorial logic of *The Cabinet of Dr. Caligari*, whose warped sets depicted the perspective of the madman narrating the film (figs. 8.19–8.22).

But *Dos monjes* is very different from *The Cabinet of Dr. Caligari*. Strip away its expressionistic production design and *The Cabinet of Dr. Caligari* is a murder mystery, predicated on identifying a serial killer, which it does in its famed final scene, which reveals the narrator to be a patient in an insane asylum. *Dos monjes*, on the other hand, is an existential mystery. It's not about *who* killed Ana—we know that, at least who fired the gun. It's about *what* killed Ana, and that question is never answered. *Dos monjes* describes a seemingly unavoidable tragedy that should have been avoided—but wasn't. It focuses on survivors living with guilt and remorse who question their fate. In these ways it's similar to de Fuentes's Revolution Trilogy. *Dos monjes* is a brooding meditation on why things happened the way they did and an inconclusive inquiry into whether they could have happened some other way.

Dos monjes: Expressionist Style in Javier's Narrative

FIG. 8.19. From his studio window, Javier spies Ana, who lives across the street, r the first time. His looking rough the obliquely angled indow slats hints at his un-balanced view of the world.

FIG. 8.20. A canted camera angle in the scene where Juan (*right*) returns after a long trip.

FIG. 8.21. In Javier's nightmare, he and Ana are engulfed in blackness.

FIG. 8.22. Javier's nightmare ends with an eerie premonition. A threat emerges out of the darkness—Juan, his best friend.

La mancha de sangre: The Dawn of Mexican Neorealism

—

Since its completion, *La mancha de sangre* has been a sui generis curiosity for historians and critics, a distinctive and confounding film that was many things at once: the only feature-length film made by a well-known artist and educator; a film banned for its nudity and frank, unsentimental depiction of prostitution; a lost film that was miraculously discovered and restored a half-century after it was made; and an inelegant mish-mash of German street film, experimental avant-garde, and the *cabaretera* genre. It is all those things—and more. The best way to approach and appreciate this film is to place it within its cultural and artistic context. It's well worth doing because properly understood, *La*

mancha de sangre reveals a lot about the cre-ative atmosphere in Mexico's artistic circles in the 1930s, and artists' links to the emerg-ing film culture. Furthermore, knowing the backgrounds of its principal filmmakers gives it a measure of coherence that it otherwise lacks and clarifies its makers' intentions and their goals for the film. It also explains why they took the artistic risks they did, despite being fully aware that their finished movie would likely encounter censorship problems.

Which it did. Because of a notorious nude scene and its unglamorous depiction of Mexico City's nightlife, complete with gangsters, pimps, and prostitutes, it caused a scandal when it was completed in 1937 and never found a distributor. In 1942, however, one enterprising exhibitor, Felipe Mier, relaunched it with a promotional campaign that was, on the whole, honest and perceptive. Though he recognized *La mancha de sangre*'s shortcomings (it was not a "great production, nor were all of its elements perfect"), he praised the director's "artistic sensibility" and the film's truthful depiction of one aspect of Mexican life, presented without the usual postcard prettification or folkloric pretense.[7] The film played for four weeks during the summer of 1943, but was ultimately banned. After that it disappeared for fifty years. A partial copy was found in Germany and restored by UNAM's Filmoteca in 1994 to its current, somewhat incomplete state—the sound for one sequence is gone (the dialogue is now shown in subtitles) and the picture for the last six minutes is missing, though the sound is intact.[8]

ADOLFO BEST MAUGARD: CHAMPION OF THE NATIONAL AESTHETIC

The creative force behind *La mancha de sangre* was artist and educator Adolfo Best Maugard (1891–1964), a fascinating figure on the Mexican cultural scene in the 1920s and 1930s. A formative early experience was his serving, in 1911, as an assistant to anthropologist Franz Boas, who had been invited to do research in Mexico by the National University. Assisting Boas in cataloguing the collection of the International School of American Anthropology and Ethnography, Best Maugard made detailed drawings of more than two thousand pre-Hispanic ceramic artworks.

Following that, the Ministry of Public Instruction and Fine Arts commissioned him to travel to Europe and make facsimile reproductions of Mexican archeological collections housed there. Upon his return to Mexico in 1915, Best Maugard joined a group of artists,

writers, and musicians "who were concerned with the creation of a new national art on the basis of popular or folkloric culture."[9] He put these ideas into practice when he taught in public schools in 1917–1918, and soon after became part of a group headed by José Vasconcelos, Mexico's secretary of education. He was one of the artists who accompanied Vasconcelos on what became a noteworthy trip to Tehuantepec, Oaxaca, in 1921, a journey "often associated by scholars with the official 'rediscovery' of Mexico's regional cultural heritage."[10] Subsequently, Vasconcelos appointed him the director of the Drawing and Handicraft Department, the art education division at the Secretariat of Public Education, a post Best Maugard held from 1921 to 1924.[11]

And it was in this capacity that he developed his method for teaching drawing. The Best system, as it was called, was based on using seven graphic design elements (the spiral, the circle, the half-circle, the S shape, the wavy line, the zigzag line, and the straight line). These seven motifs formed the basis of *la fórmula mexicana*, and by combining them, Best Maugard asserted, it was possible to produce art that would embody the essence of the Mexican national character.[12] It wasn't so much that other national traditions were forbidden, it was more the idea that Best Maugard's method gave students "the secret of their own tradition within which they could express themselves without having to look to the conventions of other countries in order to create."[13] Incorporated into the public school curriculum of Mexico City and surrounding areas from 1921 to 1924, the Best system was taught by a cadre of about 150 to 200 art instructors to approximately forty thousand students per year during that period. Some of the drawings produced by students were exhibited at home and abroad, where, according to art historian Karen Cordero Reiman, they were presented "as an example of the revolutionary nationalist art education system of Mexico."[14] As part of this pedagogical program, in 1923 the ministry of education published a drawing textbook written by Best Maugard, *Manuales y tratados—Método de dibujo: Tradición, resurgimiento, y evolución del arte mexicano* (*Manuals and Treatises—The Method of Drawing: Tradition, Resurgence, and Evolution of Mexican Art*).[15]

What Best Maugard had done was to merge the expertise he had gained cataloging ancient Mexican decorative art for Boas with his own artistic process, devising a straightforward technique for learning to draw. Moreover, Best Maugard's introductory essay presented a brief for the nationalistic art movement, arguing that the appreciation of Mexico's popular indigenous art was the first step in expressing *mexicanidad*.[16] "Popular art," he wrote, "is above all a synthetic expression of the soul of a nation, of its tastes, of its ideals, of its imagination, of its concept of life." He continued:

If any nation abruptly takes from another or others the elements necessary for expressing what it feels, what it thinks is beautiful . . . it will never be able to express itself, it will not be able to obtain the harmonious and genuine expression of its national spirit.

The only art that should interest a nation is its own because . . . it is the vibrant and characteristic representation of its race, the faithful translation of the things that the nation sees and feels; because of that, so that our art may have . . . a reason for being, it should be the continuation of our own nation's art, of popular art, which should be adopted as the foundation for future development.[17]

The anthropological urge to simplify an experience down to its essential elements and to seek out fundamental but often overlooked components that expressed what was authentically *mexicano* are two of the qualities that, in an unexpected way, would appear again in Best Maugard's only feature-length film, *La mancha de sangre*.

FROM ART TO AUTEUR

Best Maugard had long been interested in cinema. He is said to have encouraged Dolores del Río to try her luck in Hollywood, and made friends with documentary filmmaker Robert Flaherty when he visited Mexico in 1928.[18] It was Flaherty who recommended Best Maugard to Sergei Eisenstein when the Soviet filmmaker first arrived in Mexico with the idea of making a film there. He and Eisenstein became friends, and during the filming of *¡Que viva México!* Best Maugard played two seemingly conflicting roles—government censor and assistant filmmaker. The Mexican government appointed him consultant and censor on Eisenstein's film. As consultant, his job was to introduce the Russian director to the nation's culture and traditions. His mission as censor was to ensure that Mexico was depicted positively (a sensitive issue, given the stereotypical way the nation and Mexicans were often represented in many Hollywood films). At the same time, Best Maugard may have had a hand in the scripting and shooting of parts of *¡Que viva México!*—a claim he made in a letter to the editor of *Close Up* in 1933: "Eisenstein invited me to collaborate with him upon the preliminary outline of the scenario, the choice of locations and the arrangement of details. From that time our work together went as far as to my personal assistance in the shooting of the picture. I accepted this task seeing the great importance of such a work of art, and because of Eisenstein's involvement."[19] It is difficult to know for certain how involved he actually was in the making of Eisenstein's film, but based on his written reports back to the Department of Fine Arts, we do know that Best Maugard was on the set for at least one hundred days and that he documented the making of the film with still photographs and several rolls of 16mm film (shot with a movie camera provided by the government's Department of Fine Arts).[20]

After that, Best Maugard threw himself into his own filmmaking. His first film, *Humanidad* (1934), was a short promoting the work of several public institutions (the school for the blind, a children's home, La Castañeda Mental Institution, a nursing home, and the Public Welfare Vocational School) and was the first film shot by one of Mexico's leading photographers, Agustín Jiménez. Best Maugard directed another short, *Piñatas*, apparently also shot by Jiménez and about which little is known.[21] After that, the two teamed together for a feature, *La mancha de sangre*.

Ross Fisher, a veteran Hollywood cinematographer who had relocated to Mexico and had shot de Fuentes's *El prisionero 13* and *El compadre Mendoza*, was co-cinematographer. However, it is not clear who shot what, or how Fisher and Jiménez shared

responsibilities—if, for example, they worked together throughout the production, or separately, filling in when the other wasn't available. Therefore, it is entirely possible that I am giving Jiménez credit for footage that Fisher photographed. Nevertheless, I credit Jiménez to the extent I do because, as will be seen below, the daring, edgy aesthetic evident in his still photography coincides so well with Best Maugard's treatment of Mexico City nightlife in *La mancha de sangre*.

THE PRODUCTION OF *LA MANCHA DE SANGRE*

Whereas Bustillo Oro seems to have been influenced by German expressionism, Best Maugard and Jiménez appear to have drawn their inspiration from another branch of German silent cinema, *Kammerspielfilm*. These naturalistic "street films" told contemporary stories of poor or working-class characters in an unsparing and unsentimental way, and were exemplified by movies such as those by G. W. Pabst: *The Joyless Street* (1925), *Diary of a Lost Girl* (1929), *Pandora's Box* (1929), and *The Three Penny Opera* (1931).[22] In making *La mancha de sangre* (1937), Best Maugard seems to have tried to inject some of the street films' tough, realistic sensibility into Mexico's *cabaretera* genre. In the process, he created a prototype of what we might call "Mexican neorealism," years before the neorealist aesthetic was first identified in postwar Italy, and whose best-known exemplar would be Buñuel's *Los olvidados* (1950).

Jiménez's stature and his place in Mexico's avant-garde at the time is important to note because the sensibility he exhibited in his modernist photography carried over into *La mancha de sangre*. Experienced as a photojournalist and fine art photographer, by the time he began working on the films of Best Maugard and Bustillo Oro, he was recognized as one of Mexico's best still photographers, having exhibited his work in Mexico City and New York City.[23] Despite his success, his great ambition was to work in film,[24] and he took a significant step in that direction by becoming the set photographer for ¡Que viva México! Shortly thereafter he got his first chance to work as cinematographer on Bustillo Oro's Dos monjes. And although his still photography studio remained open for a time, he had in effect shifted careers and for the next four decades was one of the busiest Mexican cinematographers, photographing some 169 films.[25]

The cinematic style Best Maugard and Jiménez devised for La mancha de sangre was a fortuitous combination of their artistic backgrounds and shared sensibilities. Best Maugard wanted to make a cabaretera film that was far more realistic than Santa (1932) or La mujer del puerto (1934), the genre's two foundational films. True, those films were realistic for their time, and their candid exploration of the treatment of women within Mexican patriarchy was bitingly critical of machismo. But Best Maugard wanted to be more transgressive than that, and he set out to capture an even grittier portrayal of the ficheras' (cabaret B-girls) world. Based on a script he coauthored with Miguel Ruiz, the screenwriter of de Fuentes's El prisionero 13, he decided to cast it using a combination of unknowns and non-actors and shot much of it in an actual cabaret—"La Camelia."[26] In essence, Best Maugard introduced an uncompromising documentary style to the cabaretera genre.

And he could not have chosen a better partner for this project than Jiménez, whose modernist-realist aesthetic was perfectly suited to photographing the tough demimonde of cabarets, prostitutes, their customers and pimps. His photojournalistic background had made him adept at shooting ordinary Mexicans in their natural environment. Furthermore, he had thoroughly immersed himself in Mexico City's vibrant but clandestine nightlife by shooting a graphically realistic photo essay for the first—and only—edition of a periodical he coedited with journalist Gregorio Ortega in 1932. It was called Molino Verde, named after a popular and notorious theater that staged late-night adult variety shows.[27] "Our intention," Ortega wrote in his short introduction, "is to establish in Mexico a new kind of journalism, one which we consider to be more complete, more balanced, and more fair." They were drawn to the show, Ortega said, "because it is the only place in Mexico in which the people appear as they really are." Once the male patrons buy their tickets they become "simple men" who "lose their inhibitions and are disposed to jubilation."[28]

Ortega and Jiménez's tactic—showing things as they are with pictures, not words— was so simple it was radical. Doing anything less would be hypocritical, and bourgeois hypocrisy was the primary target of that era's avant-garde, whether in Paris or Mexico City. Since the bawdy Molino Verde spectacle was a well-known, popular entertainment, frequented by Mexico's elites, artists, and intellectuals, why pretend it didn't exist? Instead of looking the other way, as the conventional media had done, why not document it, sincerely, honestly, and free of censure or moralizing? Thus, after Ortega's brief, three-page introduction, the remainder of the *Molino Verde*'s sixty-four pages was devoted to an extended Jiménez photo essay.[29] It consisted of numerous photographs of the show's performers—comics, musicians, and scantily clad or naked female dancers in provocative poses. Perhaps the most outrageous photo of all was a picture, spread across the centerfold, of the Molino Verde's well-dressed, all-male audience. Given the notoriety their publication must have caused, it was hardly surprising that Ortega and Jiménez's venture into independent publishing came to an abrupt end when their journal was banned for obscenity.[30]

Clearly, Jiménez was familiar with the world Best Maugard set out to capture in *La mancha de sangre*. And both must have shared the *Molino Verde*'s realist, anti-hypocrisy sensibility because the film's nude dancing scene is consistent with Jiménez's photos for the notorious publication. An honest *cabaretera* film about *ficheras* working as prostitutes must depict the profession's raison d'être: the male's desire for sex. And to the extent that the film's viewers enjoyed the sexual spectacle

of the dance, they became implicated in the commerce of paying for sex. Yes, Best Maugard's film only goes halfway: a fully realistic depiction of prostitution would have shown both female and male nudity (and there were rumors of such a scene existing). But as the extended naked dance goes on, Best Maugard superimposes CUS of males locked in a lecherous male gaze, effectively illustrating the lustful desire that drives the business (fig. 8.23).

BEST MAUGARD'S NEOREALISM: FIVE DEGLAMORIZING MOMENTS

No doubt that scene was the biggest obstacle for the film finding a distributor and exhibitor, and the main reason it was eventually banned for obscenity. And, given what happened to Jiménez's *Molino Verde* venture, he and Best Maugard must have been aware of the censorship risks involved. The fact that they proceeded anyway suggests that it was a risk they were willing to take in order to make their point. But there was much more to *La mancha de sangre* than a naked female dancer; Best Maugard included other realistic elements that were in their own ways just as challenging to status quo morality—in some ways even more so.

Adding considerably to the effectiveness of Best Maugard's film was his ability to balance realism with humanism, just as the best Italian neorealist films would do a decade later. *La mancha de sangre* is filled with powerful little touches that provide a different sort of shock—a poignant jolt of humanity amidst the business of flesh. This is particularly pertinent for a picture like *La mancha de sangre*, whose originality doesn't come from its schematically simple story, but rather from the way it was told. A young *fichera*, Camelia

FIG. 8.23. *La mancha de sangre*'s nude dance.

The Classical Mexican Cinema

(Stella Inda, in her first starring role; she later played the mother in *Los olvidados*), works at a cabaret called "La Mancha de Sangre" and falls for Guillermo (José Casal), a poor young kid new to the city. When their relationship begins to eat into her earnings, her pimp, Gastón (H. G. Batemberg), demands that Camelia drop him or he'll have to "take care" of Guillermo. In the end she manages to keep Guillermo out of harm's way, and when Gastón dies in a shootout with the police, the two young lovers are free to begin a new life together.

Along the way, Best Maugard takes the time to present scenes that add little to the plot but enhance its humanism significantly and offer an unglamorous counterpoint to the film's superficial sexiness. They provide a different sort of spectacle—a quotidian chronicle of the lives of the women who work at La Mancha de Sangre, dancing, drinking, and sleeping with the male customers for a living. I will focus on five such moments. Interestingly, the first four do not advance Camelia's narrative, something typically required of scenes in the Mainstream Mexican Cinema. But for Best Maugard and his cowriter Miguel Ruiz they provided sociological, psychological, and emotional insights into the lives of the bar's *ficheras* and were therefore indispensable.

Here are the five scenes:

1. After establishing the film's central location, a cabaret named La Mancha de Sangre, the film begins with a feisty *fichera* sitting on the bar, proudly regaling two patrons with a colorful account of how she handled a tough client. There was a scuffle on the dance floor, she says, and they fell down. The man tried to get on top of her, but she kicked him in the stomach and he backed off. "And what happened to you?" she's asked. "Nothing," she says, pulling up her skirt to reveal a large bruise on her thigh, "just this" (fig. 8.24).

2. Late one night (or early one morning), the *ficheras* are leaving the cabaret. One of them kindly helps another who is too drunk to find her way home. After they clear the frame, the camera tilts down to find a cleaning woman on her hands and knees, sweeping trash from the floor by hand. When she finds a discarded flower, she rinses it in her bucket and pins it in her hair (figs. 8.25 and 8.26).

3. A young, inexperienced girl who has left her poverty-stricken family interviews for a job with the madam of the cabaret. The madam is hesitant. But the girl evidently got the job because shortly afterward she is seen sitting with an older, sympathetic customer who tells her she's too young to be working in such a place (figs. 8.27 and 8.28).

4. Camelia tidies up her flat in preparation for a visit by Guillermo. Scenes like this, of characters performing mundane activities, are usually absent or very brief in most movies, certainly in Hollywood-MMC films. A character goes through the motions for a few

FIG. 8.24. The opening scene in *La mancha de sangre*. A *fichera* shows off the bruise she got defending herself from a rowdy customer.

FIGS. 8.25 AND 8.26. *La mancha de sangre.*
The cleaning woman finds a flower in the
trash and pins it in her hair.

FIGS. 8.27 AND 8.28. *La mancha de sangre. Top,* the
young girl asks the madam for work at the cabaret.
Bottom, in the next scene, she sits with a customer,
who asks why she's working at such a place. (The
sound for this sequence is lost, so subtitles have
been inserted to provide the dialogue.)

seconds, then the scene hastily moves on to
make its plot point—a discovery, a phone call,
an encounter with another character, whatever. This scene, however, like many such
scenes in Chantal Akerman's masterpiece,
*Jeanne Dielman, 23 quai du Commerce, 1080
Bruxelles* (1975), is about housework. Its point
is to show Camelia cleaning in real time: her
cleaning lasts a full two minutes and fifteen
seconds—the final thirty-five seconds of
which are devoted to her sweeping the floor
(figs. 8.29 and 8.30).

5. Gastón orders Camelia to come to his
apartment. She doesn't want to, but in her
position she must comply. She finds him

waiting for her in bed. He explains that the
reason he's so jealous of Guillermo is because
she is special. She realizes that he wants to
have sex with her and that he has a gun to
force her to submit if necessary. He pulls her
into bed and the film fades to black. When
she returns to the cabaret (in the scene immediately following the one where the young
girl asks for a job), she is obviously shaken. "I
feel that this is killing me," she tells the other
ficheras (figs. 8.31 and 8.32).

Cinematically, *La mancha de sangre* is a
mess, obviously the work of a novice director
working with limited resources (the production was shut down for a time due to a lack

of funds).[31] The photography is rough and unsteady (in several shots in the cabaret, for instance, the microphone boom is visible at the top of the frame), the editing is choppy (usually a sign that the editor had to work with incomplete coverage), the sound is uneven, and the acting is spotty. But despite all that, Best Maugard was able to exert some lasting influences on the *cabaretera* genre formula. For one thing, he altered its dramatic structure. The seduced-and-abandoned narrative, used in both *Santa* and *La mujer del puerto*, was scrapped. In those first *cabaretera* films, the young woman protagonist is taken advantage of by an unscrupulous male, loses her virginity, and when he discards her, she's ostracized by "decent" society. That formula was a handy plot device, furnishing the narrative motivation to drive the protagonists to prostitution and at the same time critiquing patriarchal society's hypocrisy. But by avoiding it, *La mancha de sangre* introduces other, more common motivators to the mix—poverty, hunger, desperation, and the need to survive. It broadened the social criticism, altered the *cabaretera* narrative formula, and affected many films that followed, including, as we will see, *Distinto amanecer*.

FIGS. 8.29 AND 8.30. *La mancha de sangre*. Camelia (Stella Inda) sweeps her apartment before Guillermo visits. After she begins, the camera tilts down to show the broom sweeping trash on the floor for a full twenty seconds before tilting up to Camelia again.

FIGS. 8.31 AND 8.32. *La mancha de sangre. Top*, CU of Camelia when she spots the pistol under Gastón's pillow and realizes that he wants to have sex—by force if he has to. *Bottom*, at the bar afterward. "I feel that this is killing me," she says.

Another difference was its heightened degree of realism. Best Maugard's hyperrealistic approach coupled with his tendency to boil things down to their Mexican essence is similar to the Best system for drawing. In a way, it was the Best system for cinema. To truly capture *lo mexicano*, he demonstrated with *La mancha de sangre*, Mexican filmmakers needed to adopt an anthropological approach: look carefully at what Mexicans do (something he had helped Eisenstein with), take note of the telling details, and most of all do not look away. By continually and intentionally shifting the film's focus to the commonplace details of the prostitutes' lives, he launched Mexican neorealism. Just as Italian neorealism would do a few years later, *La mancha de sangre* illustrates its female characters' stark realities: *ficheras* are often boxed into prostitution for social and economic reasons over which they have no control, and they pay a physical, emotional, and psychological price for the work they do. There's trash on the floor, and someone has to clean it up.

Julio Bracho and *Distinto amanecer*
—

Julio Bracho (1909–1978) quickly established himself as a director of polished, well-made entertainments when his very first film, *¡Ay, qué tiempos, señor Don Simón!* (1941), broke box office records and received critical acclaim. Far from an overnight success, Bracho's breakthrough came after a decade-long apprenticeship in theater and screenwriting. One of the cofounders of Teatro Orientación, Mexico's first experimental theatrical company, which was supported by the government's Department of Public Education, he began directing for the stage in 1930, at

age twenty-one, mounting productions of works by John Synge and Eugene O'Neill, among others. He later founded the Workers Theater, in connection with the Fine Arts Night School for Workers, where he directed a production of O'Neill's *Lazarus Laughed: A Play for Imaginative Theatre*. In 1936, he started yet another theater troupe, Teatro de la Universidad Nacional, where he directed a number of Mexican works as well as productions of classics by Sophocles, Aristophanes, and Euripides.[32]

At the same time he was becoming interested in film and observing filmmakers in action. He visited the set of *Santa*, where he befriended its newly arrived Hollywood cinematographer Alex Phillips (who would later shoot several of his films), and saw Eisenstein at work on *¡Que viva México!*. He watched the filming of *La mujer del puerto* with particular interest, since it starred his sister, Andrea Palma (1903–1987), in the role that made her the first female superstar of Mexican cinema.

According to Bracho, he got his first professional film job by accident. When Paul Strand was preparing *Redes*, the American photographer happened to attend the premier performance of *Lazarus Laughed*, perhaps Bracho's biggest theatrical success, and met its director. Strand spoke very little Spanish and was looking for someone with directing experience to help with the filming, and he asked Bracho to codirect. Working alongside Strand and Fred Zinnemann for four of the six months *Redes* was in production proved to be a transformative experience, and convinced him to devote himself to filmmaking.[33]

Bracho wrote scripts for several films, such as the melodramas *Ave sin rumbo* and *Rapsodia mexicana* (both 1937), and sold one of his original screenplays, *¡Ay, qué tiempos, señor Don Simón!*, to Films Mundiales, a newly formed production company. Shortly thereafter he was hired to direct the film, which became the company's inaugural release. A farce with musical numbers set during the turn of the century, Bracho's debut was an enormous hit, shattering domestic box office records and playing to standing-room-only crowds.[34] (Its single-theater opening day take, 17,000 pesos, surpassed the previous record for a Mexican film by some 5,000 pesos,[35] and its initial Mexico City three-week gross totaled a record-breaking 137,000 pesos.)[36] It was a critical success as well, winning several honors from the Mexican film critics association, including best film, best director, best music, and best production design.[37] (These were the most prestigious Mexican film awards during the pre-Ariel era. The Ariel awards were instituted by the Academia Mexicana de Artes y Ciencias Cinematográficas [Mexican Academy of Cinematographic Arts and Sciences] in 1946 and first awarded in 1947.)[38]

Bracho followed up with two costume dramas for Films Mundiales. *Historia de un gran amor* (*History of a Great Love*, 1942) was a romance set in nineteenth-century Mexico and a vehicle for the rising singing star Jorge Negrete. It, too, was a commercial and critical success, winning a presidential award as the year's best Mexican film. Though his string of hits and awards ended with his next film, the poorly received *La virgen que forjó una patria* (*The Virgin Who Forged a Nation*, 1942), his first three films nevertheless demonstrated Bracho's thorough mastery of the fundamentals of the Mainstream Mexican Cinematic style that he would employ with great facility for the rest of his career.

His next film, *Distinto amanecer* (*A New Dawn*, 1943), would be a departure for Bracho in several ways. To begin with, it was a contemporary drama. And though much of its formal style was consistent with the Mainstream Mexican Cinema, it broke with it in three significant ways: in its unique combination of various genre formulas, in its explicit treatment of and sober commentary on the fate of revolutionary ideals two decades after the end of the revolution, and in its extensive experimentation with low-key lighting.

DISTINTO AMANECER: MEXICO'S DARK NIGHT OF THE SOUL

I will analyze the formal structure of Bracho's masterpiece in the next two subsections. In the first I will focus on the plotting of the script to see how he and his scriptwriting partner adapted a Spanish play and transformed it into an examination of post-revolutionary Mexico. In the second I'll examine *Distinto amanecer*'s shadowy visual style, a look that perfectly expressed its protagonist's melancholy.

Plotting the Narrative

The narrative basis for *Distinto amanecer* was a play, *La vida conyugal* (*The Married Life*), by the Spaniard Max Aub (1903–1972). One of the most prolific Spanish-language authors of the twentieth century, Aub was a novelist, essayist, playwright, screenwriter, journalist, and poet. Like his friend and fellow countryman Luis Buñuel, he emigrated to Mexico after the rise of Franco and lived there for the rest of his life, eventually becoming a Mexican citizen.[39] (Aub was an uncredited contributor to the script of Buñuel's *Los olvidados*.)[40]

La vida conyugal was a chamber play written in 1942 and first performed in Mexico City in 1944, after the release of Bracho's film.[41] Set in an unnamed port city in Spain in 1927, during the dictatorship of Miguel Primo de Rivera, the work is to an extent autobiographical, examining the difficulties of Ignacio, a writer struggling to make ends meet and support his wife and four children. At a deeper level, it depicts an artist's life under a dictatorship and investigates what happens when youthful ideals confront middle age. Its two main characters represent different responses to that question. Ignacio is a burnt-out case—disillusioned with his writing, his marriage (he has taken a mistress and considered divorce), and his life. His old friend Samuel, on the other hand, remains a true believer and resolute idealist, busily working to uncover government corruption, and hounded by the police as a result.[42]

Bracho and his screenwriting collaborator, Xavier Villaurrutia (a playwright and friend of Aub's who had previously adapted the novel *Vámonos con Pancho Villa* for de Fuentes's film), used Aub's play as the scaffolding for *Distinto amanecer*. Upon its framework they draped layers of narrative enhancements, inspired modifications that deepened the interpersonal dynamics and heightened the tension. Most importantly, they added specific references to current and recent national history and politics that gave the film an extra ideological charge by anchoring the action to the Mexican present. Let me enumerate the more salient changes they made in their plotting of *Distinto amanecer* that helped make it such a special film.

1. *They shifted the time and place to contemporary Mexico City.* True, the title card that appears immediately after the credits attempts to minimize the significance of the film's Mexican setting by proclaiming the universality of the story. "The characters in this drama have no relation with persons in real life," the prologue assures its viewers. "The dramatic conflict that is presented has universal characteristics and could therefore be situated in any contemporary city of the world." But when a disclaimer like this protests so much, it often means just the opposite.

In this case it was no doubt an attempt by Bracho and/or nervous Films Mundiales executives to avoid rankling the presidential administration of Manuel Ávila Camacho at a time when the fledgling Mexican film industry was counting on continued state support. (Indeed, President Ávila Camacho hosted the top Mexican filmmaking figures—producers, executives, film union members, stars— in December 1943, just days after *Distinto amanecer* was released. At that gathering he extolled their work and pledged his administration's continued "moral and material" backing.)[43] Unfavorable administration reaction to the film might even result in official censorship (which, as we saw in the case of *El prisionero 13*, was an all-too-real possibility). Bracho and executives at Films Mundiales had to have known how unambiguously critical their film was in its depiction of some of the realities of life in present-day Mexico. *Distinto amanecer*'s prologue, an obvious last-second adjustment hoping to deflect criticism from a film whose provocative critique might have cut too close to the bone, only confirmed what it was trying to deny. (As we saw in chapter 7, something similar happened later, with another political hot potato, Buñuel's *Los olvidados*, in 1950.)

Distinto amanecer's next few images—a series of establishing shots clearly situating the action in Mexico City—further contradict the opening title card. These include views of a statue outside the Palacio de Bellas Artes (the Palace of Fine Arts, a showcase for the arts completed in 1934 and containing murals by Diego Rivera and David Alfaro Siqueiros, among others) and exterior shots of the Palacio de Correos de México, the country's central post office, where the film's inciting incident—the assassination of a labor union leader—takes place. Later the film presents other capital city locales, such as the colonial-era cathedral (Catedral Metropolitana de la Asunción de María), whose bells announce the "new dawn" of the title, along with location shooting (impressive for its time and a selling point of the film) in the interior of the post office and the train station where the climax was shot. Despite the prologue's contention that this story could take place "anywhere in the world," the film's imagery insistently proclaims, "This is happening now in Mexico City."

And that specificity is precisely what gives the film its considerable political bite. Thus when Ignacio mentions to his friend that they live in a country where "politics drags everything down" and "where a chauffeur earns more than a teacher," the comment stands out precisely because it is such an extremely rare instance of a pointed ideological critique in the Cine de Oro. As I discuss below, there are more markers that make this a specifically Mexican tale, particularly the main characters' collegiate activism. And because the film is situated in the actual Mexican present and makes concrete references to recent events, other story details gain credibility,

immediacy, and a historical and sociopolitical edge they wouldn't otherwise possess. Story elements—governmental corruption ruthlessly enforced by the use of violence, the difficulty of making an honest living, and the desperation of women trying to hold a family together—all appear to be timely, frighteningly plausible, and distinctly Mexican.

2. *They revised and intensified the interrelationship among the three main characters.* In the play, only the writer and the activist are acquainted; in *Distinto amanecer*, all three—Ignacio (Alberto Galán), his wife, Julieta (Andrea Palma), and the activist, Octavio (Pedro Armendáriz)—know each other well, having attended university together years before. But they've drifted apart since their student days. Back then, they were active in the student movement (though it's not named, the university is presumably UNAM, the Universidad Nacional Autónoma de México (fig. 8.33).

The student strikes they recall were a series of demonstrations in the late 1920s that succeeded in winning UNAM's independence from governmental control and political influence—thus the significance

FIG. 8.33. *Distinto amanecer* (1943): Three old friends are reacquainted. *Left to right*: the writer, Ignacio (Alberto Galán); his wife, Julieta (Andrea Palma); and the union activist, Octavio (Pedro Armendáriz).

of "autonomous" in the school's name. Of course the struggle for academic autonomy wasn't anything like the actual revolution (they would have been children in the 1910s and too young to have participated), but for that generation of students it was their great cause, their way of contributing to the larger national struggle for freedom, justice, and equality. Because these events would have been relatively fresh in the minds of audiences in 1943, when the film was released, Ignacio's, Julieta's, and Octavio's college activism backstories would have provided adult Mexican viewers with specific insights into the political makeup of these characters.

Bracho and Villaurrutia further thickened the plot by creating a romantic triangle among the three. It quickly becomes evident that Ignacio and Octavio were in love with Julieta when they were students—and that both still are. Just as he was back then, Ignacio remains jealous of Octavio. The romantic dynamics are exacerbated by the fact that Ignacio and Julieta have settled into a less-than-perfect marriage. Though Julieta's younger brother lives with them, the couple is childless (she lost a child and can no longer conceive)—a change from the play that serves to underline the emptiness in their relationship. Finally, the couple lives with the fact that Ignacio has a mistress.

3. *They altered the play's dramatic structure to make Julieta, not her writer husband, the protagonist.* The film is Julieta's story, from start to finish. Where the play concentrated on the toll domesticity and conformity take on a male artist, *Distinto amanecer* focuses instead on a dissatisfied married woman at a moral and existential crossroads. It's a wrung-out Julieta that Octavio encounters at a cinema

at the beginning of the film. When she tells him that he is exactly the same as the last time they saw each other, he reflexively returns the compliment. But she doesn't accept it. "I am not the same," she says unemotionally. And then, in just a few words, Bracho and Villaurrutia economically paint a vivid picture of Julieta's desolation.

Octavio: "You say that because now you're a married woman."
Julieta: "Not just because of that."
Octavio: "You're not happy?"
Julieta: "No."
Octavio: ". . . And why aren't you happy?"
Julieta: "I don't know."

Once they arrive at the flat where she lives with her husband and brother, however, some of the sources of her unhappiness become evident. They live on the poor side of town. She has to sell their radio to pay the rent. A cynical and embittered Ignacio has taken a mistress. Octavio's appearance, however, raises the possibility of her beginning a new life with him. At the film's climax Julieta, torn between love and duty, must decide whether to start life anew with Octavio or remain in her present one with Ignacio (fig. 8.34).

4. *They accentuated the political thriller dimension.* The play contained elements of a political thriller, but Bracho and Villaurrutia intensified them in the film, and it became Hitchcockian. The action takes place in one taut thirteen-hour stretch, from the evening that Octavio accidentally bumps into Julieta in a crowded movie theater (in a reflexive move, the film playing on the screen is Bracho's blockbuster, *¡Ay, qué tiempos, señor Don Simón!*, further fixing the film's action to the Mexican present) to his leaving on the eight o'clock train the next morning. Octavio

The Classical Mexican Cinema

FIG. 8.34. *Distinto amanecer*. Julieta (Andrea Palma) hiding from the gangster pursuing Octavio. Throughout the film, Gabriel Figueroa's lighting depicts Julieta's existential dilemma as well as her divided self: whether to remain in an unhappy marriage or leave with Octavio on the morning train.

The gripping storyline is more than just suspenseful fiction cooked up by clever screenwriters. For perceptive Mexican viewers at the time, the thrills delivered by *Distinto amanecer* would likely have been as unsettling as they were entertaining because the dangers portrayed were familiar and derived directly from living in Mexico. It is the system that put these characters in peril. (Interestingly, this seems to have been recognized by at least one reviewer at the time. A highly laudatory notice in a Mexican periodical praised *Distinto amanecer* as "positively extraordinary" and "thoroughly Mexican from head to toe," and went on to say that the film raised "numerous moral, psychological, social and even economic problems.")[44]

For honest, hard-working citizens, *Distinto amanecer* says, contemporary Mexican life is like being trapped in a nightmarish thriller—no ethical way to get ahead, no one to trust, no place to hide, and nowhere to run. Each of the three principal characters represents different responses to the pressures of Mexican life. Ignacio has given up and become corrupt like the system. Octavio fights against it, but is treated like a criminal. Julieta is left to choose between them, but in fact it is no choice at all: either way leaves her having to deal with the fruits of systemic dishonesty. Stay with Ignacio and it's more of the same. Leave with Octavio and share a life on the run.

The film's thriller genre structure took the characters to an extreme, but Bracho pushed *Distinto amanecer* even further by adding elements from two more genres.

5. They made it a cabaretera movie. As if all of this weren't enough, Bracho and Villaurrutia also made *Distinto amanecer* into a *cabaretera* genre film, introducing an unexpected

works for a labor union and is on the verge of exposing a corrupt governor or two, and possibly even a government minister as well. He's being pursued by one governor's henchman, but with Julieta's help they give him the slip and she takes Octavio to the apartment she shares with Ignacio. He must retrieve some important documents (the film's MacGuffin) at the central post office, and Ignacio volunteers to get them. After he leaves, the governor's goon shows up, and when he threatens Julieta with an ax, she shoots and kills him with Octavio's pistol.

The resulting situation is one Hitchcock would have savored: unable to go to the police for help (for fear that they may be in league with the dishonest governor), Julieta and Octavio must dispose of the body, get the documents from Ignacio, avoid the governor's gunmen, and get Octavio safely off on the morning train—maybe with Julieta at his side.

FIGS. 8.35–8.37. *Distinto amanecer*. A dissolve from a wall painting to Julieta (in the same pose) waiting at the bar efficiently and economically conveys the nature of her job at Tabu.

plot twist at the film's midpoint completely absent in the play. Late at night, after her brother goes to bed and Ignacio leaves to visit his mistress, Julieta works as a *fichera* at an upscale nightclub called "Tabu." She had hoped to conceal it from Octavio, and he is stunned when he finds out. "Impossible!" he exclaims, and Julieta agrees—sometimes she too thinks it's impossible. But she was driven to it out of desperation (like the young woman in *La mancha de sangre*). After her brother fainted at school one day from hunger, she looked for work for a month. Unable to find any honest work she took the job at Tabu because, she tells Octavio, "some things, like hunger, can't wait."

As the action shifts to Tabu, a quick series of images literally paint a picture of Julieta's nocturnal life. The camera tracks from the band to a painting of a larger-than-life nude woman on one of the walls, and then there's a dissolve to Julieta standing at the bar in the same pose. Captured by cinematographer Gabriel Figueroa and executed by editor Gloria Schoemann, the transition makes the nature of her job explicit. Tabu may be a far cry from the seedy cabaret in *La mancha de sangre*, but the work is the same. She is a *fichera*, a drinking and dancing partner for the male customers, and though it's left ambiguous, quite possibly a sexual partner, too. By making it a thriller, Bracho and Villaurrutia showed how systemic corruption made Mexican life precarious. Adding the *cabaretera* dimension revealed its corrosive effect on women (figs. 8.35–8.37).

The Classical Mexican Cinema

Distinto amanecer as Film Noir:
The Figueroa Factor

The plot scripted by Bracho and Villaurrutia presented a haunting vision of postrevolutionary Mexico, made all the more disturbing by the fact that their dystopian view was moored in Mexican reality. The film's unsparing critique of contemporary Mexican life made *Distinto amanecer* the most overtly political film since de Fuentes's Revolution Trilogy. That and its unusual combination of multiple genres made it emphatically different from the MMC. But beyond the ideologically bold and narratively imaginative scripting, it was also *visually* different from any other Mexican film made up to that time, due to Gabriel Figueroa's radical low-key lighting, which pushed cinematic darkness to an extreme. Indeed, Figueroa's shadowy imagery made *Distinto amanecer* the first Mexican film noir—and possibly the first film noir period—before the term had even been coined.[45] It is almost as if Figueroa decided to make an entire film in the dusky manner he and co-cinematographer Jack Draper had created for Tiburcio's walk into the night at the end of *¡Vámonos con Pancho Villa!*

Figueroa had shot Bracho's first three films and was no doubt instrumental in helping the novice director quickly become one of the leading practitioners of the mainstream Mexican style. Very little is known about their collaboration, so it is hard to say exactly what their working arrangement was and how they arrived at the pervasive darkness of *Distinto amanecer*. Did Bracho feel the urge to break free from the Mainstream Mexican Cinema and make a more daring film—a sort of return to the experimental aesthetics of his avant-garde theater days? Was Figueroa

emboldened by Gregg Toland's recent chiaroscuro lighting for John Ford (*The Long Voyage Home*, 1940; *The Grapes of Wrath*, 1940) and Orson Welles (*Citizen Kane*, 1941)? Did the work of his Hollywood mentor spur Figueroa to test film's low-light dynamic range—the medium's ability to capture detail in the darker areas of the frame? However they arrived at the film's idiosyncratic visual style, it represented the confluence of their creative impulses.

As we saw in chapter 6, editor Gloria Schoemann described the filmmaking process established at Films Mundiales by studio head Agustín J. Fink when she and Figueroa worked with either Bracho or Fernández. Assuming that system was in place for *Distinto amanecer*, Bracho, Figueroa, and Schoemann would most likely have begun by agreeing on the overall look of the film. As I've said, the specifics of how Bracho and Figueroa came up with *Distinto amanecer*'s low-key style remain a mystery. So does the degree of freedom the cinematographer had in managing the lighting and determining the camera setups for the film. Most probably the director was actively involved, since Figueroa does not name Bracho as one of the handful of directors he worked for who allowed him a free hand at lighting design and camera placement (there were four: Fernández, Ford, Ismael Rodríguez, and Roberto Gavaldón).[46]

We do know that Figueroa—like Toland—was endlessly curious and inventive. (Recall his saying, "I was always experimenting. Toland had put this in my head.")[47] And we know that the film he and Bracho proceeded to make was not just dark, but a sort of low-key lighting limit case, one he would use to explore the bounds of the medium's ability

TOP | FIG. 8.38. Miriam Hopkins, Gary Cooper, and Fredric March in *Design for Living* (1933), a Paramount picture produced and directed by Ernst Lubitsch; cinematography by Victor Milner.

BOTTOM | FIG. 8.39. Typical high-key MMC lighting: Joaquín Pardavé and Mapy Cortés in *¡Ay, qué tiempos, señor Don Simón!* (1941), Bracho's first film and his first collaboration with Figueroa.

FIG. 8.40. Henry Fonda and John Carradine in *The Grapes of Wrath* (1940; directed by John Ford, cinematography by Gregg Toland).

to capture darkness. The result was a film that looked unlike any other Mexican film of the Golden Age and that is markedly different from almost any other film of the early 1940s, regardless of national origin. Let me illustrate how Figueroa's low-key lighting was more muted than Toland's innovations for Ford and Welles, different from the low-light style that was adopted for Hollywood film noir later in the 1940s, and from the lighting Figueroa himself would settle on afterward in films like *Río Escondido*, *Salón México*, *Víctimas del pecado*, and *Los olvidados*.

At the time, high-key lighting, in which the entire frame was evenly illuminated, was the prevailing lighting style in Hollywood and in the Mainstream Mexican Cinema. As a result of having the complementary light— the fill light—almost as bright as the primary or key light, with high-key lighting shadows were almost completely eliminated. It was ubiquitous in Hollywood and MMC movies of the 1930s and 1940s and can be seen in figs. 8.38 and 8.39. Compare the lighting in these films with the shot of Ignacio, Julieta, and Octavio around the kitchen table in fig. 8.33 and you begin to see how unusual Bracho and Figueroa's look for *Distinto amanecer* was.

Toland's method for the low-key lighting he began working on in the early 1940s, such as the memorable nighttime scene of Tom Joad (Henry Fonda) returning to a deserted home in Ford's *The Grapes of Wrath*, was to diminish the strength and spread of the key light, seemingly eliminate the fill light altogether, and allow the rest of the frame to be engulfed in pitch-black darkness (fig. 8.40).

Film noir, a kind of Hollywood expressionism, was likely influenced by lighting like this, as well as Toland's work in *Citizen Kane* and the look of German silent cinema. It came

later in the 1940s and played numerous variations on low-key lighting.[48] In the example in
fig. 8.41, from Billy Wilder's *Double Indemnity*
(1944), released a year after *Distinto amanecer*
and regarded as one of the earliest and most
influential films noir, the background lighting
is the brightest light source, and a rim light
from above catches Barbara Stanwyck's hair
and shoulders. There is no key light on the
two actors; instead a weak, diffused fill light
illuminates MacMurray and Stanwyck. It's
dark but there's still a fair amount of detail
recorded, for example, some of the pattern of
his tie, the outline of her bra straps beneath
her sweater, and the whites of her eyes, possibly lit with a muted catch light (fig. 8.41).

Figueroa's overall lighting scheme for
Distinto amanecer was radically darker. Nearly
every composition was considerably dimmer
than the low-key norms followed by Hollywood and MMC films. The result was images
that were murkier and contained far less
definition than even the example from *Double
Indemnity*, as may be seen in the examples
from the first twenty-five minutes of the film,
in figs. 8.42–8.44.

TOP | FIG. 8.42. *Distinto amanecer*. The
film opens at night, with Octavio (Pedro
Armendáriz) being followed in the streets
of Mexico City by . . .

MIDDLE | FIG. 8.43. . . . one of the hench-
men of a corrupt governor.

BOTTOM | FIG. 8.44. Julieta (Andrea Palma)
helps Octavio escape.

FIG. 8.41. Fred MacMurray and Barbara Stanwyck
in *Double Indemnity* (1944), Billy Wilder director,
John F. Seitz director of photography.

Another way to appreciate *Distinto amanecer*'s extreme darkness is to compare a production still, presumably taken by the set photographer for use on lobby cards and other kinds of promotion, with the scene as Figueroa shot it for the film (figs. 8.45 and 8.46).

Figueroa's low-key lighting was different from what Toland had been doing, from the look associated with American film noir later in the 1940s and 1950s, and from what was seen in the Mainstream Mexican Cinema. Typically, Hollywood-MMC low-key lighting and film noir were careful to keep at least one bright light source somewhere in the frame, even if it was small and contained. Large patches of darkness then surrounded that highlight (the candle flame in *The Grapes of*

Wrath shot in fig. 8.40, for example, or the light from the room behind the couple in the *Double Indemnity* still, fig. 8.41). This high-contrast, small-bright-spot-overwhelmed-by-jet-black was the low-key lighting style Hollywood preferred because it provided at least some discernible detail and definition in the frame.

From both the Hollywood and MMC perspective, then, Figueroa's subdued low-key lighting scheme for *Distinto amanecer*, seen in figs. 8.47 and 8.48, would have probably been impossible. Without a bright light source anywhere in the frame, Figueroa's lighting produced an image that was difficult to "read." Frustratingly so. Typically, actors' faces are the brightest areas in the frame, and the viewers' gaze would normally be drawn to them, and especially to their eyes. But those faces are shadowy and lack definition, and without a catch light, Andrea Palma's and Pedro Armendáriz's eyes appear dull and sunken. Furthermore, the rest of the frame is so dark that the room becomes an exceptionally undefined, ambiguous space. Those deep shadows, however, perfectly convey Julieta's no-way-out predicament.

Sadly, despite the hopefulness implicit in *Distinto amanecer*'s title, when the new dawn breaks, the morning's light does nothing to brighten Julieta's prospects. She does have it

FIGS. 8.45 AND 8.46. *Top*, a production still of Octavio and Julieta in a scene near the end of their long night together. Because it would be used for promotional purposes, most likely as a lobby card or in magazines and newspapers, the shot had to be taken using conventional high-key lighting. *Bottom*, the actual shot as it appears in the film. (As was typically the case with production stills of this era, both in Mexico and Hollywood, the exact pose seen in the photo does not occur in the film.)

The Classical Mexican Cinema

FIGS. 8.47 AND 8.48. *Distinto amanecer*. A shot/
reverse shot exchange between Octavio and Julieta
late in the film illustrates Figueroa's muted low-key
lighting. Unlike most of mainstream Hollywood's
low-key lighting, Figueroa's omitted the single
bright light source in favor of a duskier, more diffused, low contrast—and low detail—look.

better than other *cabaretera* protagonists, like
Santa and the woman in *La mujer del puerto*,
both of whom died. But Julieta dies a spiritual death. After joining Octavio on the train,
she decides at the last minute not to go with
him, and returns to her husband and brother,
waiting on the platform. As they watch Octavio's train depart, her brother asks why she
didn't leave. "I would have cried more if I had
gone," she replies. But she'll cry either way
because her situation is now even worse—
hers is a life without options. As the three
of them walk off, she turns her attention to
getting her brother off to school on time. Her
daily grind—and presumably her nightly one,
too—resumes all over again.

It's another Mexican tragedy. Fernando de
Fuentes's trilogy showed how the revolution
mangled and crushed the lives of those who
fought it. *Distinto amanecer* was a sobering
update that revealed the dispiriting effect the
revolution had on the hapless generation left
in its wake, still hoping for a new dawn.

CHAPTER 9

Conclusion

—

UIS BUÑUEL's return to European filmmaking in the 1960s was the last nail in the coffin of the CMC. Its demise was due to several factors. A major one was the pressure of market economics, a force that over the thirty-year reign of the Golden Age compelled most Mexican directors to retreat from or simply avoid risky artistic experiments and provocative ideological statements of the CMC and ease into the more sure-fire, box-office-friendly commercial projects of the Mainstream Mexican Cinema. The early career choice made by Juan Bustillo Oro in the mid-1930s, just after completing *Dos monjes*, is a prime example of this trend.

Released at the end of November 1934, *Dos monjes* was fairly well received critically. A reviewer for the popular magazine *Revista de Revistas*, for example, proclaimed it "the triumph of Mexican filmmaking."[1] But it was a box office disappointment, playing just one week in its Mexico City first run. Bustillo Oro then went to work on an adaptation of an old adventure novel set in fifteenth-century Mexico. He mentioned it to a producer who had just filmed one of his screenplays, *Tiburón* (*Shark*, 1933), who became interested in the new script because of the marketability of its title—*Monja y casada, vírgen y mártir* (*Nun and Wife, Virgin and Martyr*). Bustillo Oro saw his point, agreeing that it would be a hit if not a work of art. "Forget about art!" the producer told him. "Haven't you had enough of that with *Dos monjes?*"[2] Bustillo Oro directed the film from his script, and to improve its odds of success he changed the novel's downbeat ending (in which the heroine dies, becoming the martyr of the title) to a happy one in which the woman lives (despite the change, he kept "martyr" in the title). The producer's prediction came true: *Monja y casada, vírgen y mártir* was the biggest hit of Bustillo Oro's early career, playing four weeks in its first capital city run.

He took one last stab at art with another horror film, *El misterio del rostro pálido* (*The Mystery of the Pale Face*, 1935), a kind of disfigured face cum mad scientist horror film[3] that substituted art deco production design for German expressionism, but it was even less successful than *Dos monjes*. Thereafter, Bustillo Oro, once the energetic champion of theatrical and cinematic experimentation, sought profitability rather than cinematic innovation or political provocation. His business responsibilities as partner in the Oro Grovas studio, which he cofounded in 1937, only solidified this shift. In his 1984 memoir, he described his filmmaking transformation as the result of a synergetic collaboration he formed with producer-partner Jesús Grovas.

Don Jesús, with his knowledge of the public and his astute understanding of commerce, provided the sensible brake for my artistic extravagances. And my artistic inclinations at the very least avoided the excesses of commercial passion. The result was an equilibrium between box office success and quality.[4]

If he couldn't have art, Bustillo Oro would settle for quality filmmaking, which he defined in terms that could have been voiced by a Hollywood studio mogul: "a well-written screenplay; sparkling, ironic dialogue that was wedded to the situation; adherence to the logic of the genre; and the fluid linkage of sequences."[5] He went on to become one of the Golden Age's most prolific filmmakers, a writer-producer-director of many popular and iconic MMC films, among them Cantinflas's breakout comedy *Ahí está el detalle* (1940) and the quintessential family melodrama *Cuando los hijos se van* (1941).

A similar adjustment to commercial realities may also have altered the course of Fernando de Fuentes's career. As we noted at the end of chapter 5, after the financial disaster of *¡Vámonos con Pancho Villa!* (1936), de Fuentes shied away from the daring formal inventiveness and downbeat thematics of the Revolution Trilogy and veered toward projects with more box office potential. Just as Bustillo Oro's shift resulted in a commercial winner, so did de Fuentes's next film, *Allá en el Rancho Grande* (1936)—the biggest hit of his career and one of the most profitable Mexican films of the Golden Age. It is telling that de Fuentes was aware of the significance of the move he was making, concerned that his directing of *Allá en el Rancho Grande* might be perceived as a step down in prestige.[6] It was so successful that nobody seemed to care, and de Fuentes ended the decade still regarded as Mexico's top director. But he would never again achieve the kind of profound national soul-searching that characterized the Revolution Trilogy. Thus, after the failure of artistic projects they were

The Classical Mexican Cinema

highly invested in, both Bustillo Oro and de Fuentes opted for the safer bets of MMC filmmaking.[7]

A comparable move from art to commerce occurred at Films Mundiales just a few years later. As I related in chapter 6, the new studio was formed in 1941 as partnership among businessmen and filmmakers. The financing came from a group of French investors who lived in Mexico, and the filmmaking partners included Gabriel Figueroa, director Chano Urueta, and actor Arturo de Córdoba. According to Figueroa, the filmmakers contributed half of their salaries for a share in the studio.[8] Businessman turned talent agent turned film producer Agustín J. Fink was made company president and took charge of the day-to-day operations.[9] A gifted producer, Fink established a supportive atmosphere where directors like Emilio Fernández and Julio Bracho could do their best work. It was Fink who teamed them with talented collaborators like Figueroa, writer Mauricio Magdaleno, and editor Gloria Schoemann. Fink's nurturing of his novice directors paid off: Fernández's and Bracho's early commercial and critical triumphs got Films Mundiales off the ground.

But things at the studio changed abruptly when Fink died prematurely in 1944, at age forty-three. The businessmen took over and "they fired all of us on the spot," Figueroa recounted later. "'We don't want any geniuses here,' the new manager told Emilio Fernández, actors Dolores del Río and Pedro Armendáriz, and myself."[10] (The manager's words of farewell echo the motto adopted by RKO after Orson Welles was fired for the two flops he made following *Citizen Kane*

[1941]. The new RKO slogan, which has been understood as a slap in the face of the dismissed Welles, was "showmanship in place of genius.")

Fernández made two more films for Films Mundiales, *Las abandonadas* and *Bugambilia* (both 1945), and would later return to make *Salón México* (1949) after the studio had merged to become CLASA Films Mundiales. But the encouraging creative milieu he had enjoyed there during the Fink era was gone, and he no longer had a filmmaking "home." Fink's death and the business-oriented realignment of the studio, then, likely had an effect on the quality of Fernández's films, and it may have affected Bracho's career as well. He never made another film that matched the radical experimentation of *Distinto amanecer*, which was released just months after Fink's passing.

A second factor leading to the end of the Classical Mexican Cinema was, of course, the end of the Cine de Oro itself. As I said when discussing the postwar filmmaking decline in chapters 6 and 7, Mexican producers' strategy for competing with the postwar onslaught of Hollywood films was to make more but cheaper films. This shortsighted solution proved to be disastrous, and by the late 1950s Mexican filmmaking was in crisis and everybody knew it. Other than Buñuel, whose *Nazarín* (1959), *The Young One* (1960), the made-in-Spain *Viridiana* (1961), and *The Exterminating Angel* (1962) continued to win praise and awards at Cannes and numerous other festivals, Mexico's international presence vanished. By 1965, the year of Buñuel's last Mexican film, *Simón del desierto*, the Golden Age was over and so was the CMC.

A third factor was simply the passage of time. Established CMC filmmakers were aging, making fewer films, retiring, and dying. The revolution, the central formative event in their lives, was half a century in the past. The impetus for their filmmaking, the desire to create a national cinematic language to express *mexicanidad*, was not an all-consuming artistic concern for the next generation of filmmakers—or filmgoers.

Interestingly, though, some mid-century developments in global cinema served to validate the CMC and its filmmakers. The emergence of the French New Wave and its call for a personal, auteurist cinema was a strong if indirect vindication of CMC auteurs. Following that trend, the Grupo Nuevo Cine, a group of critics and cineastes who called for a resurgence of Mexican cinema, were positively disposed to Mexican Golden Age auteurs like de Fuentes, Fernández, and Buñuel.

Many young Mexican cineastes, however, also considered the now-canonized Golden Age films old-fashioned—the cinema of their parents and grandparents. Furthermore, the Cine de Oro was identified with the status quo. Like young New Wave filmmakers in France and around the globe, some of Mexico's young aspiring directors and critics naturally reacted against it. Worse, Golden Age cinema was considered inferior. One scathing indictment came from Carlos Monsiváis, one of Mexico's most highly regarded cultural critics. Assessing twentieth-century Mexican culture in an essay written in 1976, Monsiváis said that "the history of Mexican cinema amounts to an accumulation of aesthetic trash, the waste of economic voracity,

the defense of the most reactionary interests, depoliticization and sexism."[11]

Even the Grupo Nuevo Cine's praise for CMC auteurs and their films contained a strong negative undertow. For instance, though critics for the Grupo's journal *Nuevo Cine* (published in 1961 and 1962) were ostensibly respectful of Fernández's 1940s films, they still found ways to take swipes at them as they analyzed his more recent efforts. In a review of Fernández's *Pueblito* (1962), *Nuevo Cine* critic José de la Colina complained that the director was unable to rid himself of his "traditionally confused demagoguery." And, he went on, if "the *indios* of the village gather themselves in less statuesque attitudes" than was usual for his pictures, Fernández's "general vision continues to be folkloristic and conventional."[12] And in his review of Fernández's *Un dorado de Pancho Villa* (1966), another member of the Nuevo Cine group, Emilio García Riera, bemoaned the director's repetition of his "usual *magueys*," concluding that "the film was morose and static, like all of those by this director."[13] Clearly, Mexico was experiencing a changing of its cinematic guard, and these young cineastes were weary of the previous generation's films and ready to strike out in a new direction.

Still, while it lasted, the Classical Mexican Cinema branch of the Cine de Oro had a terrific run. For thirty-two years, from *El prisionero 13* in 1933 to *Simón del desierto* in 1965, the CMC had a positive impact on the nation's film. And its influence persisted after the CMC disappeared. In fact, traces of its innovation and creativity appear in both the Nuevo Cine movement of the 1970s and in more recent Mexican films. Though it is a mistake, I think, to look for one-to-one correspondences between post-1960s films and those made decades earlier, there are definite signs that the legacy of the Classical Mexican Cinema echoes in Mexican films made long after its demise.

For Mexico's New Wave of the 1970s and early 1980s, Nuevo Cine directors adopted the innovative, boundary-pushing spirit of the Classical Mexican Cinema to make a fresh brand of Mexican films. Three directors exemplify this trend. Paul Leduc, an early member of the Nuevo Cine group, made a revisionist, *cinéma vérité* take on the Mexican Revolution, *Reed: México insurgente* (*Reed: Insurgent Mexico*, 1970; #26 on the *Somos* poll). And Marcela Fernández Violante's very presence was a challenge to traditional Mexican filmmaking. The only female filmmaker in the Mexican film industry during the 1970s, she directed several provocative and well-received films, such as *De todos modos Juan te llamas* (*The General's Daughter*, 1974), *Cananea* (1976), and *Misterio* (*Mystery*, 1979). And Jaime Humberto Hermosillo's *Doña Herlinda y su hijo* (*Doña Herlinda and Her Son*, 1984; #65 on the *Somos* poll) harkens back almost fifty years to the boldness of Adolfo Best Maugard's *Mancha de sangre*. Hermosillo's film was radical as much for its subject matter (the most frank treatment of a gay romance that had appeared in Mexican cinema) as for its mode of production (it was produced independently by faculty and students from the School of Direction and Film Appreciation at the University of Guadalajara). I doubt if any of these directors could have made any of these films had it not been for the creative precedent established by Classical Mexican Cinema filmmakers.

More recently, I see the same sort of narrative inventiveness that was evident in *Dos monjes*—looking at the same events from different characters' points of view—in Alejandro González Iñárritu's *Amores perros* (2000). The candid look at the role of sex in Mexican life that was central to *La mancha de sangre*, *Las abandonadas*, *Salón México*, and *Pueblerina*, and all of Buñuel's films, particularly *Él*, *The Young One*, and *Ensayo de un crimen*, is not unlike Alfonso Cuarón's investigations into sex, class, gender, and machismo in *Sólo con tu pareja* (1991) and *Y tu mama también* (2001). And the questions about the nature of the Mexican character and the degree to which violence, greed, and treachery have warped it, issues that were so hauntingly explored in de Fuentes's Revolution Trilogy, are precisely the ones exposed in Gerardo Naranjo's *Miss Bala* (2011) and Luis Estrada's *La ley de Herodes* (*Herod's Law*, 1999) and *Infierno* (*Hell*, 2010).

As much as the combination of formal invention and cultural critique characterized the CMC, Mexico's revolutionary ethos defined it. Declaring its independence from Hollywood's hegemonic style, which had infected the Mainstream Mexican Cinema, the Classical Mexican Cinema was Mexico's film revolution. But unlike the bloody revolution that failed to realize its ideals, the CMC insurgency successfully produced some of the most memorable, eloquent, and evocative Mexican films ever made. Furthermore, the success of the CMC was itself the answer to the unsettling existential question its films raised about the nature of the national character. The fact that so many films of the CMC received international acclaim and rose to the top ranks of the world's cinema negated the notion that a fatal flaw forever doomed Mexicans to mediocrity and failure.

Lasting nearly three decades, the Classical Mexican Cinema was an astonishing, unprecedented achievement. Aesthetically and ideologically, it was arguably the most sustained resistance to the Hollywood paradigm of any national cinema on record. Formally, its poetics defined Mexico at home and abroad. Thematically, the CMC films were moral statements. Comprised of the films that did not look away, the Classical Mexican Cinema was nothing less than the conscience of Mexico.

Notes

CHAPTER 1

1. Eduardo de la Vega Alfaro, *Del muro a la pantalla: S. M. Eisenstein y el arte pictórico mexicano* (Guadalajara: University of Guadalajara Press, 1997).

2. Evan Lieberman and Kerry Hegarty, "Authors of the Image: Cinematographers Gabriel Figueroa and Gregg Toland," *Journal of Film and Video* 62.1–2 (Spring–Summer 2010), 31–51.

3. Patrick Keating, "The Volcano and the Barren Hill: Gabriel Figueroa and the Space of Art Cinema," in Rosalind Galt and Karl Schoonover, eds., *Global Art Cinema: New Theories and Histories* (New York: Oxford University Press, 2010), 201–217.

4. Kristin Thompson, *Breaking the Glass Armor: Neoformalist Film Analysis* (Princeton, NJ: Princeton University Press, 1988).

5. See, for example, Kristin Thompson, *Storytelling in the New Hollywood: Understanding Classical Narrative Technique* (Cambridge, MA: Harvard University Press, 1999), and *Storytelling in Film and Television* (Cambridge, MA: Harvard University Press, 2003); David Bordwell, *Figures Traced in Light: On Cinematic Staging* (Berkeley: University of California Press, 2005), *On the History of Film Style* (Cambridge, MA: Harvard University Press, 1997), *The Way Hollywood Tells It: Story and Style in Modern Movies* (Berkeley: University of California Press, 2006), and *Poetics of Cinema* (New York: Routledge, 2008); see also Thompson and Bordwell's *Minding Movies* (University of Chicago Press: 2011); Thompson and Bordwell both contribute to David Bordwell's website on cinema, http://www.davidbordwell.net/blog/.

6. David Bordwell, *Ozu and the Poetics of Cinema* (Princeton, NJ: Princeton University Press, 1988), *The Films of Carl-Theodor Dreyer* (Berkeley: University of California Press, 1981). *Ozu and the Poetics of Cinema* is available for download online at https://

www.cjspubs.lsa.umich.edu/electronic/facultyseries
/list/series/ozu.php.

7. "Konban-wa, Ozu-san" (undated new introduction to Bordwell's book on Ozu), https://www
.cjspubs.lsa.umich.edu/electronic/facultyseries/list
/series/ozu.php.

8. See, for example, Ira Bhaskar, "'Historical Poetics,' Narrative, and Interpretation," in Toby Miller and Robert Stam, eds., *A Companion to Film Theory* (Malden, MA: Blackwell, 1999), 387–412; and Berys Gaut, "Making Sense of Films: Neoformalism and Its Limits," *Forum for Modern Language Studies* 31.1 (1995), 8–23.

9. David Bordwell, "Historical Poetics of Cinema," in R. Barton Palmer, ed., *The Cinematic Text: Methods and Approaches*, Georgia State Literary Studies no. 3 (New York: AMS Press, 1989), 369–398. In this essay, Bordwell wrote a concise definition of the method and its goals:

> A historical poetics of cinema produces knowledge in answer to two broad questions:
>
> 1. What are the principles according to which films are constructed and by means of which they achieve particular effects?
>
> 2. How and why have these principles arisen and changed in particular empirical circumstances?

Bordwell revised this essay, "almost out of recognition" he says on his blog, in *Poetics of Cinema*. There, he elaborated a bit more on the relation between the close reading of a film and the film's context. It is worth quoting in full, since it aligns well with the aims of my study:

> As I conceive it, a poetics of cinema aims to produce reliable knowledge by pursuing questions within two principal areas of inquiry. First is what we might call *analytical* poetics. What are the principles according to which films are constructed and through which they achieve particular effects? Second, there's *historical* poetics, which asks, How and why have these principles arisen and changed in particular empirical circumstances? In my view, poetics is characterized by the phenomena

it studies (films' constructional principles and effects) and the questions it asks about those phenomena—their constitution, functions, purposes, and historical manifestations. (23)

10. Bordwell, *Ozu and the Poetics of Cinema*, chapter 8; Bordwell also discusses neoformalism and ideological analysis in "Konban-wa, Ozu-san."

11. Charles Ramírez Berg, *Latino Images in Film: Stereotypes, Subversion, and Resistance* (Austin: University of Texas Press, 2002), 42–54.

12. Robin Wood, *Hitchcock's Film Revisited*, rev. ed. (New York: Columbia University Press, 2002); Dolores Tierney, *Emilio Fernández: Pictures in the Margins* (Manchester and New York: Manchester University Press, 2007). Early in his career, Wood's books were mainly auteurist, though several of them were revised, including the one on Hitchcock, which I have quoted here. In all, he published works on Howard Hawks (1968, 1981, 2006), Ingmar Bergman (1969), Arthur Penn (1969), Claude Chabrol (1970, with Michael Walker), Michelangelo Antonioni (1971), and Satyajit Ray's Apu Trilogy (1971). The Hitchcock book, originally published in 1965, was revised and reprinted several times (in 1969, 1977, 1989, and 2002), and the introductions he wrote for the various editions are a chronicle of Wood's evolving rethinking of his auteurist stance and his critical methodology.

13. Wood, *Hitchcock's Film Revisited*, 9.

14. Tierney, *Emilio Fernández*, 50.

15. Wood, *Hitchcock's Film Revisited*, 5.

16. Aurelio de los Reyes, *Medio siglo de cine mexicano (1896–1947)* (Mexico City: Editorial Trillas, 1987), 119.

17. Carl J. Mora, *Mexican Cinema: Reflections of a Society, 1896–1980* (Berkeley: University of California Press, 1982), 7–27.

18. María Luisa Amador and Jorge Ayala Blanco, *Cartelera cinematográfica, 1930–1939* (Mexico City: Filmoteca UNAM, 1982), 272–276.

19. See Bordwell's "Part One: The Classical Hollywood Style, 1917–1960" in David Bordwell, Janet Staiger, and Kristin Thompson's *The Classical Hollywood Cinema: Film Style and Mode of Production to 1960* (New York: Columbia University Press, 1985), 1–84.

20. For a more detailed analysis of the way Mexican cinema blended Hollywood with *lo mexicano*, see my *Cinema of Solitude: A Critical Study of Mexican Film, 1967–1983* (Austin: University of Texas Press, 1992), chapter 2.

21. David Bordwell, "The Bounds of Difference," in Bordwell, Staiger and Thompson et al., *The Classical Hollywood Cinema*, 81.

22. Bordwell, Staiger, and Thompson, *The Classical Hollywood Cinema*.

23. *Somos*, Edición Especial, Las 100 mejores películas del cine (Special Edition, The 100 Best Films) 5.100 (July 16, 1994). The 100 Best Mexican Films can also be found at the Más de Cien Años de Cine Mexicano website: http://cinemexicano.mty .itesm.mx/pelicula1.html.

24. Quoted in Emilio García Riera, *Fernando de Fuentes* (Mexico City: Cineteca Nacional, 1984), 28. Unless otherwise noted, all translations from the Spanish are mine.

25. Fernández interviewed by Beatriz Reyes Nevares, *The Mexican Cinema: Interviews with Thirteen Directors*, trans. Carl Mora and Elizabeth Gard (1974; rpt. Albuquerque: University of New Mexico Press, 1976), 15. Figueroa interviewed by Eugenia Meyer, ed., *Testimonios para la historia del cinema mexicano*, Cuadernos de la Cineteca Nacional no. 3 (Mexico City, Secretaria de Gobernación, 1976), 45–46.

26. John Baxter, *Buñuel* (New York: Carroll and Graf, 1998), 207.

27. Luis Buñuel, *My Last Sigh: The Autobiography of Luis Buñuel* (New York: Alfred A. Knopf, 1983), 107.

CHAPTER 2

1. Ron Tyler, ed., *Posada's Mexico* (Washington, DC: Library of Congress, 1979), 300–302, appendices 2, 3.

2. Arsacio Vanegas Arroyo, the grandson of Antonio Vanegas Arroyo, the publisher of many of Posada's etchings, claimed that some of the published ballads sold millions of copies. One children's game illustrated by Posada, "La oca" ("The Goose"), is said to have sold as many as 5 million copies throughout Mexico. This astounding market saturation would make Posada without a doubt the best-known artist in Mexico at the time. See Arroyo, "José Guadalupe Posada," in *José Guadalupe Posada: 36 grabados* (Mexico City: Ediciones Arsacio Vanegas Arroyo, 1943).

3. Appendices 2 and 3 in Tyler, *Posada's Mexico*, 300–302, list selected penny newspapers and give their prices. Most sold for one centavo, though some sold for two centavos, with an occasional one selling for three or five. Some of the broadsides in the Edward Larocque Tinker collection of the Humanities Research Center at the University of Texas, Austin, had prices of five and ten centavos.

4. Fernando Gamboa, "José Guadalupe Posada: The Man, His Art, His Times," in *Posada, Printmaker to the Mexican People* (Chicago: Art Institute of Chicago, 1944), 16.

5. See especially John L. Fell, *Film and the Narrative Tradition* (Norman: University of Oklahoma Press, 1974), and Fell, "Cellulose Nitrate Roots: Popular Entertainments and the Birth of Film Narrative," in *Before Hollywood: Turn-of-the-Century American Film* (New York: Hudson Hills Press, 1987), 39–49. Charles Musser makes references to other image media throughout his excellent study, *The Emergence of Cinema: The American Screen to 1970* (New York: Charles Scribner's Sons, 1990). His first chapter is a very useful survey of pre-cinematic media. Similarly, Musser's *Before the Nickelodeon* (Berkeley: University of California Press, 1991) makes several mentions of comic strips and newspapers in relation to early U.S. cinema.

6. See de los Reyes, *Medio*; Charles Ramírez Berg, "The Cinematic Invention of Mexico: The Poetics and Politics of the Fernández-Figueroa Style," in Chon A. Noriega and Steven Ricci, eds., *The Mexican Cinema Project* (Los Angeles: UCLA Film and Television Archive, 1994), 13–24. Aurelio de los Reyes looks briefly at Posada's programs for early film exhibitions in his monograph on the artist's illustrated poster announcements for entertainment shows, *¡Tercera llamada, tercera! Programas de espectáculos ilustrados por José Guadalupe Posada* (Aguascalientes: Instituto Cultural de Aguascalientes, 2005), 22–34. De los Reyes also mentions Posada's film poster programs for early films in his *Cine y sociedad en México, 1896–1930: Vivir de Sueños* (Mexico City: UNAM,

1983), 63, 99. Finally, there is this tantalizing comment in Roberto Berdecio and Stanley Appelbaum, *Posada's Popular Mexican Prints* (New York: Dover, 1972): "The relationship between popular [Mexican] graphic art . . . and the imaginative inventions of the earliest film-makers was strong in all countries, and there must have been cross-fertilization from the very beginning" (152, note 174).

7. The note to figure 234 in Tyler, *Posada's Mexico*, 297, argues that the first estimates of Posada's output numbering twenty thousand prints gave Posada credit for all the images produced at the Vanegas Arroyo print shop. It is now generally agreed that other artists produced some of the prints originally attributed to Posada, not the least of whom was Posada's mentor, Manuel Manilla (who died in 1893). Another early estimate was fifteen thousand prints, made by Frances Toor, in Toor, Paul O'Higgins, and Blas Vanegas Arroyo, eds., *Monografía: Las obras de José Guadalupe Posada, grabador mexicano*, introduction by Diego Rivera (Mexico City: Mexican Folkways, 1930). This fifteen thousand estimate also appears in Hannes Jähn, *The Works of Guadalupe Posada* (Frankfurt, Germany: Produktion Greno GmbH, Obertshausen, 1976, 12), though Jähn estimates that Posada created that many for Vanegas Arroyo *alone*, arguing that Posada's total output was therefore much higher. Patrick Frank in *Posada's Broadsheets: Mexican Popular Imagery, 1890–1910* (Albuquerque: University of New Mexico Press, 1998), 239, attributes the fifteen thousand number to Diego Rivera and regards the estimates of fifteen to twenty thousand as too high, citing two thousand as a more realistic figure. Since most of Posada's work has been lost, we will never know the exact tally. Nevertheless, in more than forty years of constant work Posada must have created several thousand prints—still a tremendous number.

8. Tyler, *Posada's Mexico*, 5–6.

9. David Elliott, "Orozco: A Beginning," in David Elliott, ed., *¡Orozco! 1883–1949* (Oxford: Museum of Modern Art, 1980), 11.

10. de los Reyes, *Medio*, 22.

11. Kristin Thompson, "From Primitive to Classical," in Bordwell, Staiger, and Thompson, *The Classical Hollywood Cinema*, 159–160; Eileen Bowser, "The Films: Alternate Scenes," in Charles Harpole,

ed., *The Transformation of Cinema: 1907–1915* (New York: Charles Scribner's Sons, 1990), 53–72; Musser, *Emergence*, chapter 11.

12. de los Reyes, *Medio*, 25–27.

13. This was, in fact, a popular tactic of itinerant Mexican filmmakers. They would visit a town and announce that they would photograph the congregation leaving the next Sunday's mass. A crowd would gather to be captured by their camera the next Sunday, and the following Monday the same crowd would attend the screening of this local *actualité*, a French term coined by the Lumière brothers for such mini-documentaries. See de los Reyes, "The Silent Cinema," in Paulo Antonio Paranagua, ed., *Mexican Cinema* (London: BFI, 1995), 64–65.

14. Patrick Romanell, *Making of the Mexican Mind: A Study in Recent Mexican Thought* (Lincoln: University of Nebraska Press, 1952), 29–53.

15. de los Reyes, "Silent," 65.

16. de los Reyes, *Medio*, 35–38.

17. de los Reyes, *Medio*, 17–22.

18. de los Reyes, *Cine y sociedad*, 202.

19. de los Reyes, *Medio*, 68–72.

20. That only about one thousand Posada prints survive is the general consensus. Jähn, however, who claims that his book "offers the most comprehensive collection, so far, of Posada's work" (p. 9), reproduces 1,699 illustrations. The problem, of course, which may never be solved, is ascertaining how many of them were made by Posada.

21. David Bordwell, *Narration in the Fiction Film* (Madison: University of Wisconsin Press, 1985), xi.

22. de los Reyes, *¡Tercera llamada, tercera!*, 28–34.

23. In one form or another, I believe I have seen most if not all of the approximately one thousand extant Posada prints. To assemble this list of cinematic techniques, I made use of the following collections of Posada's art: several hundred images in the Edward Larocque Tinker collection of the Humanities Research Center at the University of Texas at Austin; numerous illustrations in rare books and periodicals held in the Nettie Lee Benson Latin American Collection at the University of Texas at Austin; the 272 illustrations collected in Berdecio and Appelbaum's *Posada's Popular Mexican Prints*; the 1,699 illustrations reproduced by Jähn; the several hundred Posada

images in Tyler's *Posada's Mexico*, the catalogue of an exhibition of Posada's work held at the Library of Congress in 1980; and the 138 digitized Posada prints posted online by the Library of Congress at http://www.loc.gov/pictures/related/?fi=name&q=Posada%2C%20Jos%C3%A9%20Guadalupe%2C%201852–1913.

24. There are numerous other examples of larger etchings and engravings being cut down to smaller compositions, evidently depending on what was needed by the layout artist at the time.

25. Joyce Waddell Bailey, "The Penny Press," in Tyler, *Posada's Mexico*, 116.

26. Tyler, *Posada's Mexico*, 230.

27. Frank, *Posada's Broadsheets*, 19.

28. Margarita de Orellana, "Words Regarding Images: An Interview with Gabriel Figueroa," *Artes de Mexico*, "El Arte de Gabriel Figueroa," no. 2 (Winter 1988), 89.

CHAPTER 3

1. Emilio García Riera, *Historia del cine mexicano* (Mexico City: Secretaria de Educación Pública, 1986), 45.

2. Gabriel Ramírez, *Crónica del cine mudo mexicano* (Mexico City: Cineteca Nacional, 1989), 117.

3. de los Reyes, *Cine y sociedad en Mexico, 1896–1930*, 245; Federico Serrano and Antonio Noyola, "Nota a *El automóvil gris*," in Federico Serrano and Fernando del Moral, eds., *El automóvil gris*, Cuadernos de la Cineteca Nacional no. 10 (Mexico City: Cineteca Nacional, 1981), 10.

4. The prologue title card reads as follows: "The story that is presented here takes place in the same locations where the events actually took place. The scenes of the robberies, the homes where the criminals lived, and the locations where they were apprehended or where they confessed their guilt are rigorously authentic. The action takes place in 1915."

5. de los Reyes, *Medio*, 75–76.

6. *Excelsior*, January 25, 1920, rpt. in Luis Reyes de la Maza, *Salón rojo (programas y crónicas del cine mudo en México), vol. 1 (1895–1920)*, Cuadernos de Cine no. 16 (Mexico City: Dirección General de Difusión Cultural, UNAM, 1968), 230. The newspaper

El Universal reported on December 11, 1919, that on the opening day of the film in Mexico City, it premiered at eighteen theaters; rpt. in Helena Almoina, *Notas para la historia del cine en México (1896–1925)*, vol. 2 (Mexico City: Colección Documentos de Filmoteca, UNAM, 1980), 100. Ramírez reports that on one afternoon after its premiere it showed at twenty-three theaters; Ramírez, *Crónica del cine mudo*, 119.

7. Emilio García Riera and Fernando Macotela, *La guia del cine mexicano: De la pantalla grande a la televisión* (Mexico City: Editorial Patria, 1984), 36; Ramírez, *Crónica del cine mudo*, 121.

8. de los Reyes, *Cine y sociedad*, 256; Federico Dávalos Orozco and Esperanza Vázquez Bernal, *Filmografía general del cine mexicano (1906–1931)* (Puebla: Universidad Autónoma de Puebla, 1985), 55–56.

9. I wrote about the thematic darkness that pervades sound-era revolutionary films in *Cinema of Solitude*, 201–202. David Maciel has argued that one of the defining features of Mexican filmmaking of the late 1980s and 1990s is that its filmmakers have at long last been able to shake off this languishing post-revolutionary guilt. See his "El imperio de la fortuna: Mexico's Contemporary Cinema, 1985–1992," in Chon A. Noriega and Steven Ricci, eds., *The Mexican Cinema Project* (Los Angeles: UCLA Film and Television Archive, 1994), 33–44.

10. For a discussion of the state's support of Mexico's Golden Age cinema, see my *Cinema of Solitude*, 12–15; for the effect it had on the Golden Age's decline, see 37–42; for an account of state support in the post–Golden Age era, see 44–54. See also Maciel, "El imperio de la fortuna."

11. Kristin Thompson, "From Primitive to Classical," in Bordwell, Staiger, and Thompson, *The Classical Hollywood Cinema*, 159–160. See also Bowser, "The Films."

12. de los Reyes, *Medio*, 36.

13. de los Reyes, *Cine y sociedad*, 202.

14. For example, an early Mexican film critic, Silvestre Bonnard (Carlos Noriega Hope), asked that Mexico's Department of Censorship step up its protests of Hollywood's anti-Mexican filmmaking. See "La censura de las películas cinematográficas ¡Es necesario hacer algo!" ("Film Censorship: It's Time to

Do Something!"), published in *El Universal*, February 17, 1920; rpt. in Almoina, *Notas para la historia del cine*, 132–135. See also an unsigned, undated article, presumably published in a Mexico City newspaper in 1920, that complained about the denigrating representation of Mexico in U.S. films; rpt. in Reyes de la Maza, *Salón rojo*, 227–228.

15. de los Reyes, *Medio*, 66; de los Reyes, *Cine y sociedad*, 204.

16. Dávalos Orozco and Vázquez Bernal, *Filmografía general del cine*, 25–52. See also Moisés Viñas, *Índice cronológico del cine mexicano* (Mexico City: Dirección General de Actividades Cinematográficas, UNAM, 1992).

17. de los Reyes, *Cine y sociedad*, 176–177.

18. However, other opportunistic criminals are suspected of having imitated the method of *la banda del automóvil gris*, and similar robberies probably occurred during the nine-month period. Even after six members of the gang were executed, some copycat crimes were reported.

Except where noted, this section summarizes the historical research published by Aurelio de los Reyes in the chapter entitled "Gangsters contra churros" ("Gangsters versus Cowboys") in *Cine y sociedad*, 174–191.

19. See Ricardo Pozas Horcasitas, "Del infierno al purgatorio, del fin de la dictadura a la promesa de la democracia (1910–1920)," in *Filmoteca 1: El cine y la revolución mexicana* (November 1979), 4–21; Jan Bazant, *A Concise History of Mexico: From Hidalgo to Cardenas, 1805–1940* (Cambridge: Cambridge University Press, 1979), 123–146; Anita Brenner, *The Wind That Swept Mexico*, 2nd ed. (Austin: University of Texas Press, 1971), 3–61.

20. de los Reyes, *Cine y sociedad*, 243.

21. Ramírez, *Crónica del cine mudo*, 117. Five years after the crimes, and after the opening of the film, Higinio Granda declared that he had not acted alone in committing the crimes, and that "high officials" had been his accomplices; de los Reyes, *Cine y sociedad*, 243.

22. Kristin Thompson and David Bordwell, *Film History: An Introduction* (New York: McGraw-Hill, 1994), 58. See also Angela Dalle Vache, *Diva: Defiance and Passion in Early Italian Cinema* (Austin: University of Texas Press, 2008), and Peter Bondanella, *A History of Italian Cinema* (New York: Continuum, 2009), 12–14. According to Dávalos Orozco and Vázquez Bernal, *Filmografía general del cine*, 30–40, all five of the Derba-Rosas films were "in the Italian style."

23. de los Reyes, *Cine y sociedad*, 202–208; Dávalos Orozco and Vázquez Bernal, *Filmografía general del cine*, 18–19, 33–48.

24. Ramos was one of the most prolific screenwriters and filmmakers of Mexican silent cinema. Among his script credits are *Tepeyac* (which he codirected; 1917), *Confesión trágica* (1919), *Viaje redondo* (which he also directed; 1919), *Hasta despues de la muerte* (1919), *El zarco* (which he directed; 1920), *Carmen* (1920), *Amnesia* (1921), and *La parcela* (1921). He even adapted the script for the film that competed with *El automóvil gris*, called *La banda del automóvil* (*La dama enlutada*). See Serrano and Noyola, "Nota a *El automóvil gris*," 11, 14.

25. See de los Reyes, *Cine y sociedad*, 245–246. Likewise, the credit page for the film in the published screenplay gives Rosas sole credit as director; see *El automóvil gris*, 119.

26. García Riera, *Historia del cine mexicano*, 46.

27. de los Reyes, *Cine y sociedad*, 248.

28. de los Reyes, *Cine y sociedad*, 247–256.

29. Ramírez, *Crónica del cine mudo*, 118–119. Rosas's choice to make a serial rather than a feature in the first place may seem unusual today, but for more than a decade after the inception of the form in 1913, the serial was extremely popular. In 1922, for example, 35 percent of movie theaters in the United States were exhibiting them. See Anthony Slide, *Early American Cinema* (Cranbury, NJ: Barnes, 1970), 157–170; and Richard Koszarski, *An Evening's Entertainment: The Age of the Silent Feature Picture, 1915–1928* (New York: Charles Scribner's Sons: 1990), 164–166. Moreover, a serial is sensible in that it was a useful bridge between the short film and the feature (p. 164). For an international perspective on silent serials, see "The Brief Heyday of the Serial," in Thompson and Bordwell, *Film History*, 61–62.

30. de los Reyes, *Cine y sociedad*, 246–247; on Ramos's participation, see note 24. See the various announcements for and newspaper criticism of the film in Almoina, *Notas para la historia del cine*, 59–72, and Serrano and Noyola, "Nota a *El automóvil gris*," 15.

31. de la Maza, *Salón rojo*, 215–216; Ramírez, *Crónica del cine mudo*, 114.

32. See Kristin Thompson's chapters (14–17) in Bordwell, Staiger, and Thompson, *The Classical Hollywood Cinema*.

33. An impressionistic insight into one Mexican viewer's estimation of Italian silent cinema may be found in director Juan Bustillo Oro's memoirs, *Vida cinematográfica* (Mexico City: Cineteca Nacional, 1984), 33–35. Among the more memorable elements of silent Italian cinema noted by Bustillo Oro were the "idyllic and sometimes licentious" stories, the historical spectacle of early epics such as *The Last Days of Pompeii* (1913), *Quo Vadis?* (1913), and *Cabiria* (1914), and the beauty of Italian film actresses. Another gauge of the impact on Mexican cinema is to note that many of the films produced in Mexico in 1917, the first year of sustained Mexican narrative filmmaking, were inspired by Italian melodramas. The first Mexican narrative feature, *La luz* (*The Light*, 1917) was a remake of the Italian film *Il fouco* (1916). In addition, the five Rosas-Derba films made that year were in the "Italian style." See Dávalos Orozco and Vázquez Bernal, *Filmografía general del cine*, 30–40.

However, both Italian and French films were popular in Mexico in the 1910s, though their prominence gradually gave way to Hollywood cinema, especially during and after World War I. Bustillo Oro imagined a "battle" between Italian and French cinemas over the Mexican movie market. According to him, the French cinema dominated the marketplace early in the decade, until Italian spectacles and melodramas rose in popularity. The French "countered" with detective serials such as Feuillade's. The prominence of both French and Italian cinema in Mexico is evident in the newspaper accounts of the day and is chronicled in both de la Maza's and Almoina's compilations.

34. See Kristin Thompson, chapters 14–17, and David Bordwell, chapters 1–7, in Bordwell, Staiger, and Thompson, *The Classical Hollywood Cinema*; and chapter 2, on the films of Louis Feuillade, in Bordwell, *Figures Traced in Light*.

35. "*El automóvil gris*: Argumento original," in Serrano and del Moral, *El automóvil gris*, 19–57.

36. de los Reyes, *Cine y sociedad*, 231.

37. de los Reyes, *Cine y sociedad*, 254.

38. Bordwell, *Figures*, 46–47.

39. Bordwell, *Figures*, 47.

40. Mick Hurbis-Cherrier, *Voice and Vision: A Creative Approach to Narrative Film and DV Production* (Burlington, MA: Focal Press, 2007), 60.

41. "Enrique Rosas: Nota biofilmografica," in Serrano and del Moral, *El automóvil gris*, 121.

42. Bonnard, "*El automóvil gris*," 103.

43. Bustillo Oro, *Vida cinematográfica*, 44.

44. Dávalos Orozco and Vázquez Bernal, *Filmografía general del cine*, 19.

45. Ramírez, *Crónica del cine mudo*, 121.

46. This view is elaborated in Ella Shohat and Robert Stam, *Unthinking Eurocentrism: Multiculturalism and the Media* (New York: Routledge, 1994), 27–31.

CHAPTER 4

1. María Luisa Amador and Jorge Ayala Blanco, *Cartelera cinematográfica 1920–1929* (Mexico City: UNAM, 1999), 469.

2. Moisés Viñas, *Indice cronológico del cine mexicano (1896–1992)* (Mexico City: UNAM, 1992), 25; Eduardo de la Vega Alfaro, "Mexican Feature Film Production: 1906–1991," in Paolo Antonio Paranguá, ed., *Mexican Cinema*, 303; Amador and Ayala Blanco, *Cartelera cinematográfica, 1920–1929*, 465–469; María Luisa Amador and Jorge Ayala Blanco, *Cartelera cinematográfica, 1930–1939* (Mexico City: Filmoteca UNAM, 1980), 272–273; and Eduardo de la Vega Alfaro, *La industria cinematográfica mexicano: Perfil histórico-social* (Guadalajara: University of Guadalajara Press, 1991), 23–24. The figures vary slightly from source to source, however the total number of films produced in the period from *El automóvil gris* to the release of *Santa* in 1932 are consistently very low, regardless of source.

3. Bustillo Oro, *Vida cinematográfica*, 44.

4. Bordwell, *Figures*, 73.

5. Bordwell, *Figures*, 83.

6. For a comprehensive list of Mexicans in Hollywood in the 1920s and early 1930s, see Emilio García Riera, *Historia documental del cine mexicano*, vol. 1 (Guadalajara: University of Guadalajara Press, 1993), 26–30, and Luis Reyes and Peter Rubie, *Hispanics*

in Hollywood: An Encyclopedia of Film and Television (New York: Garland, 1994), 10–15.

7. García Riera, *Historia documental del cine mexicano*, vol. 1, 45.

8. Eduardo de la Vega Alfaro, "Origins, Development and Crisis of the Sound Cinema (1929–1964), in Paulo Antonio Paranaguá, ed., *Mexican Cinema* (London: British Film Institute, 1995), 81.

9. Estimates place the amount of film that Eisenstein shot at between 175,000 to 200,000 feet. See Isabel Arredondo's review of Masha Salazkina's *In Excess: Sergei Eisenstein's Mexico*, *The Americas*, 66.4 (April 2010), 584.

10. Sinclair sold some of the footage to Bell and Howell, and it was used to make five educational shorts and a feature. At least one of the shorts, *Mexico Marches* (1942), was used to promote the Good Neighbor Policy with Mexico. See Jesse Lerner, "Proletkult Meets Vanguardismo: The Jiménez/Eisenstein Exchange," in *Agustín Jiménez: Memoirs of the Avant-Garde* (Mexico City: Museo de Arte Moderno, 2008), 53; García Riera, *Historia documental del cine mexicano*, vol. 1, 45–46; David Bordwell, *The Cinema of Eisenstein* (Cambridge, MA: Harvard University Press, 1993), 19–21.

11. Bustillo Oro, *Vida cinematográfica*, 38.

12. de los Reyes, *Medio*, 119.

13. Notes for online films are available on the UNAM film archive website at http://www.filmoteca.unam.mx/cinelinea/intro.html.

14. Preserved by the University of Mexico (Universidad Nacional Autónoma de México, or UNAM) film archives and available at http://www.filmoteca.unam.mx/cinelinea/silente/silente_ini.html.

15. Notes for *El tren fantasma* (1926), http://www.filmoteca.unam.mx/cinelinea/silente/silente_tren_cap.html. *El tren fantasma*, *El puño de hierro*, and *Tepeyac* (1917) are available for viewing at http://www.filmoteca.unam.mx/cinelinea/silente/silente_ini.html.

16. William M. Drew and Esperanza Vázquez Bernal, "*El Puño de Hierro*, a Mexican Silent Film Classic," Cine Silente Mexicano, http://cinesilentemexicano.wordpress.com/2010/10/03/el-puno-de-hierro-a-mexican-silent-film-classic/. Reprinted from the *Journal of Film Preservation* 66.10 (2003), 10–21.

17. de la Vega Alfaro, *La industria*, 23.

18. See Reyes and Rubie, *Hispanics in Hollywood*, 10–15; Emilio García Riera, "Cine Hispano," in *Historia documental*, vol. 1, 38–44; Carl J. Mora, *Mexican Cinema: Reflections of a Society: 1896–2004*, 3rd ed. (Jefferson, NC: McFarland, 2005), 30–38; Rogelio Agransanchez Jr., *Mexican Movies in the United States: A History of the Films, Theaters and Audiences, 1920–1960* (Jefferson, NC: McFarland, 2006), 4–5; and de la Vega Alfaro, "Origins," 79.

19. de la Vega Alfaro, *La industria*, 25. See also de los Reyes, *Medio*, 114–117.

20. Michael Curtin, "Thinking Globally: From Media Imperialism to Media Capital," in Jennifer Holt and Alisa Perren, eds., *Media Industries: History, Theory, and Method* (Malden, MA: Wiley-Blackwell, 2009), 111.

21. It is unclear where they worked, or whether the discrepancy is due to the fact that they may have worked at several different moving picture–related companies. José Rodríguez said in an interview that he and his brother were working at Consolidated labs when they developed their sound system. See interview with José de Jesús Rodríguez Ruelas in Eugenia Meyer, ed., *Testimonios para la historia del cinema mexicano*, vol. 2, Cuadernos de la Cineteca Nacional no. 2 (Mexico City: Secretaria de Gobernación, 1976), 74.

22. Pepe Romay, "Joselito Rodríguez 'Padre de la Cinefonia Nacional,'" *80 Años cine sonoro México* (*80 Years of Sound Film in Mexico*), http://www.80cinesonoromexico.com.mx/joselito-rodriguez-padre-de-la-cinefonia-nacional/#more-576. See also de la Vega Alfaro, *La industria*, 25.

23. García Riera, *Historia documental del cine mexicano*, vol. 1, 48.

24. Arturo Agramonte and Luciano Castillo, *Ramón Peón: El Hombre de los Glóbos Negros* (Havana, Cuba: Editorial de Ciencias Sociales, 2003), 43–45; Mildrey Ponce, "The Cuba Griffith: Ramón Peón and the Dream of Film-making," trans. Adriana Pinelo Avendaño, CUBANOW.net, http://www.cubanow.net/pages/articulo.php?sec=40&t=2&item=9163; Josefina Ortega, "Ramón Peón: El Deseo Compulsivo de Filmar," *La Jiribilla*, http://www.lajiribilla.cu/2002/n84_diciembre/memoria.html.

25. Nelson Carro, "Film-makers," in Paranaguá, *Mexican Cinema*, 293–294.

26. de los Reyes, *Medio*, 121; *Historia documental del cine mexicano*, vol. 1, 49–50.

27. José de Jesús Rodríguez Ruelas in Meyer, *Testimonios*, 76. See also (José) Pepe Romay, "Joselito Rodríguez"; "Rodríguez Ruelas, José de Jesús, 'Joselito,'" Escritores de Cine Mexicano, UNAM, http://escritores.cinemexicano.unam.mx/biografias/R/RO DRIGUEZ_ruelas_jose_de_jesus_joselito/biografia .html. Romay is the son of Joselito Rodríguez. "Rodríguez Ruelas, Roberto," Escritores de Cine Mexicano, UNAM, http://escritores.cinemexicano.unam .mx/biografias/R/RODRIGUEZ_ruelas_roberto/ biografia.htmlhttp://escritores.cinemexicano.unam .mx/biografias/R/RODRIGUEZ_ruelas_roberto/ biografia.html; Hugo Chavez Lara, "80 años del cine sonoro mexicano," http://www.80cinesonoromexico .com.mx/category/historia/. See also de los Reyes, *Medio*, 126.

28. García Riera, *Historia documental del cine mexicano*, vol. 1, 50, 52.

29. Adolfo Fernández Bustamante, "Eisenstein, orientador," *El (Universal) Ilustrado*, July 16, 1931, quoted in de los Reyes, *Medio*, 121.

CHAPTER 5

1. Vega Alfaro, "Origins," 83.

2. Juan Bustillo Oro, *Ilustrado*, no. 841 (June 22, 1933), rpt. in García Riera, *Fernando de Fuentes*, 94.

3. The 100 Best Mexican Films can also be found at the Más de Cien Años de Cine Mexicano website: http://cinemexicano.mty.itesm.mx/pelicula1.html.

4. de Fuentes's biographical information in this paragraph and the following two is summarized from Emilio García Riera's *Fernando de Fuentes*, 13–17.

5. Agramonte and Castillo, *Ramón Peón*, 73.

6. Quoted in García Riera, *Fernando de Fuentes*, 17.

7. Masha Salazkina, *In Excess: Sergei Eisenstein's Mexico* (Chicago: University of Chicago Press, 2009), 22–23.

8. de los Reyes, *Medio*, 110.

9. de los Reyes, *Medio*, 111–114. For a list of publications that covered *¡Que viva México!* see Harry M. Geduld and Ronald Gottesman, eds., *Sergei Eisenstein and Upton Sinclair: The Making and Unmaking of "Que Viva México"* (Bloomington: Indiana University Press, 1970), 430–431. For reproductions of pages of some of these photo essays see Emilia García-Romeu, "Sergei Eisenstein's *¡Que viva México!*," in Salvador Albiñana and Horacio Fernández, eds., *Mexicana: Fotografía moderna en México, 1923–1940* (Valencia, Spain: Institut Valencià d'Art Modern, 1998), 90–101, 261–263.

10. María Luisa Amador and Jorge Ayala Blanco, *Cartelera cinematográfica, 1930–1939* (Mexico City: UNAM, 1960), 147.

11. Mora, *Mexican Cinema*, 33, 38.

12. García Riera, *Fernando de Fuentes*, 42.

13. García Riera, *Fernando de Fuentes*, 46.

14. Emma Roldán, Cuadernos de la Cineteca Nacional, no. 6 (Mexico City, Cineteca Nacional, 1976), 18–19; also quoted in García Riera, *Fernando de Fuentes*, 19–20.

15. "El estreno de 'El prisionero 13' ¡Un suceso!" *El Cine Gráfico*, June 4, 1933, 2, 8. This review includes a synopsis and provides the following account of the film's ending on p. 8: "But the father and mother arrive late; when they get to the [place of the] execution, the innocent [boy] falls, [his body] riddled with bullets." Another review, "El abate Casanova opina acerca del "Prisionero numero trece," published on May 31, 1933, also states that the innocent prisoner is a fatal victim. Note: both reviews were found in Fernando de Fuentes's scrapbook, cut out from the original publications and pasted to its pages. In the case of the second, the name of the publication and the page number were not visible.

16. Luz Alba, *Ilustrado*, June 8, 1933, quoted in García Riera, *Fernando de Fuentes*, 93; Roldán, *Cuadernos*, 18–19; also quoted in García Riera, *Fernando de Fuentes*, 19–20. See also John Mraz, "How Real Is Reel?" in Ann Marie Stock, ed., *Framing Latin American Cinema: Contemporary Critical Perspectives* (Minneapolis: University of Minneapolis Press, 1997), 94–95.

17. See Mraz, "How Real Is Reel?," for a discussion of the two endings and whether there might have been censorship by the Cárdenas regime, or it was simply de Fuentes's artistic choice; 108–109.

18. This is because in scanning a composition, the viewer's eye goes to the area of highest luminance first. See Jacqueline B. Frost, *Cinematography for Directors: A Guide for Creative Collaboration* (Studio City, CA: Michael Wise Productions, 2009), 103.

19. García Riera, *Fernando de Fuentes*, 20.

20. Vega Alfaro, *Del muro a la pantalla*, 11–13.

21. Anita Brenner, *Idols behind Altars*, originally published in 1929 (rpt. New York: Biblo and Tannel, 1967).

22. Aurelio de los Reyes, "Eisenstein y la Revolución Mexicana," in Fernando Fabio Sánchez and Gerardo García Muñoz, eds., *La luz y la guerra: El cine de la Revolución Mexicana* (Mexico City: Dirección de Publicaciones del Consejo Nacional para la Cultura y las Artes, 2010), 169–205.

23. Bordwell, *The Cinema of Eisenstein*, 195; Salazkina, *In Excess*, 9–11.

24. Years after de Fuentes's death, director Juan Bustillo Oro wrote an article recounting their first meeting at a screening of Murnau's *Faust* at the Cine Olimpia, which de Fuentes was managing at the time. During their conversation it became clear that de Fuentes liked Murnau's film quite a bit. Quoted in García Riera, *Fernando de Fuentes*, 16.

25. L. Kip Wheeler, "Freytag's Pyramid," http://web.cn.edu/kwheeler/freytag.html.

26. Quoted in García Riera, *Fernando de Fuentes*, 28.

27. García Riera, *Historia documental del cine mexicano*, vol. 1, 128, 131; rpt. in García Riera, *Fernando de Fuentes*, 140.

CHAPTER 6

1. I am not counting the film John Ford made in Mexico, *The Fugitive* (1947), produced by Argosy Pictures and distributed by RKO Radio Pictures, which Fernández and Figueroa both worked on. Figueroa was the film's director of photography and Fernández is officially credited as associate producer. Emilio García Riera agrees with that assessment; Emilio García Riera, *Emilio Fernández, 1904–1986* (Guadalajara: University of Guadalajara Press, 1987), 104; therefore he does not list *The Fugitive* in Fernández's filmography, 315–326. In her biography of Fernández, however, his daughter Adela Fernández calls him the film's codirector; Adela Fernández, *El Indio Fernández: Vida y mito* (Mexico City: Panorama Editorial, 1986), 46, 238.

2. See, for example, de los Reyes, *Medio*, 96–113, 184–198. See also García Riera, *Historia documental del cine mexicano*; see his discussions of *¡Que viva México!* (vol. 1, 18–19), *Redes* (vol. 1, 69–72); and individual entries for each of the Fernández-Figueroa films. See also García Riera, *Emilio Fernández*; Jorge Ayala Blanco, *La aventura del cine mexicano* (Mexico City: Editorial Diana, 1975), 31–39, 84–97; Jean Franco, "*Flor silvestre* y *Enamorada* de Emilio El Indio Fernández," in Fernando Fabio Sánchez and Gerardo García Muñoz, eds., *La luz y la guerra: El cine de la Revolución Mexicana* (Mexico City: Dirección de Publicaciones del Consejo Nacional para la Cultura y las Artes, 2010), 365–390; Zusana Pick, "Gabriel Figueroa: La 'mística de Mexico' en *El fugitivo* (John Ford, 1947)," *El Ojo Que Piensa* 3.6 (July–December 2012), http://www.elojoquepiensa.net/06/index.php/modules-menu/gabriel-figueroa-la-mistica-de-mexico-en-el-fugitivo-john-ford-1947; Paco Ignacio Taibo I, *El Indio Fernández: El cine por mis pistolas* (Mexico City: Joaquín Mortiz/Planeta, 1986); on the collaboration of Fernández and Figueroa, see 77–80 (on individual films, see the comments throughout the book; also see eight still photographs from various Fernández-Figueroa films that Taibo uses to illustrate the Fernández-Figueroa visual style, grouped at the end of the book under the heading "The Aesthetics of Fernández-Figueroa").

In English, see *Artes de México* 2 (Winter 1988), a bilingual edition devoted entirely to Figueroa, which includes an interview with Figueroa and essays by, among others, Carlos Monsiváis and Carlos Fuentes. See also Kirk Ellis, "Stranger Than Fiction: Emilio Fernández's Mexico," *Journal of Popular Film and Video* 10.1 (Spring 1982), 27–36; John King, *Magical Reels: A History of Cinema in Latin America* (New York: Verso, 1990); Mora, *Mexican Cinema*, 3rd. ed.; Armond White, "Figueroa in a Landscape," *Film Comment* (January–February 1992), 60–63. See also two articles by Tom Dey: "Gabriel Figueroa: Mexico's Master Cinematographer," *American Cinematographer* (March 1992), 34–40, and "ASC Hails Career of Gabriel Figueroa," *American Cinematographer* (March

1995), 40–48. Both are brief but salient accounts of Figueroa's career that provide illuminating technical discussion of his style. See also Julia Tuñon, "Emilio Fernández: A Look behind the Bars," in Paranaguá, *Mexican Cinema*, 179–192; Claudia Monterde, *Under the Mexican Sky: Gabriel Figueroa, Art and Film* (Mexico City: Fundación Televisa, 2013). Finally, Dolores Tierney's *Emilio Fernández* is a masterful textual analysis of Fernández's key films.

3. "The Cinematic Invention of Mexico: The Poetics and Politics of the Fernández-Figueroa Style" (Los Angeles: UCLA Film and Television Archive, 1994), 13–24. This essay is a revised version of one that had appeared earlier: "Figueroa's Skies and Oblique Perspective: Notes on the Development of the Classical Mexican Cinematographic Style," *Spectator* 13.1 (Fall 1992), 24–41.

4. Evan Lieberman and Kerry Hegarty, "Authors of the Image: Cinematographers Gabriel and Gregg Toland," *Journal of Film and Video* 62.1–2 (Spring–Summer 2010), 31–51.

5. Keating, "The Volcano and the Barren Hill."

6. Tierney, *Emilio Fernández*, 55–57; and see her analysis of the serenade scene in *Enamorada*, 108–111.

7. Claudia Monterde, ed., *Luna Córnea, No. 32: Gabriel Figueroa* (Mexico City: CONACULTA/Centro de la Imagen, 2008); see especially José Antonio Rodríguez, "Modernas sombras fugitivas: Las construcciones visuales de Gabriel Figueroa," 232–289; Ceri Higgins, "Transitando *lo mexicano*," 88–113 ("Transiting the National," 593–605).

8. Ceri Higgins, *Gabriel Figueroa: Nuevas perspectivas* (Mexico City: CONACULTA, 2008).

9. Higgins, *Gabriel Figueroa*, 13.

10. *Río Escondido* (1948), for example, in many ways the quintessential example of the Fernández-Figueroa style, won eight Silver Ariels for best direction, best cinematography, best original story (Fernández and Mauricio Magdaleno), best musical score, three acting awards, and an honorary award as a film of "special national interest." In addition, Fernández won the highest honor given for film in Mexico, the Golden Ariel. Other Fernández films from this period were similarly honored: *Enamorada* (1946) won seven Silver Ariels (among them best direction, best cinematography, best actress

[María Félix], best editing [Gloria Schoemann], and a Golden Ariel for Fernández) and *La perla* (1947) won five (best direction, another Golden Ariel for Fernández, another best cinematography award for Figueroa, plus two acting awards). Figueroa won yet another director of photography Ariel for the Fernández-directed *Pueblerina* (1948). In addition, all of his international awards were for his work with Fernández during the 1940s: Cannes, 1946 (*María Candelaria*); Golden Globe, 1947 (*La perla*); Locarno, 1947 (*María Candelaria*); Venice, 1947 (*La perla*), (*La malquerida*, 1949).

11. Taibo, *El Indio Fernández*, 116.

12. García Riera, *Historia del cine mexicano*, 177.

13. Fernández quoted in Julia Tuñon, *En su propio espejo: Entrevista con Emilio "El Indio" Fernández* (Mexico City: UNAM, 1988), 28. There were only a few films that Fernández felt were truly Mexican: de Fuentes's *El prisionero 13*, for example, which Fernández considered the best Mexican film ever made; *El compadre Mendoza*; and Arcady Boytler's *La mujer del puerto* (*Woman of the Port*, 1934).

14. Fernández quoted in Beatriz Reyes Nevares, *The Mexican Cinema: Interviews with Thirteen Directors*, trans. Carl J. Mora and Elizabeth Gard (1974; rpt. Albuquerque: University of New Mexico Press, 1976), 15.

15. Fernández quoted in Tuñon, *En su propio espejo*, 65.

16. Quoted in Taibo, *El Indio Fernández*, 51.

17. Quoted in Taibo, *El Indio Fernández*, 81.

18. See García Riera, *Emilio Fernández*, 12–15; Tierney, *Emilio Fernández*, 63–64; Adela Fernández, *El Indio Fernández*, 33–55; Taibo, *El Indio Fernández*, 19–35.

19. García Riera, *Emilio Fernández*, 15; Taibo, *El Indio Fernández*, 44.

20. See individual entries in Reyes and Rubie, *Hispanics in Hollywood*; see also Taibo, *El Indio Fernández*, 40–60; García Riera, *Emilio Fernández*, 15–16; Adela Fernández, *El Indio Fernández*, 50–58.

21. Adela Fernández, *El Indio Fernández*, 56–58; García Riera, *Emilio Fernández*, 15–17; Taibo, *El Indio Fernández*, 55.

22. Adela Fernández, *El Indio Fernández*, 61.

23. Taibo, *El Indio Fernández*, 45.

24. García Riera, *Emilio Fernández*, 17–24; Adela Fernández, *El Indio Fernández*, 60.

25. Reyes Nevares, *The Mexican Cinema*, 14.

26. Interview with María Luisa Algarra, quoted in García Riera, *Emilio Fernández*, 27.

27. *Medalla Salvador Toscano al Merito Cinematográfico: Gloria Schoemann* (program notes) (Mexico City: Cineteca Nacional, Dirección General de Radio, Television y Cinematográfica de la Secretaria de Gobernación, Dirección de Cinematográfica, April 23, 1993), n.p.

28. *Medalla Salvador Toscano*, n.p.

29. Interview with Gloria Schoemann, in Meyer, *Testimonios*, 74–75.

30. Schoemann in Meyer, *Testimonios*, 75.

31. Quoted in Taibo, *El Indio Fernández*, 81. See also Gabriel Figueroa, *Gabriel Figueroa: Memorias* (Mexico City: UNAM, 2005), 51.

32. Schoemann in Meyer, *Testimonios*, 78–79.

33. Interview with Mauricio Magdaleno, in Meyer, *Testimonios*, 28.

34. García Riera, *Emilio Fernández*, 36.

35. Quoted in Andrew Sarris, *Interviews with Film Directors* (New York: Avon Books, 1970), 244.

36. See Ernest Lehman's commentary on the writing of *North by Northwest*, "Destination Hitchcock: The Making of North by Northwest" (2000) on Alfred Hitchcock's *North by Northwest* DVD, Turner Entertainment Co. and Warner Bros. Entertainment Inc., 2009. Another example of this took place during the writing of Hitchcock's *To Catch a Thief* (1955). According to Steven DeRosa, after scriptwriter John Michael Hayes had worked out the film's romantic plotline, "the director conceived several of those dazzling Hitchcockian set pieces for Hayes to weave into the story." See Steven DeRosa, *Writing with Hitchcock: The Collaboration of Alfred Hitchcock and John Michael Hayes* (London: Faber and Faber), 96.

37. Interview with Magdaleno, in Meyer, *Testimonios*, 31.

38. Taylor quoted in DeRosa, *Writing with Hitchcock*, 84.

39. Interview with Magdaleno, in Meyer, *Testimonios*, 31.

40. Meyer, *Testimonios*, 29.

41. Taibo, *El Indio Fernández*, 89.

42. Tuñon, *En su propio espejo*, 39.

43. Figueroa quoted in Elena Feder, "A Reckoning: Interview with Gabriel Figueroa," *Film Quarterly* 49.3 (Spring 1996), 10.

44. Tuñon, *En su propio espejo*, comes to the same conclusion, 39.

45. Magdaleno quoted in Taibo, *El Indio Fernández*, 115.

46. Taibo, *El Indio Fernández*, 126.

47. Margarita de Orellana, "Words regarding Images: An Interview with Gabriel Figueroa," *Artes de México* 2 (Winter 1988), trans. Margarita Mansilla, 88–89; Alberto Isaac, *Conversaciones con Gabriel Figueroa* (Guadalajara: University of Guadalajara Press, 1993), 20. See also "Candilejas," 12–18; and Elisa Lozano, "Figueroa antes de Figueroa," 19–26, both in Monterde, *Luna Córnea*. Higgins also covers his early career in *Gabriel Figueroa*, 15–16.

48. See Eduardo de la Vega Alfaro, "Gabriel Figueroa, *stillman*, o la génesis de una estética (1932–1935)," in Monterde, *Luna Córnea*, 31–53.

49. Isaac, *Conversaciones con Gabriel Figueroa*, 17–24, 125.

50. Interview with Figueroa in Meyer, *Testimonios*, 40. Isaac, *Conversaciones con Gabriel Figueroa*, 24; for more on Figueroa in Hollywood and his associations with other Mexicans in the movie business there, see Héctor Orozco, "Cuando viajan las estrellas," in Monterde, *Luna Córnea*, 54–57. Figueroa refers to his studies with Toland in several interviews: Isaac, *Conversaciones con Gabriel Figueroa*, 24–26; Meyer, *Testimonios*, 40, 44–45; Feder, "A Reckoning," 3–4; de Orellana, "Words regarding Images," 89–90. See Figueroa's complete filmography in Isaac, *Conversaciones con Gabriel Figueroa*, 125–130. On the founding of CLASA, see García Riera, *Fernando de Fuentes*, 33–40.

51. On Figueroa's award for best cinematography, see García Riera, *Fernando de Fuentes*, 44. On Figueroa and *Allá en el Rancho Grande*, see Higgins, *Gabriel Figueroa*, 115–147.

52. Figueroa in Meyer, *Testimonios*, 45–46.

53. Linda B. Hall, "Dolores del Río, Films Mundiales, and the Mexican Revolution," paper delivered at the XIII Reunión de Historiadores de México, Estados Unidos y Canadá, October 28, 2010, 7–8, http://13mexeuacan.colmex.mx/Ponencias%20PDF/Linda%20B.%20Hall.pdf.

54. Feder, "A Reckoning," 4.

55. Meyer, *Testimonios*, 48.

56. de Orellana, "Words regarding Images," 92. In another interview, Figueroa said that he and Fernández developed their working relationship on their second film: "From the very beginning, when we shot the opening scene of *María Candelaria*, where she [Dolores del Río] holds the piglet in her arms, Fernández told me to place the camera wherever I wanted. He couldn't believe his eyes when he saw the rushes; they went beyond his wildest imagination. Since that point I had complete freedom to continue developing my own style." Feder, "A Reckoning," 5.

57. Feder, "A Reckoning," 4–5. See also Meyer, *Testimonios*, 50.

58. de la Vega Alfaro, "Origins," in Paranaguá, *Mexican Cinema*, 85–86. Much of the information in this section comes from de la Vega Alfaro's essay, 85–90.

59. García Riera, *Historia documental del cine mexicano*, vol. 10, 13–14.

60. Table 6.2 information is culled from individual film entries in various volumes of García Riera's *Historia documental del cine mexicano*: vol. 2, 23, 270; vol. 3, 17, 66, 156, 196, 254, 291; vol. 4, 59, 144, 202, 263, 285; vol. 5, 50, 99, 122, 173, 225, 288, 336; vol. 6, 50, 72, 104, 206; vol. 7, 17, 46, 96, 126, 179, 279; vol. 8, 162, 220, 268; and from García Riera's *Emilio Fernández*, 63; for Félix's salary on *Enamorada*, see p. 92. The length of the first run of *La isla de la Pasión* is from María Luisa Amador and Jorge Ayala Blanco, *Cartelera cinematográfica, 1940–1949* (Mexico City: UNAM, 1982), 111.

61. See David Bordwell, "Exceptionally Exact Perceptions: On Staging in Depth," in *On the History of Film Style*, 158–271.

62. Quoted in Hannes Jähn, *The Works of José Guadalupe Posada* (Frankfurt, Germany: Greno GmbH, 1978), 13.

63. Quoted in Dey, "ASC Hails" (see note 2), 42, and also in Feder, "A Reckoning," 13; and Meyer's interview of Figueroa, *Testimonios*, 46.

64. Tyler, *Posada's Mexico*, 275.

65. It is a commonly understood aspect of film language that low-angle shots confer their subjects with power, and we know that Figueroa was conscious of this because he explicitly mentions it. See Feder, "A Reckoning," 6.

66. Quoted in Tuñon, *En su propio espejo*, 51.

67. Agustín Velásquez Chávez, *Contemporary Mexican Artists* (New York: Golden Eagle Press, 1937), 45.

68. Antonio Luna Arroyo, *El Dr. Atl: Sinopsis de su vida y su pintura* (Mexico City: Editorial Cultura, 1952), 145.

69. For a good introduction to Dr. Atl, his art, his revolutionary aesthetic stance, and his influence on the next generation of artists, especially José Clemente Orozco, see Jesse Lerner, "The Artist as Volcano," *Cabinet* 17 (Spring 2005), http://www.cabinetmagazine.org/issues/17/lerner.php.

70. de Orellana, "Words regarding Images," 89.

71. Quoted in Dey, "Master," 36–37.

72. The credits for *Redes* were a matter of controversy and dispute—at least as far as Strand was concerned. The usual listings for the film, produced by the Secretaria de Educación Pública, identify the directors as Fred Zinnemann and Emilio Gómez Muriel, with Paul Strand as director of photography and script by Agustín Velásquez Chávez and Strand, adapted by Gómez Muriel, Zinnemann, and Henwar Rodakiewicz. García Riera, *Historia documental del cine mexicano*, vol. 1, 127. Strand always contested this, saying he had far more input and claiming that he was the film's creator, from original concept to photography. See James Krippner, *Paul Strand in Mexico* (New York: Aperture Foundation, 2010), 69–95. See also Charles Ramírez Berg, "El cine mexicano," in *Martin Scorsese's World Cinema Project*, Criterion DVD box set no. 684 (New York: Criterion Collection, 2013).

73. Dr. Atl quoted in Luna Arroyo, *El Dr. Atl*, 154–155.

74. Quoted in Feder, "A Reckoning," 5.

75. Feder, "A Reckoning," 5–6.

76. de Orellana, "Words regarding Images," 92.

77. de Orellana, "Words regarding Images," 89; Isaac, *Conversaciones con Gabriel Figueroa*, 108; Dey, "Master," 36.

78. Dey, "Master," 40; Dey, "ASC Hails," 48. Also mentioned in Isaac, *Conversaciones con Gabriel Figueroa*, 112.

79. Quoted in de Orellana, "Words regarding Images," 90.

80. Taibo, *El Indio Fernández*, 82–83.

81. Isaac, *Conversaciones con Gabriel Figueroa*, 33–34; García Riera, *Historia documental del cine mexicano*, vol. 4, 60.

82. de la Vega Alfaro, "Origins," 91.

83. García Riera, *Emilio Fernández*, 127.

84. For details on the postwar downturn in Mexican cinema, see Eduardo de la Vega Alfaro, "The Decline of the Golden Age and the Making of the Crisis," 165–191, and Seth Fein, "From Collaboration to Containment: Hollywood and the International Political Economy of Mexican Cinema after the Second World War," 123–164, both in Joanne Hershfield and David R. Maciel, eds., *Mexican Cinema: A Century of Film and Filmmakers* (Wilmington, DE: SR Books, 1999).

85. Taibo, *El Indio Fernández*, 144.

86. Quoted in Isaac, *Conversaciones con Gabriel Figueroa*, 111.

87. Isaac, *Conversaciones con Gabriel Figueroa*, 111–112. See also Feder, "A Reckoning," 11.

88. Feder, "A Reckoning," 12.

89. Feder, "A Reckoning," 11–12.

90. Quoted in an article originally published in *Esto*, January 21, 1956, reproduced at length in García Riera, *Emilio Fernández*, 239–241.

91. Taibo, *El Indio Fernández*, 154–156.

92. Taibo, *El Indio Fernández*, 185–188.

93. Isaac, *Conversaciones con Gabriel Figueroa*, 117.

CHAPTER 7

1. Quoted in Baxter, *Buñuel*, 207.

2. *Somos*, 12–13, 18–19, 20, 34–35, 58, 62, 63, 101. The 100 Best Mexican Films can also be found at the Más de Cien Años de Cine Mexicano website: http://cinemexicano.mty.itesm.mx/pelicula1.html.

3. See Emilio García Riera's commentary on the Mexican films of Buñuel in vols. 4–12 of his *Historia documental del cine mexicano*.

4. Eduardo Lizalde, *Luis Buñuel: Odisea del demoledor* (Mexico City: Dirección de Difusión Cultural, UNAM, 1962).

5. Freddy Buache, *The Cinema of Luis Buñuel*, trans. Peter Graham (New York: A. S. Barnes, 1973).

6. Raymond Durgnat, *Luis Buñuel* (Berkeley: University of California Press, 1977).

7. Francisco Aranda, *Luis Buñuel: A Critical Biography* (New York: Da Capo Press, 1985).

8. Baxter, *Buñuel*.

9. Victor Fuentes, *Buñuel en Mexico* (Teruel, Mexico: Instituto de Estudios Turolenses, 1993); Iván Humberto Ávila Dueñas, *El cine mexicano de Luis Buñuel: Estudio analítico de los argumentos y personajes* (Mexico City: Dirección General de Publicaciones del Consejo Nacional para la Cultura y las Artes [CONACULTA] and the Instituto Mexicano de Cinematografía [IMCINE], 1994).

10. Ernesto R. Acevedo-Muñoz, *Buñuel and Mexico: The Crisis of National Cinema* (Berkeley: University of California Press, 2003), 13.

11. Durgnat, "Style and Anti-Style," in his *Luis Buñuel*, 15–21.

12. David Thomson, "Luis Buñuel," in *The New Biographical Dictionary of Film* (New York: Alfred A. Knopf, 2004), 120–122.

13. Thompson and Bordwell, *Film History*, 383–385.

14. David Ramón, *Somos*, 58.

15. Sarris, "Luis Buñuel," in his *Interviews with Film Directors*, 70.

16. Thomson, "Luis Buñuel," 120–121.

17. Buñuel quoted in José de la Colina and Tomás Pérez Turrent, *Objects of Desire: Conversations with Luis Buñuel* (New York: Marsilio, 1992), 175.

18. Buñuel quoted in Aranda, *Luis Buñuel*, 136.

19. Buñuel, *My Last Sigh*, 143.

20. Buñuel, *My Last Sigh*, 143–145; Buache, *The Cinema of Luis Buñuel*, 40–42; Acevedo-Muñoz, *Buñuel and Mexico*, 35–43; Baxter, *Buñuel*, 149–157, 167–201; Barry Jordan and Mark Allinson, *Spanish Cinema: A Student's Guide* (London: Hodder Arnold, 2005), 83–86.

21. Buñuel, *My Last Sigh*, 145.

22. Mark Polizzotti, *Los olvidados* (London: British Film Institute, 2006), 21.

23. Buñuel quoted in de la Colina and Pérez Turrent, *Objects of Desire*, 37.

24. Buñuel, *My Last Sigh*, 198.

25. García Riera, *Historia documental del cine mexicano*, vol. 10, 13–15.

26. Acevedo-Muñoz, *Buñuel and Mexico*, 44–46.

27. Buñuel quoted in Aranda, *Luis Buñuel*, 136; Victor Fuentes, "Confluences: Buñuel's Cinematic Narrative and the Latin American New Novel," *Discourse* 26.1 and 26.2 (Winter and Spring 2004), 92.

28. María Luisa Amador and Jorge Ayala Blanco, *Cartelera cinematográfica, 1950–1959* (Mexico City. UNAM, 1985), 364–365. The exact figure is 74 percent.

29. For details of the postwar crisis in Mexican cinema see Eduardo de la Vega Alfaro, "The Decline of the Golden Age and the Making of the Crisis," 165–191, and Seth Fein, "From Collaboration to Containment," 123–164, both in Hershfield and Maciel, *Mexican Cinema*.

30. J. M. Ferrer and Martí Rom, excerpts from "An Interview with Pere Portabella" (one of *Viridiana*'s producers), MoMA.org, http://www.moma .org/interactives/exhibitions/2007/portabella/inter view.html; Andrew Whittaker, *Speak the Culture: Spain* (London: Thorogood, 2008), 225. The two Spanish companies that joined together to produce *Viridiana* were Portabella's Films 59 and UNICNCI, a company founded by emerging postwar filmmakers Carlos Saura, Juan Antonio Bardem, and Luis García Berlanga. See also Tatjana Pavlovic, Immaculada Alvarez, Rosana Blanco-Cano, Anitra Grisales, Alejandra Osorio, and Alejandra Sánchez, *100 Years of Spanish Cinema* (West Sussex, UK: Wiley-Blackwell, 2009), 97–98.

31. Aranda, *Luis Buñuel*, 190–205; Bill Krohn, *Luis Buñuel: The Complete Films* (Köln, Germany: Taschen, 2005), 126. The account of the origin of *Viridiana* in Ado Kyrou, *Luis Buñuel: An Introduction* (New York: Simon and Schuster, 1963), 77–80, appears to be mostly fanciful.

32. André Breton, "Manifesto of Surrealism," http://www.tcf.ua.edu/Classes/Jbutler/T340/Sur Manifesto/ManifestoOfSurrealism.htm.

33. Luis Buñuel, *My Last Sigh*, 107.

34. Buñuel, *My Last Sigh*, 104.

35. Buñuel quoted in de la Colina and Pérez Turrent, *Objects of Desire*, 175.

36. Buñuel quoted in de la Colina and Pérez Turrent, *Objects of Desire*, 109.

37. Buñuel quoted in de la Colina and Pérez Turrent, *Objects of Desire*, 63.

38. Buñuel, *My Last Sigh*, 199–200.

39. Quoted in Aranda, *Luis Buñuel*, 137.

40. "Why does he remember his mother?" Buñuel said. "I don't know. That is how I felt it." Buñuel quoted in de la Colina and Pérez Turrent, *Objects of Desire*, 58

41. Aranda, *Luis Buñuel*, 141–142.

42. Quoted in Aranda, *Luis Buñuel*, 137–138. In *My Last Sigh*, 200, Buñuel says the orchestra idea was for another scene, of the blind man being beaten. See also Baxter, *Buñuel*, 210.

43. In comedies, direct address, visually or verbally, is rare, but acceptable. For example, Groucho Marx in *Horse Feathers*, Woody Allen in *Annie Hall*, Matthew Broderick in *Ferris Bueller's Day Off*. But in a drama, particularly a social melodrama like *Los olvidados*, it's unheard of.

44. Baxter, *Buñuel*, 205–206.

45. Buñuel, *My Last Sigh*, 190.

46. Baxter, *Buñuel*, 94, 210, 212, 216, 218. Buñuel claimed *Los olvidados* was shot in twenty-one days; *My Last Sigh*, 200.

47. Baxter, *Buñuel*, 205.

48. Buñuel quoted in de la Colina and Pérez Turrent, *Objects of Desire*, 70.

49. Buñuel quoted in de la Colina and Pérez Turrent, *Objects of Desire*, 230.

50. As an example, here are the timings for scenes near the end of *Casablanca* (1942), directed by one of the fastest working and efficient directors of Hollywood's Golden Age, Michael Curtiz:

- the scene where Ilsa comes to Rick's apartment to beg for the letters of transit, 3:29
- the next scene, where they discuss what they will do now that they have kissed and revealed their love to each other, 2:30
- the scene where Rick explains his plan to escape with Ilsa and hand her husband, Victor Laszlo, over to the Nazis, to Captain Renault, 2:29
- the farewell scene between Rick and Ilsa at the airport, 2:23

51. Buñuel quoted in de la Colina and Pérez Turrent, *Objects of Desire*, 230.

52. Buñuel quoted in de la Colina and Pérez Turrent, *Objects of Desire*, 214–215.

53. J. Francisco Aranda, "The Passion according to Buñuel," in *The Exterminating Angel, Nazarin and Los Olvidados: Three Films by Luis Buñuel* (New York: Simon and Schuster, 1972), 108; García Riera, *Historia documental del cine mexicano*, vol. 11, 157; García Riera, *Historia documental del cine mexicano*, vol. 9, 246.

54. Quoted in Buache, *The Cinema of Luis Buñuel*, 126.

55. Buñuel quoted in de la Colina and Pérez Turrent, *Objects of Desire*, 115.

56. Buñuel quoted in de la Colina and Pérez Turrent, *Objects of Desire*, 152.

57. Buñuel quoted in *Cinéastes de notre temps*, directed by Robert Valey, produced by Jannine Bazin and André Labarthe; originally broadcast on French television, April 4, 1964; included on the Criterion DVD of Viridiana, no. 332 (New York: Criterion Collection, 2006).

58. Buñuel quoted in de la Colina and Pérez Turrent, *Objects of Desire*, 139.

59. Baxter, *Buñuel*, 212–213; Buñuel quoted in de la Colina and Pérez Turrent, *Objects of Desire*, 61.

60. The alternative happy ending can be found on the Alter Films, S.A./Televisa DVD of *Los olvidados*, released in 2004.

61. According to James Steffen, "Los Olvidados," a Turner Classic Movies film article available at http://www.tcm.com/this-month/article/93547%7Co/Los-Olvidados.html. Who directed the alternative ending is unclear. However, in an interview with Mejía published in *Vanguardia* and available at http://www.vanguardia.com.mx/unolvidadoensaltillo-643875.html, the actor claims that Dancigers had Buñuel write the happy ending. Though the director was loath to do it, he ultimately complied.

CHAPTER 8

1. Bustillo Oro, *Vida cinematográfica*, 39.

2. Bustillo Oro, *Vida cinematográfica*, 36–39. Aurelio de los Reyes concurs, suggesting that for Mexican film critics writing in the 1920s, the German silent cinema, by virtue of its artistic superiority, challenged existing notions of film. See "El cine alemán y el cine soviético en México en los años veinte," *Journal of Film Preservation* 60–61 (2000), 53.

3. Bustillo Oro, *Vida cinematográfica*, 100–104.

4. Bustillo Oro, *Vida cinematográfica*, 112–115.

5. Bustillo Oro, *Vida cinematográfica*, 112–115.

6. Charles Ramírez Berg, "A Taxonomy of Alternative Plots in Recent Films: Classifying the 'Tarantino Effect,'" *Film Criticism* 31.1–2 (Fall–Winter 2006), 33–38.

7. Quoted in García Riera, *Historia documental del cine mexicano*, vol. 1, 288.

8. García Riera, *Historia documental del cine mexicano*, vol. 1, 288–289; Luis Recillas Enecoiz, "El cine maldito de Adolfo Best Maugard," *Cine silente mexicano* (July 20, 2010), http://cinesilentemexicano.wordpress.com/2009/07/20/el-cine-maldito-de-adolfo-best-maugard/; Arturo Garmendia, "La mancha de sangre de Adolfo Best Maugard," *Dicine* 63 (July–August 1995), http://www.imagenmedica.com.mx/portal/index.php?option=com_content&view=article&id=85:la-mancha-de-sangre&catid=35:notas-cine.

9. Karen Cordero Reiman, "The Best Maugard Drawing Method: A Common Ground for Modern Mexicanist Aesthetics," *Journal of Decorative and Propaganda Arts* 26 (June 2010), 51–53.

10. Cordero Reiman, "The Best Maugard Drawing Method," 52.

11. Cordero Reiman, "The Best Maugard Drawing Method," 51–52; Rita Pomade, "From a Mexican Perspective: The Vision of Adolfo Best Maugard," Arts of Mexico, Mexconnect, http://www.mexconnect.com/articles/1080-from-a-mexican-perspective-the-vision-of-adolfo-best-maugard.

12. Pedro Henriquez Ureña, "Arte mexicano," afterword to Best Maugard, *Método de dibujo: Tradición, resurgimiento y evolución del arte mexicano* (Mexico City: Departamento Editorial de la Secretaria de Educación, 1923), 132.

13. Pomade, "From a Mexican Perspective."

14. Cordero Reiman, "The Best Maugard Drawing Method," 45.

15. Best Maugard, *Método de dibujo*.

16. Best Maugard, *Método de dibujo*, 1–18.

17. Best Maugard, *Método de dibujo*, 14.

18. The information in this paragraph comes from Aurelio de los Reyes, "Informes de Adolfo Best Maugard al jefe del Departamento de Bellas Artes de la Secretaria de Educación Pública, sobre su trabajo de supervision y censure a Sergei Eisenstein, durante el rodaje de *¡Que viva México!* en 1930," *Anales del Instituto de Investigaciones Estéticas* 81 (2002), 161–172.

19. de los Reyes, "Informes," 161–162.

20. Adolfo Best Maugard, letters to the Department of Bellas Artes, in de los Reyes, "Informes," 168–169.

21. Elisa Lozano, "Agustín Jiménez: His Moving Images," in *Agustín Jiménez: Memoirs of the Avant-Garde* (Mexico City: Museo de Arte Moderno, 2008), 50–53.

22. According to Eduardo de la Vega, in *La mancha de sangre*, Jiménez "applied an aesthetic rooted in certain examples of *Kammerspielfilm*, or German realist cinema of the 1920s, by filmmakers such as Lupu Pick, Leopold Jessner, Paul Leni, Georg Wilhelm Pabst, Karl Grüne and Ewald A. Dupont." Quoted in Lozano, "Agustín Jiménez," 54.

23. Agustín Aragón Leiva, "Photography and Photography in Mexico," reprinted in Lozano, *Agustín Jiménez*, 177–179. According to Aragón Leiva, Manuel Álvarez Bravo and Agustín Jiménez were "the two Mexico photographers who have stood out most in these first years of our photography" (178). See also "Biography," in Lozano, *Agustín Jiménez*, 68.

24. Carlos del Río, "Agustín Jiménez: A Rebel," *Resista de Revistas*, February 21, 1932, reprinted in Lozano, *Agustín Jiménez*, 179. "Your ambition?" del Río asked him, and Jiménez replied with one word— "cinema." It was, del Río wrote, "an ambition which possesses and masters him, which torments him and fills him with . . . a perfect joy."

25. Salvador Albiñana, "Agustín Jiménez," in Horacio Fernández and Salvador Albiñana, eds., *Mexicana: Fotografía moderna en México, 1923–1940* (Valencia, Spain: Generalitat Valenciana, Conselleria de Cultura, Educación y Ciencia, IVAM Centre Julio González, 1998), 106.

26. Stella Inda, interview in Meyer, *Testimonios*, 119; García Riera, *Historia documental del cine mexicano*, vol. 1, 288.

27. José Antonio Rodríguez, "Molino Verde," in Lozano, *Agustín Jiménez*, 136.

28. "Molino Verde, Espejo y Sombra" ("Molino Verde: Mirror and Shadow"), unsigned introduction to *Molino Verde*, in Lozano, *Agustín Jiménez*, 136 (English translation), 138, 140 (original Spanish).

29. According to author Miguel Angel Morales, writing in the blog *Fotografía en México* (January 23, 2009), the entire monograph of *Molino Verde* is reproduced in Lozano, *Agustín Jiménez*, where it can be found on pp. 137–151, http://miguelangelmorales-fotografos.blogspot.com/search/label/JIM%C3%89NEZ%20%28AGUST%C3%8DN%29.

30. Albiñana, "*Agustín Jiménez*," 121.

31. Stella Inda interview in Meyer, *Testimonios*, 119.

32. Emilio García Riera, *Julio Bracho: 1909–1978* (Guadalajara: University of Guadalajara Press, 1986), 19–22; Jesús Ibarra, *Los Bracho: Tres generaciones de cine mexicano* (Mexico City: UNAM, 2006), 100–104.

33. García Riera, *Julio Bracho*, 26; Ibarra, *Los Bracho*, 104.

34. García Riera, *Julio Bracho*, 23–32. On the founding of Films Mundiales and the decision to make *¡Ay, qué tiempos, señor Don Simón!* its first film, also see Figueroa, *Memorias*, 45–49.

35. *El Universal*, September 18, 1941, quoted in García Riera, *Julio Bracho*, 31.

36. García Riera, *Historia documental del cine mexicano*, vol. 2, 194.

37. García Riera, *Historia documental del cine mexicano*, vol. 2, 182.

38. "Historia del Ariel," Academia Mexicana de Artes y Ciencias Cinematográficas website, http://www.academiamexicanadecine.org.mx/historiaAriel.asp.

39. Eric Lee Dickey, "Los Campos de la Memoria: The Concentration Camp as a Site of Memory in the Narrative of Max Aub," (PhD diss., University of Minnesota), 52–67, https://conservancy.umn.edu/bitstream/54165/1/Dickey_umn_0130E_10532.pdf.

40. Though Aub's name did not appear on the screen credits, most sources acknowledge his contribution to the script for *Los olvidados*. In interviews, Buñuel himself confirmed Aub's participation. See Aub's book-length series of interviews with the director, his relatives, associates, and friends,

Conversaciones con Buñuel (Madrid: Aguilar, 1985), in which Buñuel confirms Aub's collaboration on the script, 118; see also de la Colina and Pérez Turrent, *Objects of Desire*, 53.

41. Domingo Adame, "Max Aub en el contexto del teatro contemporáneo en México," in James Valender and Gabriel Rojo, eds., *Homenaje a Max Aub* (Mexico City: El Colegio de México, 2005), 139.

42. Max Aub, *Obras completas de Max Aub: La vida conyugal; Cara y cruz* (Mexico City: Joaquín Mortiz, 1966), 9–69.

43. The meeting is referenced in an editorial in *México Cinema*, December 1943, reprinted in García Riera, *Julio Bracho*, 46–48.

44. Efraín Huerta, *Esto*, January 7, 1944, quoted in García Riera, *Julio Bracho*, 44–45.

45. That *Distinto amanecer* might be the first film noir is also expressed in a brief entry on the film on the blog Caffè Noir, August 28, 2011, http://mexnoir.blogspot.com/2011_08_01_archive.html.

46. Feder, "A Reckoning," 7.

47. Dey, "Gabriel Figueroa," 39.

48. See Janey Place and Lowell Peterson, "Some Visual Motifs of *Film Noir*," in Alain Silver and James Ursini, eds., *Film Noir Reader* (New York: Limelight Editions, 2000), 65–76.

CHAPTER 9

1. Letrois Parish, "Un verdadero triunfo de la cinematográfica mexicana," *Revista de Revistas*, January 13, 1935 (n.p.), reprinted in Elisa Lozano, "Agustín Jiménez: His Moving Images," in *Agustín Jiménez: Memoirs of the Avant Garde* (Mexico City: Museo del Arte Moderno, 2008), 48.

2. Bustillo Oro, *Vida cinematográfica*, 130–131.

3. For an analysis of the 1930s Mexican horror film cycle, see Gary D. Rhodes, "Fantasmas del cine mexicano: The 1930s Horror Film Cycle of Mexico," in Steven Jay Schneider, ed., *Fear without Frontiers: Horror Cinema across the Globe* (Godalming, England: FAB Press, 2003), 92–103.

4. Bustillo Oro, *Vida*, 176.

5. Bustillo Oro, *Vida*, 176.

6. Bustillo Oro, *Vida*, 153.

7. Emilio García Riera, *Fernando de Fuentes, 1894–1958* (Mexico City: Cineteca Nacional, 1984), 58.

8. Feder, "A Reckoning," 4.

9. García Riera, *Historia documental del cine mexicano*, vol. 2, 194; García Riera, *Julio Bracho*, 29. For Figueroa's recounting of the partnership, see Feder, "A Reckoning," 4. Also see Hall, "Dolores del Río," 7–8.

10. Feder, "A Reckoning," 4. See also Isaac, *Conversaciones con Gabriel Figueroa*, 31.

11. Carlos Monsiváis, "Notas sobre la cultura mexicana en el siglo XX," in Daniel Cosío Villegas, ed., *Historia general de México*, vol. 4 (Mexico City: El Colegio de México, 1976), 435–436; quoted in Tierney, *Emilio Fernández*, 39–40.

12. José de la Colina, quoted in García Riera, *Emilio Fernández*, 257.

13. Quoted in García Riera, *Emilio Fernández*, 275.

Index

Note: Italic page numbers refer to figures.

Maugard, 181–182, 188; and Bracho, 188; Buñuel compared to, 148; de la Vega Alfaro's critical study of, 2; dialectical montage of, 84, 85; as influence on de Fuentes, 65, 66, 74, 81–85, 105; as influence on Emilio Fernández, 65, 66, 84, 96, 109, 120; as influence on Mexican cinema, 61–62, 65, 74; and low-angle shots, 108, 109; and maguey plant, 85, 105, 107, 108; Posada as influence on, 14, 65, 83; ¡Que viva México!, 14, 55, 65–66, 82–84, 83, 84, 85, 96, 106, 107, 108, 114, 119, 120, 181–182, 188, 214n9, 214n10; and Rivera, 65, 66; and Soviet filmmaking style, 55

Él (This Strange Passion, 1953): and Buñuel's critique of machismo, 172; critical acclaim for, 8; and Figueroa, 153; frame-within-the-frame composition in, 149, 150, 150, 151; narrative structure of, 167–168; poetics of, 137; role of sex in, 205; running time of, 155; shooting schedule of, 153; and Somos poll, 134

El Trio Calaveras, 123

Enamorada (A Woman in Love, 1946): awards of, 217n10; diagonal composition in, 121; expressionistic lighting in, 118–119, 118; and Emilio Fernández's borrowing plot lines from Hollywood films, 124; foregrounding in, 109; frame-within-the-frame composition in, 109; low-angle shots in, 111, 112, 112; and Somos poll, 93; z-axis angle in, 121

Enemigos (1934), 105

Ensayo de un crimen (The Criminal Life of Archibaldo de la Cruz, 1955), 134, 137, 162, 165, 205

entering narrative space, Posada's use of, 23

Epstein, Jean, 54

Esquivel, Ángel, 43

Estrada, Luis: Infierno (Hell, 2010), 205; La ley de Herodes (Herod's Law, 1999), 205; and Nuevo Cine, 1

Euripides, 188

European cinema: documentaries of, 40; Mexican cinema distinguished from, 48; and Mexican movie market, 141; and narrative film, 16, 35, 40, 41; production system of, 98; and serial films, 40; and tableau style, 42, 44, 46, 81, 85, 153. See also French cinema; Italian cinema

extreme long shots (ELSs): in The Grapes of Wrath, 111, 111; in Río Escondido, 111, 111

Fairbanks, Douglas, 95

Falling Down (1992), 3

El fantasma del convento (The Phantom of the Convent, 1934), 65, 174

Le fantôme de la liberté (The Phantom of Liberty, 1974), 134, 168

Félix, María: awards of, 217n10; in Doña Barbara, 102; in Enamorada, 121, 124; in Río Escondido, 108, 110, 111, 113, 120, 127, 127, 128

Fernández, Adela, 216n1

Fernández, Emilio "El Indio": awards of, 93, 128, 217n10; borrowing plot lines from Hollywood films, 99, 100, 105, 124–128; box office performance of films, 103, 105; budgets and lengths of Golden Age films, 103, 104, 105, 129, 140; cinematic legacy of, 93; and Classical Mexican Cinema, 89, 91, 93, 94, 105, 128, 172, 217n13; critical appreciation of, 204; decline of filmmaking unit style, 94, 128–131, 136; as director, 94, 95–97, 99–100; domestic reception of films, 8–9; Eisenstein as

influence on, 65, 66, 84, 96, 109, 120; and expressionism, 56, 117; and expression of mexicanidad, 58, 136; Figueroa on, 131–132, 195; filmmaking unit of, 9, 10, 50, 56, 61, 91, 92, 94–102, 105, 173; and Films Mundiales, 97, 102, 195, 203; and Ford, 117, 216n1; and frame-within-the-frame composition, 47, 74–75; Hollywood experience of, 54, 66, 95, 96; Kikapú Indian ancestry of, 5, 95; maguey plant as visual motif, 107, 204; and Mexican film culture, 7, 102–103; nationalistic cinematic style developed by, 10, 11, 50, 91, 93–94, 96, 100, 102, 106–107, 109, 125, 127, 128, 129, 131, 172; personal life of, 131–132; and Phillips, 60; poetics of filmmaking unit, 92, 105–107, 109, 111–128, 136, 160, 172; Posada's influence on, 5, 14, 29, 30, 106; and reopening of global markets after World War II, 5–6; and screen credit, 100; song and dance used by, 122–123; stylistic differences in films, 4, 5, 91, 94, 129–130; Tierney's study of, 4, 92; and tragic stories, 117–118, 160, 165, 168

Fernández, Emilio "El Indio," works: Bugambilia (1945), 203; Un dorado de Pancho Villa (1966), 204; El impostor (1960), 130; La isla de la Pasión (Passion Island, 1942), 96, 103; La malquerida (The Unloved Woman, 1949), 93, 105, 117, 123; Nosotros dos, 129; Pueblito (1962), 130, 204; El rapto (1953), 130; La rebelión de los colgados (1954), 129, 130, 131; Reportaje (1953), 130; Rosa blanca, 129; La Tierra de Fuego se apaga, 129, 130; Una cita de amor (1956), 130; Víctimas del pecado (1951), 93, 129, 196. See also

Gable, Clark, 124

Galán, Abraham, 70

Galán, Alberto, 191, *191*

Galindo, Alejandro, 97

Gamboa, Federico, 17, 60

Gance, Abel, 54, 81

Garbo, Greta, 60

Garcés, Delia, *150*, 167

García Berlanga, Luis, 221n30

García Lorca, Federico, 138

García Moreno, Gabriel: *El puño de hierro* (*The Iron Fist*, 1927), 52, 56–57, *57*, *58*, *59*; *El tren fantasma* (*The Phantom Train*, 1927), 56

García Riera, Emilio: on analog montage, 79; on Buñuel, 135; on de Fuentes's *Allá en el Rancho Grande*, 67, 88; on Emilio Fernández, 93, 124, 204, 216n1; on Hollywood influence on *Santa*, 61; on influence of Soviet filmmaking, 55; on Mexican film production, 139–140

The Gaucho (1927), 95

Gavaldón, Roberto, 54, 96, 97, 195

Gentil Arcos, María, *158*

German cinema: expressionism, 55, 56, 173, 174, 182, 202; as influence on Bustillo Oro, 56, 174, 202; as influence on Mexican cinema, 55, 56, 73, 173; *Kammerspielfilm*, 182, 223n22; low-key lighting of, 73–74, 196; and silent films, 54, 182, 196, 222n2

glance-object editing, 23

globalization, of media, 57–58

Golden Age Mexican films: and *Allá en el Rancho Grande,* 67, 89, 101; annual film production during, 103, *103*, 129, *139*; and *El automóvil gris,* 34, 41, 51; character actresses of, 96; critical study of, 1; development of, 35, 55–56; and distinctive stylistic structure, 8; Eisenstein as influence on, 82, 83; ending of, 168, 201, 203, 204; and expressionism, 56; Emilio Fernández's Golden Age films, 104, *104*; and Hollywood film aesthetic, 7, 12, 35; ideological critique of, 191; and Magdaleno, 98; and musical performances, 122; poetics of, 2; Posada's influence on, 28–31; and Schoemann, 97; and sound films, 61; status quo identified with, 204. *See also* Classical Mexican Cinema (CMC); Mainstream Mexican Cinema (MMC)

Gómez Muriel, Emilio, 54, 219n72

González, Carlos E., *49*

González, Pablo, 37–39

González, Vicente, 38, 44, 46

González Iñárritu, Alejandro: *Amores perros* (2000), 205; and Nuevo Cine, 1

Good Neighbor Policy, 102, 129, 214n10

Granat, Jacobo, 40

El gran calavera (*The Great Carouser*, 1949), 137, 140, 157, 164, 168

Gran casino (1947): budget of, 157; irrational elements in, 143, *143*, 144; long take in, 153, *154*; narrative structure of, 160; poetics of, 137, 138

Granda, Higinio, 37, 38, 39, 44, 46, 47, 212n21

The Grapes of Wrath (1940): chiaroscuro lighting of, 195; low-key lighting in, 196, *196*, 198; musical interludes in, 123; and Toland, 101, 109, *110*, 111, *111*, 195, *196*

Gray Car Gangster robberies, 33–34, 36–38, 39, 42, 125–126, 212n18, 212n21

The Great Train Robbery (1903), 24

Griffith, D. W., 42, 60

Grovas, Jesús, 202

Grüne, Karl, 223n22

Guerrero, Carmen, 69

Guillén, Ernesto (Donald Reed), 60

Hakim, Raymond, 168

Hakim, Robert, 168

Haller, Magda, 175

Hawks, Howard, 208n12

Hayes, Helen, 99, 125

Hayes, John Michael, 218n36

Hegarty, Kerry, 2, 92

Hermosillo, Jaime Humberto, *Doña Herlinda y su hijo* (*Doña Herlinda and Her Son*, 1984), 205

Higgins, Ceri, 92

La hija del engaño (*Daughter of Deceit*, 1951): critique of *machismo*, 29, *29*; direct address in, 147; frame-within-the-frame composition in, 151, *152*; narrative structure of, 162–165; poetics of, 137; shooting schedule of, 153

Historia de un gran amor (*History of a Great Love*, 1942), 189

Hitchcock, Alfred: as influence on *Distinto amanecer,* 192, 193; and screenwriters, 98–99, 218n36; style of, 136, 148, 155; Wood on, 4, 208n12

Hollywood: Buñuel in, 138; Buñuel's use of style, 142, 145, 147, 150, 153, 160, 162, 165, 167; continuity style of, 42, 44, 45, 46, *46*, 47, 51, 54, 56–57, 60, 61–62, 81, 205, 206; and expressionism, 56; Emilio Fernández's borrowing plot lines from Hollywood films, 124–128; film aesthetic of, 6–7, 8, 10, 11, 20, 35, 41, 53, 58, 61, 63, 65, 205; high-key lighting of, 196, *196*; homogeneous filmmaking of, 8; as influence on *El automóvil gris,* 35; as influence on Classical Mexican Cinema, 7, 8, 11, 31, 58; low-key lighting of, 197, 198; Mexican filmmakers' relationship to, 4, 6, 7, 10, 48; and Mexican movie market, 5–6, 7, 8, 36, 53, 56, 57, 129, 130, 141, 203; and Mexico–USA pact, 103, 129;

Mundiales, 102, 203; and Now
Theater, 174; as screenwriter,
98–100
maguey plant: as compositional
feature of Posada's work, 14;
de Fuentes's use of, *85*, 105;
Eisenstein's use of, *85*, 105, 107,
108; Emilio Fernández's use of,
107, 204; as symbol for Mexican
people, 106–107
Mainstream Mexican Cinema
(MMC): and *El automóvil gris*,
51; Bracho's use of style of, 189,
195; Buñuel's use of style of, 10,
137, 138, 142, 145, 147, 148, 150,
153, 160, 162, 165, 167; Bustillo
Oro's use of style of, 202; Classical Mexican Cinema compared
to, 9–11, 12, 63; and commercial
films, 8, 9, 201; de Fuentes's
use of style of, 89, 203; Emilio
Fernández's criticism of, 124;
high-key lighting of, 196, *196*;
and Hollywood film aesthetic,
7, 8, 10, 11, 12, 15, 35, 53, 61,
63, 65, 205; implicit ideology
of, 11, 195; low-key lighting of,
197, 198; narrative structure of,
165–167, *166*; production of,
140; scenes advancing narrative,
185–186
La malquerida (*The Unloved Woman*,
1949), 93, 105, *117*, 123
La mancha de sangre (*The Blood Stain*,
1937): and avant-garde experimentation, 173, 179; censorship
of, 179, 180, 184; cinematography of, 186–187; *Distinto
amanecer* compared to, 194; *Doña
Herlinda y su hijo* compared to,
205; funding of, 141; humanism
in, 184, 185–186; hyperrealistic
approach of, 188; and Jiménez,
182–183, 184, 223n22; nude
dancing scene of, 184, *184*;
opening scene, 185, *185*; production of, 182–184; as prototypical neorealist *cabaretera* film,

50, 173, 179, 182, 183, 184–188;
scenes enhancing humanism of,
185–186, *185*, *186*, *187*
Manilla, Manuel, 210n7
Mann, Anthony, 106
Mano a mano (*Hand to Hand*, 1932),
64–65
María Candelaria (1943): budget
of, 103; critical acclaim for,
5, 8, 91; domestic reception
of, 9; and Emilio Fernández's
borrowing plot lines from Hollywood films, 124; and Emilio
Fernández's collaboration with
Figueroa, 91, 103, 219n56;
lack of song and dance in, 123;
low-angle shots in, *110*; low-key
lighting in, 118, *118*; narrative
structure of, 160, 165; and *Somos*
poll, 93
María Elena (1936), 101
Marqués, María Elena, *110*
Marx Brothers, 95
Más de Cien Años de Cine Mexicano, 215n3
match-action cutting, in *El puño*
hierro, 56, 59
Mathé, Édouard, *44*
Maugham, W. Somerset, 128
McCay, Winsor, 15
media imperialism theory, 51
medium close-ups (MCUs):
Buñuel's use of, 145, 157, *161*;
Rosas's use of, *44*, *45*, 46
medium long shots (MLSs), Rosas's
use of, *44*, *45*, 46, *46*
medium shots (MSs): Buñuel's use
of, 148, 157, *161*, *171*; definition
of, 19; and off-screen space, 23;
and partial-figure representations, 20; Posada's use of, 20,
21–22; in *El puño de hierro*, *57*;
Rosas's use of, *44*, *45*, 46, *47*
Meersman, Kay, *149*
Mejía, Alfonso, 144, 167, 222n61
Memory of the World Program
Registry, 134
Mendoza, Victor Manuel, *158*

Mercadante, Rafael, 37, 38, 46
Mexican art: and Best Maugard,
180–181; and film culture, 179;
Posada's influence on, 93, 106;
postrevolutionary nationalism of, 10–11, 14, 17, 34, 65,
112–113
Mexican cinema: adoption of Hollywood filmmaking paradigm,
6–7, 54, 56–57, 60–62; changes
in industry, 128, 129–130, 131;
collapse of 1960s, 141; critical
study of, 1–2; culture of 1920s,
6, 41, 53–54, 56, 213n2; culture
of 1930s, 66–67; culture of
late 1940s and 1950s, 139–141,
203; culture of World War II,
102–103, 105, 129; development
of, 15–16, 31, 34, 35–36, 55,
66–67; documentary film stage,
16–18, 31, 34, 35–36, 38, 40,
41, 48, 210n13; and journalism,
16, 17, 33, 40, 41; and narrative
films, 16, 17–18, 36, 38, 40–42;
and nationalism, 17, 36, 48;
Nuevo Cine, 1, 97, 204–205;
poetics of, 2; Posada's influence on, 2, 5, 13–16, 28–31, 54;
production system of, 97, 98,
129, 134, 140, 142; resurgence
of, 204; silent films, 2, 6, 33, 51,
74, 105, 212n24; sound films, 54,
55, 57, 58–61, 63, 64, 66; state
involvement in, 34, 67, 68, 140,
181, 190; style in, 2, 3. *See also*
Golden Age Mexican films
mexicanidad (Mexicanness): and
Best Maugard, 181; and Classical
Mexican Cinema, 9, 11, 30, 204,
205–206; in *El compadre Mendoza*, 74; in de Fuentes's work,
136; in Eisenstein's work, 55; in
Emilio Fernández's work, 58,
136; in Posada's work, 14
lo mexicano (Mexicanness): and
Doctor Atl, 113, 114; and Best
Maugard, 188; and Buñuel, 136;
and Classical Mexican Cinema,

196; frame-within-the-frame composition in, *149*; funding of, 140; irrational elements in, 143, 144, *144*; narrative economy in, 155, *156*; narrative structure of, 165–167, 168, 172; and neorealism, 182; one-shot scene in, 157, *159*; poetics of, 137; running time of, 155; script for, 143, 189, 224n40; sexual desire in, *156*; shooting schedule of, 153, 155, 221n46; and *Somos* poll, 9, 134; surrealism of, 137; surrealist sequences in, 145–147, *145*, *146*, 221n43

O'Neill, Eugene, *Lazarus Laughed,* 188

Oro Grovas, 202

Orozco, José Clemente: and Eisenstein, 65; as influence on Figueroa, 118; low-angle perspectives used by, 109; nationalism of, 66, 101; Posada's influence on, 5, 14, 106, 107

Orozco, José Clemente, works: *Dos magueyes and dos mujeres* (*Two Magueys and Two Women*, 1929), 107, *107*; *Magueyes, nopal y figuras* (*Magueys, Cactus, and Figures,* 1929), 107, *107*; *Requiem* (1928), 118, *118*

Ortega, Gregorio, 183–184

Ozu, Yasujiro, 2, 3

Pabst, Georg Wilhelm, 182, 223n22

Pacheco, Guillermo, *58*

Palacio de Bellas Artes (Palace of Fine Arts), 191

Palacio de Correos de Mexico, 191

Palma, Andrea, 188, 191, *191*, *193*, *197*, 198

Palou, Matilde, 157, *158*

Paramount Pictures, 138

Paramount Studios, 64

partial-figure representations, Posada's use of, 20–22, 27–28

Penn, Arthur, 208n12

penny press, and Posada, 15–16, 29, 34, 41, 106, 209n2, 209n3

Peón, Ramón, 60

Pérez, Ismael, *117*

Pérez Turrent, Tomás, 156

La perla (*The Pearl*, 1947): awards of, 217n10; diagonal composition in, 119, *120*; and Emilio Fernández's borrowing plot lines from Hollywood films, 124; foregrounding in, *108*; low-angle shots in, *110*; and *Somos* poll, 93; song and dance used in, 123

Phillips, Alex, 54, 60, 101, 188

Phonofilm, 59

Pick, Lupu, 223n22

Pinal, Sylvia, *161*

Piñatas, 182

Porfiriato (1876–1910), 67, 86, 163

Porter, Edwin S., 24

Posada, José Guadalupe: audience of, 66; *calaveras* of, 14, 15, 16, 20, 21–22; cinematic qualities of images, 14, 15; cinematic techniques used by, 19–28; collections of art, 210–211n23; editing of prints, 22, 211n24; Eisenstein's study of, 14, 65, 83; influence on Classical Mexican Cinema, 13, 14, 15, 28–31, 51; influence on Figueroa, 5, 14, 30, 94, 106; influence on Mexican art, 93, 106; influence on Mexican cinema, 2, 5, 13–16, 28–31, 34, 54, 106; journalism of, 14–16, 29, 34, 41, 50; length of career, 15–16; Mexican imagery of, 14, 28, 106, 107; and narrational representation, 18, 23, 40; and nationalism, 11, 28, 41; number of images created by, 16, 18, 106, 210n7; poster programs for film exhibitions, 18–19, 209n6; and social variety of nation, 79; survival of prints, 18, 210n20

Posada, José Guadalupe, works: *Alegoría de revolucionarios* (*Allegory of the Revolutionaries*, no date), 23, *23*; Aurelia the fish vendor, 21, *21*; *Calavera de cupido* (1913), 22; *La catrina*, 21, *22*; *Corrido aquí la calavera está, señores, de toditos los buenos valedores* (*Here Is the Calavera, Gentlemen, of All the Good Friends*, 1910), 21–22, *22*; *De nuestros dibujantes, momentos antes de los acontecimientos* (*From Our Artists, Moments before the Event*, 1903), 27, *27*; Doña Antonia the butcher, 21, *21*; Don Chepito declares his love, 26, *26*; Don Chepito is accosted by the woman's husband, 26, *26*; Don Chepito taken to jail, 26, *26*; engraving showing the coup de grâce, 50, *50*; *El fenómeno* (*The Phenomenon*, no date), 22, *23*; *Fusilamiento del capitán Calapiz* (*Execution of Captain Calapiz*), 29–30, *30*; *Gran chasco que se pegó Don Chepito Mariguana* (*The Great Joke Played on Don Chepito Mariguana*, no date), 26, *26*; *Gran Fandango y Francachela de Todas las Calaveras* (*Happy Dance and Wild Party of the Skeletons*, no date), 20, *20*, 24; handbill promoting *La poule aux oeufs d'or*, 18, *19*; *Jurado* (*Trial*, no date), 24, 27, 28; *Los patinadores* (*The Street Cleaners*, 1890), 24, *24*; placing viewers inside narrative space, 23, 24; *Un sentenciado en capilla* (*A Prisoner in Solitary Confinement*, no date), 25, *25*; *Sorprendente Milagro* (*Amazing Miracle*), 14, *14*, 107, *107*; *¡Terribles y espantosísimos estragos!* (*Terrible and Frightful Ravages*, 1893), 24, *25*; *Tristísimas lamentaciones de un enganchado para el Valle Nacional* (*Very Sad*

El río y la muerte (*The River and Death*, 1954), 137, 162, 165
Ripstein, Alfredo, Jr., 131
Rivera, Diego: and Eisenstein, 65, 66; as influence on Figueroa, 94, 101; mural in *Río Escondido*, 127; murals of, 191; Posada's influence on, 5, 14, 106; on Posada's output, 210n7
RKO studios, 140, 203
Robinson Crusoe (1954), 9, 137, 153, 160, 165
Robles, Fernando, 98
Rodakiewica, Henwar, 219n72
Rodríguez, Ismael, 60, 195
Rodríguez, José Antonio, 92
Rodríguez, Joselito, 59–60, 61, 214n21
Rodríguez, Roberto, 59–60, 61
Rodríguez Sound Recording System, 59–60, 61
Roland, Gilbert, 95
Roldán, Emma, 54, 68, 96
Rosas, Enrique: and analytical editing, 42, 44, 46; and Azteca Films, 38; death of, 51; documentaries of, 17, 35, 38–39, 40, 49–51, 50, 54; and Feuillade's crime serials, 42–43; frame-within-the-frame composition used by, 47, 48, 49, 74; and Hollywood continuity style, 42, 44, 45, 46, 46, 47, 51, 54; influence of, 54; and locations, 48, 49; melodramas of, 41; and Mexican film aesthetic, 51; and narrative film, 23, 36, 38; and nationalism, 11, 34, 48; poetics of, 2, 42–51; style of, 31, 33, 34; and tableau style, 42, 44, 46, 47, 48, 51. See also *El automóvil gris* (*The Gray Automobile*, 1919)
Ruiz, Miguel, 183, 185

Salazkina, Masha, 84
Salón México (1949): *Distinto amanecer* compared to, 173; and expressionism, 56; and Figueroa, 196; and Films Mundiales, 203; Magdaleno's script for, 100; Mexican references in, 61; narrative structure of, 160, 165; role of sex in, 205; and *Somos* poll, 93; *Víctimas del pecado* compared to, 129
San Francisco (1936), 124
Santa (1918), 17, 60
Santa (1932): Bracho visiting set of, 188; and *cabaretera* genre, 61, 125, 183, 187, 199; de Fuentes's work on, 64; and Hollywood continuity system, 60; as sound film, 53, 58, 60–61; success of, 66
Sarris, Andrew, 136
Saura, Carlos, 221n30
The Scarlet Runner (1916), 40
Schoemann, Gloria: awards of, 97, 217n10; as editor, 97–98, 126, 194; and Fernández's filmmaking unit, 9, 92, 94–95, 97–98, 105, 130, 131; and Figueroa, 195; and Films Mundiales, 97, 195, 203; in Hollywood, 54, 97
Scott, Zachary, 150
Sequeyro, Adela, 67, 68, 74
Seton, Marie, 55
Sevilla, Ninón, 129
sexism, Emilio Fernández's critique of, 91, 125, 126, 127
Shakespeare, William, 85, 86, 86, 87, 89
Sherlock Jr. (1924), 145
shot duration: in Hollywood film aesthetic, 7. See also long shots (LSs)
shot progressions: in *El automóvil gris*, 44, 45, 46, 46, 47; de Fuentes's use of, 81; and Hollywood continuity style, 56; in *El puño de hierro*, 58
Sight and Sound critics' poll, 134
Silberman, Serge, 168
silent films: and American cinema, 54, 60, 95; and French cinema, 54; and German cinema, 54;

182, 196, 222n2; and guiding-eye composition, 74, 75; and Mexican cinema, 2, 6, 33, 51, 74, 105, 212n24; poetics of, 106; and Soviet cinema, 54. See also *El automóvil gris* (*The Gray Automobile*, 1919)
Simón del desierto (*Simon of the Desert*, 1965), 7, 137, 144, 168, 203
Sinclair, Upton, 55, 65, 66, 214n10
Sindicato de Trabajadores de la Producción Cinematográfica Mexicana, 139–140
The Sin of Madelon Caudet (1931), 99, 124, 125–126
Siqueiros, David Alfaro: and Eisenstein, 65; murals of, 191; nationalism of, 66, 101; Posada's influence on, 5, 14, 106
Solares, Gilberto Martínez, 54, 96, 97
Soler, Domingo, 70
Soler, Fernando, 151, 156, 160
Sólo con tu pareja (1991), 205
Somos magazine, poll of top one hundred films, 9, 12, 64, 93, 94, 134, 136, 205
Sophocles, 188
Soviet cinema: ideological critique in, 55; as influence on Mexican cinema, 55, 56; and montage, 81; and silent films, 54
Soy puro mexicano (1942), 97
Spanish cinema, 103, 129, 141
The Spanish Dancer (1924), 60
Staiger, Janet, 6–7, 8
Stanwyck, Barbara, 197, 197
Star Wars IV, 87, 166
Strand, Paul, *Redes* (*The Wave*, 1934), 54, 114, 114, 188, 219n72
Subida al cielo (*Mexican Bus Ride*, 1952), 137, 149, 150, 151, 155, 164, 168
Susana (1951): frame-within-the-frame composition in, 149, 150–151, 151; narrative structure of, 160, 162, 162, 200; one-shot scene in, 157, 158;